THE THEOLOGY OF PETER DAMIAN

THE THEOLOGY OF PETER DAMIAN

"Let Your Life Always Serve as a Witness"

PATRICIA RANFT

THE CATHOLIC UNIVERSITY OF AMERICA PRESS
Washington, D.C.

The author gratefully acknowledges financial support of this work by the Camaldolesan and Sky Farm hermitages.

The paper used in this publication meets the minimum requirements of American National Standards for Information Science—Permanence of Paper for Printed Library Materials, ANSI Z39.48-1984.
∞

LIBRARY OF CONGRESS CATALOGING-IN-PUBLICATION DATA
Ranft, Patricia.
The theology of Peter Damian : "let your life always serve as a witness" / Patricia Ranft.
p. cm.
Includes bibliographical references (p.) and index.
ISBN 978-0-8132-1997-4 (cloth : alk. paper)
1. Peter Damian, Saint, 1007?–1072. 2. Peter Damian, Saint, 1007?–1072—Correspondence. I. Title.
BX4700.P77R36 2012
230'.2092—dc23 2012010575

To Óddur and to Amanda

For all the happiness they have brought to our family

and

To Ólafur, Finnur, and August West

The next generation of medieval scholars

CONTENTS

ABBREVIATIONS

AASS	*Acta Sanctorum*
ANF	*The Ante-Nicene Fathers*
B	*Die Briefe des Petrus Damiani*
CCCM	*Corpus Christianorum, Continuatio Mediaevalis*
L	*The Letters of Peter Damian*
Mansi	*Sacrorum conciliorum nova et amplissima collectio*
MGH	*Monumenta Germaniae Historica*
PG	*Patrologicae cursus completus, series graeca*
PL	*Patrologicae cursus completus, series latina*
S	*Sancti Petri Damiani Sermones*

THE THEOLOGY OF PETER DAMIAN

Vitae poro tuae semper habeto testem.

(Moreover, let your life always serve as a witness.)

—Peter Damian, *Briefe* 50:75

INTRODUCTION

While our knowledge of the Middle Ages has increased dramatically during the last century, there are still riches to discover. Peter Damian is one such treasure. Born in Ravenna in 1007, Damian's life and writings are relatively unexplored and greatly underappreciated. The goal of this book is to remedy this regrettable situation.

Modern neglect is at least partially due to the sorry state of his writings until recently. Thanks to the Herculean efforts of a few scholars we now have critical editions of all letters and sermons.[1] Unfortunately, secondary sources have been slow to follow.[2] There

1. The neglect continued even after the revival of medieval studies at the end of the nineteenth century; Damian was still "virtually neglected for the fifty years prior to World War II," says Owen Blum, in intro., *The Letters of Peter Damian,* tr. Owen Blum (vols.1–3, 5) and Irven Resnick (vols. 6–7), Fathers of the Church, Mediaeval Continuation (Washington, D.C.: The Catholic University of America Press, 1989–2005), 1:3; hereafter cited as L. While Kurt Reindel is the only editor of the critical edition listed by publishers, in the foreword he acknowledges Owen Blum's collaboration in producing the critical edition of Damian's works: *Die Briefe des Petrus Damiani,* ed. Kurt Reindel, 4 vols., MGH, Briefe der deuschen Kaiserzeit (Munich: 1983–93); hereafter cited as B. For sermons, see *Sancti Petri Damiani Sermones,* ed. Ioannis Lucchesi, CCCM 57 (Turnhout: Brepols, 1983); hereafter cited as S.

2. Rather than include an incomplete historiography in the text, I refer the reader to the notes and bibliography herein, particularly the works by Nicolangelo D'Acunto, Guiseppe Fornasari, Benedetto Calati, Paolo Golinelli, Kurt Reindel, Michel Grandjean, Stephen Freud, Irven Resnick, and myself. For older works still of value, see Owen Blum, Jean Leclercq, Jean Gonsette, and dissertations by John Oostermann, Ronald Osborn, Kennerly Woody, and John Wang.

is no modern biography.[3] Perhaps a bigger reason for his neglect is his rhetoric. Greatly admired by his contemporaries for his skill in the art, today many passages seem inappropriately vitriolic.[4] Undue focus on select passages perpetuates misinterpretations.[5] Once the entire corpus is mastered, however, one realizes that his rhetorical extremes are comparatively few. Instead, what one is struck by is the balance and common sense that permeate the works. Here is a man of profound insight. He offers practical advice, analyzes complex situations, promotes rational thought, resolves conflicts, comforts the grieving, provides leadership, settles civic unrest, admonishes the powerful, encourages the powerless, preaches personal and social responsibility, demands equity before the law, reveres creation, promotes individualism, and reinforces the bonds of community. Damian is not the voice of intemperance; he is the voice of reason. Even when his righteous anger flares forth, he pursues a moderate course. He has little tolerance for clerical misconduct, for exam-

3. The main source for Damian's life is John of Lodi, *Vita B. Petri Damiani,* PL 144, 113–46; and *Vita Petri Damiani,* MGH, Studien und Texte (Hanover: Hahn, 1995). Three other medieval monks wrote versions of Damian's life, but they vary little from John's account; see PL 144, 1452–80. Raphaelis Foglietti, *Sancti Petri Damiani Ecclesiae Doctoris Autobiographia* (Turin: A. Baglione, 1899), tried, unsuccessfully, to construct a biography from Damian's own comments. For other biographical works of varying worth, see bibliography for Franz Neukirch, Jacob Loderchius, A. Vogel, L. Guerrier, and M. J. Kleinermanns. For the best reconstruction of Damian's chronology, see Giovanni Lucchesi, "Per una Vita di San Pier Damiani," in *San Pier Damiani nel IX Centario della Morte (1072–1972),* 4 vols., (Cesna: Centro Studi e ricerche sulla antica provincia ecclesiastica ravennate, 1972–78), 1:13–180; 2:13–160, with a summary and table at 2:148–59. See also Fridolin Dressler, *Petrus Damiani: Leben und Werk,* in *Studia Anselmiana* 34 (1954).

4. For example, Damian's rejection of ancient philosophers in Letter 28.4, in L, 1:257; B, 1:251–52. [All citations to Damian's works will be in this form; for example, this one should be read: Letter 28, paragraph 4, in Blum, *The Letters of Peter Damian,* vol. 1, p. 257, and in Reindel, *Die Briefe des Petrus Damiani,* vol. 1, pp. 251–52.]

5. One infamous example is Lester K. Little, "The Personal Development of Peter Damian," in *Order and Innovation in the Middle Ages,* ed. William Jordan, Bruce McNab, and Teofilo Ruiz, 317–41 (Princeton, N.J.: Princeton University Press, 1976). Concentrating on a handful of citations and with no regard for context, Little constructs a pop-psychologist's profile of Damian as "a seriously disturbed personality" (337), "filled with an obsessively controlled anger and sexual drive" (336). On the basis of one sentence in one source he claims Peter suffered permanent psychological damage because his mother had an argument with another son when Peter was a day old!

ple, but is lenient in his treatment of all but recalcitrant offenders.[6]

Damian is a prolific writer, "a compulsive letter writer."[7] We have one hundred eighty extant letters of his, for he kept copies in his monastery. In his critical edition of Damian's letters, Kurt Reindel designated all Damian's *epistolae* and *opuscula* ("little works," or books) as letters, arranged them in chronological order, and assigned them consecutive numbers.[8] The letters date from 1040/1041 to 1070; letters 171 to 180 are undatable.[9] His instructions to friends Theodosius, Rodulfus, Gebiza, Tebaldus, and John of Lodi to censor and edit his letters speak to Damian's desire for the works to reach the widest possible audience.[10] He begs one addressee "not to let this short letter be destroyed but copy it in one of your books," a request evidently denied, for no letters outside of his own collection at Fonte Avellana have been found.[11] Some letters bear fictitious names and addresses, indicating that he used the epistolary form to expound his ideas.[12] He is extremely conscious of the literary demands of letter writing, to the point of near obsession, and his writings are replete with apologies and explanations for any apparent or real shortcoming he might be guilty of.[13] This is probably because of critics who, according to

6. See Letter 31.65, in L, 2:45; B, 1:322, where he encourages the sinner to "not be depressed and utterly despair." His works are filled with compassion.

7. Blum, intro., 12, in L, 1:12. Damian was also most diverse in content; see J. Joseph Ryan, *Saint Peter Damiani and His Canonical Sources* (Toronto: Pontifical Institute of Medieval Studies, 1956), xvii.

8. This organization overrides Constantine Gaetani's seventeenth-century presentation of Damian's opus in PL. There is also John of Lodi's *Collectanea,* PL 145, 987–1170, an anthology of sorts of Damian's exegesis and excerpts from letters that have not survived elsewhere. Some texts have been placed in their proper position in *Briefe,* but there is no complete critical edition or translation of *Collectanea* (sometimes called *Liber testimonium*). The manuscript tradition is discussed in Reindel, "Studien," and intro., B, 1:17–39. See also Letter 1.20–27, in L, 1:49–56; B, 1:75–80.

9. Most letters were dated by Franz Neukirch, *Das leben des Petrus Damiani: Leben und Werk,* in *Studia Anselmiana* 34 (1954).

10. See also Letter 58.6, in L, 2:393; B, 2:194: "I request that this letter be made public."

11. Letter 37.5, in L, 2:72; B, 1:347.

12. See Blum, intro., 20, in L, 1:16; and Reindel, "Petrus Damiani und seine Korrespondenten," *Studi gregoriani* 10 (1975), 203–20.

13. He comments on his writing over one hundred times. He is particularly conscious of the demands for epistolary brevity and of transgressing those requirements.

Damian, were plentiful: "I am quite well aware that when my letter gets into the hands of secular grammarians" they search it feverishly for "errors" or lack of "artistic style."[14] His letters are addressed to a wide array of peoples and discuss a vast assortment of topics.[15] Damian also wrote seven vitae (some included in the body of letters), and a few hymns, poems, and prayers.[16] His hymns and poems have received more attention than his letters and are of impressive quality.[17] Most of the hymns are dedicated to male saints and were likely written for their offices. His prayers include liturgical and devotional supplications and express themes consistent with his other writings.[18]

Damian is also a conscientious scholar: "When I am writing something that I especially wish to preserve, surrounded by an extensive library of various volumes, I call to mind the opinions of masters and always resort, when necessary, to their works."[19] He made a partial list of those works in his monastery's library, telling us that he even "corrected a number of those codices, according to my capacity."[20] The repeated requests of Hildebrand for Damian to compile all canonical texts on Roman primacy suggest that Damian is a noted canonical au-

14. Letter 21.1, in L, 1:197; B, 1:203.

15. See appendix 2.

16. Vitae are those of Romuald, found in PL 144, 953–1008; AASS Feb. 2, 104–24; and *Petri Damiani vita Beati Romualdi,* ed. Giovanni Tabacco, in *Fonti per la storia d'Italia* 94 (1957); and *The Life of Blessed Romuald,* in *The Mystery of Romuald and the Five Brothers,* tr. Thomas Matus (Big Sur, Calif.: Source Books and Hermitage Books, 1994), hereafter cited as VR. For Odilonis, see AASS Jan. 1, 71–77; and PL 144, 925–44. For Dominici Loricati, see Letter 109.9–28, in L, 5:211–26; and AASS Oct. 6, 143–51. For Rodulfi, see Letter 109.2–8, in L, 5:207–11; and AASS Oct. 8, 194–97. For Lucilliae et Florae, see PL 144, 1025–32; and AASS July 7, 24–27. For Mauri, see PL 144, 945–52. For Mariani et Jacobi, see PL 144, 1031–36. For hymns and prayers, see Stephen Hurlburt, *The Songs of S. Peter Damian* (Washington, D.C.: St. Albans Press, 1928); Hurlburt, *Hortus Conclusus* (Washington, D.C.: St. Albans Press, 1936); and Margareta Lokrantz, "L'opera poetica di S. Pier Damiani," *Studia Latina Stockholmensia* 12 (1964).

17. Owen Blum, *St. Peter Damian: His Teaching on the Spiritual Life* (Washington, D.C.: The Catholic University of America Press, 1947), 49, 50–55. They are found in G. M. Dreves and C. Blume, *Analecta hymnica medii aevi* (Leipzig: Fues's, 1905), 48:29–78. See also A. Wilmart, "Le recueil des poèmes et des prières de saint Pierre Damien," *Revue bénédictine* 41 (1949), 342–57; and F. J. E. Raby, *A History of Christian-Latin Poetry* (Oxford: Oxford University Press, 1927), 250–56.

18. See A. Wilmart, "Les prières de saint Pierre Damien pour l'adoration de la croix," *Auteurs spirituels et textes dévots du moyen âge latin* (Paris, 1932), 138–46; and Blum, *St. Peter,* 46–49.

19. Letter 141.2, in L, 6:112; B, 3:488.

20. Letter 18.20, in L, 1:169; B, 1:178.

thority.[21] He denounces sources he judges spurious, admits when he has been unable to check a source for accuracy, and states whether he is citing from memory or notes; in short, he makes "intelligent and conscientious use" of quotes.[22] His mastery of the literary arts is apparent, many believing that he was the best Latinist and leading Italian poet of the day, whose "language and rhetoric [was] deployed so brilliantly" and whose "talent for lyricism was unrivalled."[23] His hymn *De gaudio Paradisi* is one of the most copied texts of the medieval period.[24] Few if any medieval writers employ irony and sarcasm to better advantage, and to this he added "sustained and balanced arguments."[25] The breadth of his knowledge is intimidating. His contemporary Bonizo of Sutri writes that Damian is "a man endowed with every kind of knowledge."[26] Some historians judge him to be "a prodigious repository of biblical, natural, classical, dogmatic, and canonical learning," one who "exhibits real competence as a commentator [and] knows how to subject a text to a careful grammatical analysis."[27] Likewise is his com-

21. Letter 65.2, in L, 3:25; B, 2:229. See also Ryan, *Canonical Sources,* 10, 15, and 166, n. 34; and H. E. J. Cowdrey, *Pope Gregory VII, 1073–85* (Oxford: Clarendon Press, 1998), 40.

22. Letter 31.32, in L, 2:24–25; B, 1:304, especially: "Now, therefore, that we have eliminated from the canons this dramatic nonsense . . . I will now set before you canons whose fidelity and authority there can be absolutely no doubt"; Letter 91.18, in L, 5:13, B, 3:10: "This statement, however, cannot be found in [Jerome's] exposition of the faith, at least not in that version which I read"; and Letter 141.7, in L, 6:115; B, 3:491: "But even though the body of canons is presently not at my disposal, I will not hesitate to cite certain statements of the Fathers, either those that were oft repeated from memory, or that can be found in some old sheets of parchment that are on hand." Quote is from Ryan, *Canonical Sources,* 139.

23. See Blum, *St. Peter,* 55, and Marvin Becker, *Medieval Italy* (Bloomington: Indiana University Press, 1981), 65. See also Irven Resnick, *Divine Power and Possibility in St. Peter Damian's "Divine Omnipotentia"* (Leiden: Brill, 1992); and Jean Leclercq, *Saint Pierre Damien: ermite, et homme d'èglise* (Rome: Edizione di Storia e Letteratura, 1960), 172.

24. Leclercq, ibid., 73. He also says that Damian's use of Latin gave hymns "a profundity of vocabulary, a musical rhythm which makes them all but untranslatable."

25. Ryan, *Canonical Sources,* 138. One must always remember the ancient and medieval love of literary exaggeration and judge Damian's writing accordingly.

26. Bonizo of Sutri, *Book which is entitled "To A Friend,"* Bk. 6, in *The Papal Reform of the Eleventh Century,* tr. I. S. Robinson (Manchester: Manchester University Press, 2004), 203. Latin in found in *Liber ad Amicum,* ed. Ernest Dummler, MGH, Libelli de lite imperatorum et pontificum (1891), 1:568–620. One should not forget that Dante chose Damian to represent the ideal man. See Dante, *The Comedy of Dante Alighieri the Florentine: Cantica III Paradise,* tr. Dorothy Sayers and Barbara Reynolds (Harmondsworth: Penguin, 1986), Canto 21, 241–45.

27. Cowdrey, *Pope Gregory,* 39; and Ryan, *Canonical Sources,* 139.

petence in philosophical analysis; his investigation into divine omnipotence gave rise to a concept of possibility distinct from the Greek idea and one that is as essential to Western intellectual history as the principle of plenitude.[28] He embraces interdisciplinary approaches: Letter 86 uses *Physiologus* and *Bestiarius* as the basis for a mystical interpretation of creation; Letter 49 is a commentary on the physical aspects of creation; and Letter 108 is concerned with the material and spiritual ecology of the world.

His scriptural exegesis is consistent with that of his patristic predecessors. Citations pervade both letters and sermons (Blum says his work "almost flounders beneath the mass of scriptural quotations"), but he rarely employs the same passage more than twice.[29] Those few passages he does cite frequently say much about the focus of his thought.[30] Similarly, his repetition of certain nonscriptural terms in both letters and sermons, such as *humanis generis, testimonium* and its derivatives, *martyrium, exemplum,* and *imitatio,* indicates his main concerns.

While he considers letter writing his particular apostolate, he also preached frequently. Unfortunately, only a sampling of sermons has survived, but even these reflect his diverse interests. Their length varies, and if and how much the recorded version varies from the original is hard to ascertain. Likewise, Damian's audience cannot always be ascertained; the only words of address he uses are the indeterminate *dilectissimi* and *fratres carissimmi.* Sometimes the body of a sermon re-

28. Francis Oakley, *Omnipotence, Covenant and Order* (Ithaca, N.Y.: Cornell University Press, 1984), 41–45.

29. Blum, *St. Peter,* 38. As Heinrich Fichtenau, *Heretics and Scholars in the High Middle Ages 1000–1200,* tr. Denise Kaiser (University Park: Pennsylvania State University Press, 1998), 136, observes, a transition was taking place in the era; a laity which had traditionally been expected to memorize only the Lord's Prayer and the Creed was increasingly being familiarized with Scripture via sermons. In this Damian helps usher in what Brian Stock calls a more "literate way of thinking." *Implications of Literacy* (Princeton, N.J.: Princeton University Press, 1983), 455.

30. See appendix 4. In Letters 1–30 he cites the Old Testament 413 times; only fifteen passages are cited more than once. In his sermons he cites the Old Testament 669 times; only 72 of those citations appear more than twice. Hence when we see Damian cite 1 Tm 2:5 (Christ as mediator between God and man) twelve times in his sermons and Mt 11:10–12 (the witness of John the Baptist) ten times, we can assume that these verses are central to his thought.

veals that he is addressing laity or clergy, and we know he preached to crowds.[31] Fifty-two sermons, mostly ones commemorating saints, have survived, along with four fragments.[32] Certain differences between the sermons and letters are apparent. The sermons concentrate heavily on the Incarnation and theological themes that emphasize the human and the divine.[33] *Mediator Dei et hominum* is Damian's most frequently used designation for God in the sermons. Mary is often discussed, as is the Body of Christ and the Eucharist.[34] *Humanis generis* and *humanae conditionis* are other favorite terms.[35] There is no mention of monastic problems or practices, but the sermons do discuss labor, marriage, virginity, *fragilior sexus,* lay pietistic devotions, love of community, and *Redemptor noster.*[36] Closing words most often include strong moral exhortations. The sermons are, generally, more compassionate and inspiring than chastising and condemnatory. They reveal a preacher concerned with guidance in everyday life.

On the one hand, the sermons contain little rational argumentation and rarely discuss the liberal arts, clerical abuses, church reform, penitential practices, or eschatology—all of which are favorite

31. See Letter 65.4–8, in L, 3:27–29; B, 2:232–36. He includes his sermon in the letter and tells us that afterwards they "with one voice promised to carry out anything I should enjoin them."

32. Of these, eight sermons are divided in the manuscripts in two parts; two sermons are in three parts. The occasion for most sermons was feast days. See appendix 3.

33. See, for example, S, 3:191–99; 4:7–40; 5:95; 14:26; 17.2:14, 60; 20:70; 21:59; 22:30; 25:169; 30:105; 31:35; 39:221–; 45:13–, 64, 155, 387; 53:261; 65:1–30; 66:169; 67:124; 72:119; and sermons 18, 48, 61, 63, and 64, passim.

34. For Mediator see, for example, S, 4:18; 5:95; 6:337; 17.1:335; 17.2:391; 34:56; 44:114, 198; 46:317; 49:66, 209; 53:87; and 63:87. Examples for Mary are sermons 45, 46 (passim), 63, and 67 (passim), and S, 24:23; 36:85; 49:200; 53:233; 64:90–; 65:23–. For Body of Christ see S, 2:5–7; 3:5; 6:135, 212; 18:367; 21:69; 38:134; 45:107; and 72:118. For Eucharist, see S, 10 (passim); 33:170–; 39:240; 46:1; 61:49; and 66:59. These phrases and topics are, of course, present in the letters but are proportionately less visible.

35. *Humanis generis* is found in S, 20:2; 25:8; 45:130, 169; 46:148, 177; 48:89; 50:167; 51:111, 244; 66:51; 67:16, 139; and 68:188. For *humanis conditionis* see S, 17.1:129; 17.2:303; 18:1–; 24:2, 30; 25:167; 32:263–88; 46:537, 587; 48:280; 66:61–103; and 74:75. Again, they are proportionately less visible. The exception might be Letter 81 where *mediator Dei et hominum* and *humanis conditionis* are plentiful.

36. For marriage, see S, 4:12–34; 28:90ff; 66:23; and 73:298. For virginity, S, 34; 67; and 68. For women, S, 4:121–49, 165–75, 180; 6:284, 293–95; 34:154; 35:18; 66:67–89; and 68. For devotions, S, 18 and 48. For labor, S, 4:87–93; 233–35; 5:63; 6:152, 330; 8:13–15; 13:164, 183; 22:35–39; 34:129, 152; 35:277; 37:207; and 53:254.

themes in the letters. The letters are often pastoral in tone and intent, and they contain more reasoned explanations of his guidance. *Eadem veritas* is Damian's favorite nomenclature for God here, while *Petrus peccator* is what he calls himself.[37] The letters discuss a broader range of topics, provide a more comprehensive look at Damian's mindset, and are much more numerous than the sermons. In presentation and format they are not innovative. Their content, however, is not typical; it is exceptional. In many, many areas they express thoughts that break with precedent, introduce new perspectives, depart from old methods, and establish fresh approaches to social realities. The letters are, therefore, indispensable to Damian research. I rely on them almost exclusively in this study.

The theology articulated in the letters is profound in its simplicity. Damian begins with the Incarnation. He sees paradox, that baffling reality so perfectly embodied by the Incarnation, as the defining mystery of life, and he understands life within this paradigm. One must engage the world while withdrawing from it, pursue contemplation in the midst of activity, reject cultural determinism while shaping culture, promote faith through reason, discover individualism amidst community, elevate the body by focusing on the soul, and champion rational thought while criticizing it. Most importantly, one must change the temporal world to ready it for the world of eternity. Damian recognizes the purpose of the Incarnation paradox; it is to save, not confuse. It is through the paradoxical union of the divine and the human in the Word Incarnate—*mediator Dei et hominum*—that salvation comes to all.

This realization brings Damian to the keystone of his theology, the concept of witness. It has always surprised me that historians have not spent more time exploring the impact this concept had on Western society. The esteemed M. D. Chenu is the exception. Long ago he told us that, for medieval people, "personal witness was the only

37. The designation is a favorite throughout his career. It is found in his first letter (Letter 1:49, in L, 1:67; B, 1:89), written 1040–41, and in his last datable letter (Letter 170.8, in L, 7:250; B, 4:252–53), written in 1070.

suitable communication," and that the evangelical movement of the twelfth century was the result of "the concomitant effect of Christian witness as such."[38] He documented how "the evangelical shock reverberated throughout the Christian body of the church wherever it encountered the world, especially at those points where laymen bore witness in secular society" and of the power of "this interaction of thought and behavior."[39] He observed how preaching doctrine was often sterile, while "authorized witness within the apostolic movement ... became a vehicle for the religious and social expression of the new Christianity."[40] In the new world medieval society was birthing, "mere moral purification inspired by the zeal for personal reform was not by itself enough." What was needed instead "was the church's encounter with the world, an encounter to be accomplished by a pure and forthright witness, but one sensitive to the values of the new society."[41] For the movement to succeed "its dynamics had to be: witness to the faith."[42] So persuasively did Chenu write about twelfth-century witness that he motivated me to research it further. What I found, however, was that the medieval rediscovery of witness started before the twelfth century. It began with Peter Damian. True, Chenu granted Damian proper attention for his overall role in medieval reform, but, being a historian of the twelfth century, Chenu did not research Damian's role specific to witness. If he had, he would have found Damian's theology of witness and recognized its legacy in the thought of the twelfth-century reformers.

This is not to say that Damian's theology is easy to find. He never offers a formal description or analysis of *testimonium* or its derivatives. He rarely talks explicitly about witness. Yet it is there. It is everywhere. It permeates his thoughts, actions, and words. It is

38. "The Evangelical Awakening," in M. D. Chenu, *Nature, Man and Society in the Twelfth Century,* tr. Jerome Taylor and Lester Little (Chicago: University of Chicago Press, 1968), 247–48; French edition published in 1957.

39. Ibid., 259.

40. Ibid., 261.

41. "Nature and Man—The Renaissance of the Twelfth Century," in ibid., 38.

42. "Monks, Canons and Laymen in Search of the Apostolic Life," in ibid., 217.

the lens through which he sees and judges all. It is a way of life, a rule directing his behavior, an all-inclusive demand for consistency in mind and body, a responsibility that shaped every aspect of his being. For Damian, witness is the link that binds thoughts to actions, individuals to community, religious to society. It is *the* vehicle for the religious and social expression that Chenu talks about.

Damian's reflection on the power and need for witness is not radical in itself. It is, after all, a scriptural concept with a long, rich history. It begins with Yahweh's call to Israel to make known to other nations its experience of the divine: "Let all the nations gather together, let the people assemble! . . . You are my witnesses, says the Lord, my servants whom I have chosen to know and believe in me and understand that it is I" (Is 43:9–10). This witness is to encompass Israel's whole existence. Everything it says and does is to reflect the message of Yahweh. When John the Baptist transmits the Old Law to the New, the obligation to witness is included. He is the first to bear witness to Jesus: "Now I have seen for myself and have testified, 'This is God's Chosen One'" (Jn 1:34). Jesus himself discusses the importance of John's witness and of witness in general. It is essential in salvation history.

> If I witness on my behalf, you cannot verify my testimony; but there is another who is testifying on my behalf, and the testimony he renders me I know can be verified. You have sent to John, who has testified to the truth. (Not that I myself accept such human testimony—I refer to these things only for your salvation.) He was the lamp, set aflame and burning brightly, and for a while you exulted willingly in his light. Yet I have testimony greater than John's, namely, the works the Father has given me to accomplish. (Jn 5:31–38)

Without works, witness is inferior. Without witness, Jesus' life defies comprehension, for Christianity is first and foremost a historical religion with an incarnate God: "The way we came to understand love was that [Jesus] laid down his life for us" (1 Jn 3:16). Humans need the testimony of others in order to believe. Once the witness of John convinced the first Christians of Jesus' truth, they had an obligation to add their witness to John's. Nowhere is this mandate more plainly stated than in the very last command of Jesus while on earth: "'You are to be my witnesses in Jerusalem, throughout Judea and Samaria, yes, even to the ends of the earth.' No sooner had he said this than he was lifted up before their eyes in a cloud which took him from their sight" (Acts 1:8–9). That the disciples understood the seriousness of this final mandate is manifest throughout Acts, where the apostles refer to themselves in the post-Resurrection world as witnesses more frequently than any other designation.[43] It is an inclusive title used to express the totality of their faith and their social responsibility.

Herein lies the historical significance of witness. It mandates a relationship between the individual and the community. It is a demanding relationship of communication and interdependence: to be saved, one must save others. Moreover, it involves the whole person and all society, for witness is comprehensive, not selective. It encompasses body and soul, at all times, in all places, and to all peoples. It is how Jesus bore witness. The first Christian community was quick to recognize the power of witness (Acts 4:32–33) and the efficacy of witness through actions as well as words. As the centuries passed, Christians continued to bear witness, particularly through personal example, but they rarely reflected upon the concept or their obligation to bear witness.[44] This led to the regrettable situation whereby the relationship established by witness between the individual and society was gradually forgotten, and with it, the need to have lives reflect beliefs. Good Christians still bore witness to Christian beliefs, but it was seldom intended or consciously given. Disparity increased between the truths of Christianity and the message communicated by the Church and its members. Exacerbating the problem was neglect of the principle of adaptability inherent in witness. Witness is communication, and, as such, the articulator must speak in a language the audience understands and adapt the medium of the mes-

43. It is used twenty-four times in Acts alone, and considering the medieval emphasis on *vita apostolica,* this is highly noteworthy. See Allison Trites, *The Concept of Witness in New Testament Thought* (Cambridge: Cambridge University Press, 1977), and discussion below in chap. 1.

44. The exception is Rule of St. Augustine. See my "The Rule of St. Augustine in Medieval Monasticism," *Proceedings of the PMR Conference* 11 (1986), 143–50.

sage appropriately when necessary for comprehension. By the time we get to the late tenth century, these essentials were neglected and the obligation to bear witness often forgotten.

This is where Damian comes into the picture. His theology of witness is a shift in emphasis, one that gives him a perspective on eleventh-century life that few had and many needed. He saw a society whose actions were not in harmony with its stated beliefs. He observed a church behaving in ways that contradicted its teachings. He was aware of a vast chasm between principles and performance. He recognized the Church's unwillingness to adapt its witness when and where needed. With this new vision Damian gave birth to numerous concepts, notions, attitudes, and even institutions that would eventually become part of the fabric of Western culture. The common thread running through all of Damian's contributions is this: witness. Caroline Walker Bynum once commented that "the years between 1050 and 1215 saw a fundamental change in men's basic conceptions of the Christian life."[45] I believe that Damian's insistence on witness was the snowball that started the avalanche.

It is hard to exaggerate Damian's influence on eleventh-century society, religious life, papal politics, and intellectual activity. We have in Damian's writings an opportunity to explore the inner workings of a century, "arguably the greatest turning point in the history of Christianity" and in the development of Western culture.[46] If this study provides a better grasp of eleventh-century life, it has achieved much. It can also serve another purpose. There is a timelessness about Damian's theology. It transcends the eleventh century. It is *catholic* in the deepest sense of the word. Its principles are as applicable to our world as to his. I leave it up to the readers to perform this last task, and I predict that if they do allow Damian's insights to shine light on modern problems, the rewards will be plentiful.

45. Caroline Walker Bynum, "The Spirituality of Regular Canons in the Twelfth Century: A New Approach," *Medievalia et humanistica,* n.s. 4 (1973), 3.

46. Phyllis Jestice, *Wayward Monks and the Religious Revolution of the Eleventh Century* (Leiden: Brill, 1997), 12.

One

ITALY AT THE MILLENNIUM

"Scarcely five years before I was born, Otto III passed away," Peter Damian writes to Duke Godfrey of Tuscany.[1] This, the only reference Damian makes to the date of his birth, would be 1007, and most scholars accept the date as valid.[2] Peter held Emperor Otto III in high regard, for both had a special relationship with Ravenna, a northern Italian city of ancient Roman glory and Peter's birthplace. It was in Ravenna in 996 that the Roman ambassador first greeted Otto and his army after he took over the reins of the empire, and it was here that Otto nominated his cousin Bruno of Corinthia to be the first German pope (Gregory V). Of greater consideration to Damian, though, was Otto's relationship to the nascent eremitic movement stirring throughout Italy and centered around one monk in particular, Romuald of Ravenna. Damian knew well the stories concerning Otto and Romuald. In his vita of Romuald Damian records two encounters these leaders had in Ravenna in 998. In the first, "the young emperor Otto, wishing to reform the abbey [of Sant' Apollinare in Classe at Ravenna], gave the monks the faculty to freely elect whomever they would choose. Without hesitation and unanimously they asked for Romuald."[3] Romuald accepted reluctantly but re-

1. Letter 67.20, in L, 3:78; B, 2:288.
2. A thorough discussion of the birth year is found in Little, "Personal Development."
3. VR 22 (203).

signed a year later; he spend the rest of his days alternately as a hermit and as an advocate and founder of monastic communities. In the second encounter we see how personal Otto III's interest in monasticism was. While staying at Sant' Apollinare, Otto "followed the monastic regime of fasting and prayer" and "even promised Romuald to abdicate his imperial crown for a monk's cowl."[4] Otto's death at age twenty-one eliminated that possibility, but we have no reason to question the sincerity of his youthful promise.

This was Damian's world, a world with undefined boundaries between *regnum* and *sacerdotium*. One day living the austere life of a monk, another day enjoying the sumptuous court life at his palace on Aventine Hill, Otto felt no contradiction, nor did his contemporaries accuse him of any. Romuald considered himself first and foremost a hermit, yet frequented imperial courts, socialized with nobility, preached to crowds, and negotiated political settlements; he was not accused of hypocrisy.[5] Throughout the early Middle Ages both worlds were so intertwined that it is misleading to discuss them as separate worlds, yet by the thirteenth century there is a clear distinction. The eleventh century, especially eleventh-century Italy, is when and where the transition begins. Historians describe this transition in various ways. It was "the time when European civilization, as we know it, was created."[6] It was also a time of challenges and possibilities; the demise of charismatic culture and the introduction of an intellectual one; the "mutation de l'an mil"; a transforming period; a turning point in Western history; a pivotal epoch.[7] And so on. When all is said and done, however, there is basic agreement: the eleventh century is of great historical consequence.

4. VR, 26 (210).

5. For example, see ibid., 35 (229–30); 40 (237); 22 (204); 23 (205–6); and 23 (206).

6. Kathleen Cushing, *Papacy and Law in the Gregorian Revolution* (Oxford: Clarendon Press, 1998), 14, summarizing the thesis of "French historians over the past two generations."

7. Becker, *Medieval Italy*, 59–98; Stephen Jaeger, *The Envy of Angels* (Philadelphia: University of Pennsylvania Press, 1994); Jean-Pierre Poly and Eric Bournazel, *La Mutation féodale Xe-XIIe siècles*, 2nd ed. (Paris: Pressus Universitaires de France, c. 1980); G. Bois, *The Transformation of the Year 1000*, tr. J. Birrell (Manchester: Manchester University Press,

The Basics

Northern Italy, with its great plain surrounded by the Alps and its Po, Adege, and Reno valleys, was the richest region of early medieval Italy. Only Rome and Naples could compete with the northern cities of Milan, Pavia, Verona, and Ravenna in population or political importance. The Apennines border the Po plain on the south and form a natural barrier between the north and the rest of Italy. These mountains split Italy down the middle of central and south Italy, where, by mid-tenth century numerous river valleys supported a growing network of cities and rural communes. Rome was by far the most important. In southern Italy the Apennines are not as high as in central Italy, but there are fewer fertile plains to support cities. The region's main cities—Capua, Naples, Benevento, Salerno, and Amalfi—clustered around the middle of the Campagna plain. They served as the Mediterranean trading center for the rest of Italy; in mid-eleventh century Damian's friend Abbott Desiderius of Monte Cassino traveled to Amalfi to buy Byzantine silk and silver vessels for an anticipated visit from Emperor Henry IV.[8]

For all its prestige, Rome at the millennium was not a thriving city. Estimates place its population at twenty-five thousand to thirty thousand people.[9] There was little commerce in the city, and its main source of income was pilgrims, who, besides being the mainstay of the Roman economy, served as cultural conduits between Italy and the rest of the West.[10] Only powerful Roman families were able to provide Rome with a stable government and military defense, but these necessities came with the exorbitant price of corruption and violence. In the rural areas surrounding Rome monasteries and epis-

1992); Horst Fuhrmann, *Germany in the High Middle Ages, 1050–1200,* tr. Timothy Reuter (Cambridge: Cambridge University Press, 1986); Cushing, *Papacy,* 14.

8. Henry Willard, *Abbot Desiderius and the Ties between Montecassino and Amalfi in the Eleventh Century,* Miscellanea Cassinese 37 (Badea de Montecassino, 1973), 42–43.

9. Becker, *Medieval Italy,* 15, estimates the population for all Italy at 4.5 million in 700, 5.5 million in 950, and 10 million in 1200. It had 262 settlements in the ninth century, 552 in the tenth, 945 in the eleventh, and 1014 in the twelfth.

10. See G. T. Radan, "The Beginning of Eremitical Architecture in Tuscany," *Augustiana* 53.1 (2003), 296–97.

copal sees dominated. During the tenth century the families, monasteries, and bishops engaged in *incastellamento,* whereby villagers were moved to hilltop *castelli* enclosed by a stone wall. It is unclear whether the motive for these fortified settlements was defense against the Saracens, land clearance, or exploitation. Regardless of the motive, these new villages, each of which could support between two hundred and three hundred inhabitants, resulted in internal colonization and created production centers with considerable economic freedom. They increased population and forced cooperation among the inhabitants. The villagers were responsible for village defense, assessed taxes, and maintained the walls, bridges, and roads.[11] Contracts established rents, which were fairly low. Social mobility was possible. Some villagers became lords of their *castelli,* while merchants and artisans were elevated in stature. In the south, fortified villages brought stability of tenure and free status; only the establishment of rural communes at the end of the eleventh century provided peasants with better conditions. *Incastellamento* gave large landowners the means to reorganize their holdings for more efficient management and a leading role in determining the development of the region.[12]

Not all would agree with such a rosy assessment of *incastellamento.* Peasants were coerced into leaving ancient family homes and forced into artificial social networks complete with new sources of tension and dispute. Familial ties were broken, and centuries-old customs and patterns of civility abandoned.[13] The line between protection and the exercise of authority was often hard to find. Social mobility gave the violent as well as the able ready access to positions of power. Land prices fluctuated to the benefit of the few and detriment of the many.[14]

11. Becker, *Medieval Italy,* 93–95. He notes that before 1000 eleven fortified villages were established, 52 by 1050, and 130 by 1100.

12. See John Howe, *Church Reform and Social Change in Eleventh-Century Italy: Dominic of Soro and His Patrons* (Philadelphia: University of Pennsylvania Press, 1997), 10–12.

13. Chris Wickham, *Early Medieval Italy* (Ann Arbor: University of Michigan Press, 1981), 165–67.

14. R. I. Moore, "Family, Community and Cult on the Eve of the Gregorian Reform," *Transactions of the Royal Historical Society,* n.s. 5, 30 (1980), 58–59.

Despite the deficiencies present in tenth-century Italy, it was the most advanced region in the West and well poised to lead the way in economic, civic, and educational developments. Towns began to grow, and markets became more numerous. By the end of the tenth century Venice, Pisa, Ostia, Genoa, and Amalfi were established port cities. Milan, which was probably the largest northern Italian city throughout the early Middle Ages, had a thriving commerce. With it came an increase in stature and wealth for merchants, who used both to become powerful landowners within the city boundaries. Some cities, such as Pavia, where trade was surging, became intellectual centers. In the opening decades of the eleventh century the ancient and rigid *ministeria* organization of artisans, craftsmen, and merchants was replaced with a new business model, freer and more competitive. Changes in vocabulary, "the beginnings of a new language, that of the scholastic," followed quickly upon the heels of these social and economic developments.[15] Intellectual activity increased. Since the ninth century, northern Italy had had a unique group of literate legal professionals serving as judges and notaries, and by mid-eleventh century the region was a known center for the study of law in the West. Around 1020 the earliest glosses of the Lombard code appeared in Pavia, and by mid-century Justinian's works were in circulation.[16] Western physicians traveled to Salerno as early as the tenth century to study medicine, and in the eleventh century the city drew students from Byzantium and the Muslim world. The rhetorical arts found a home in Pavia, Parma, and Milan.

Southern Italy was all that remained of Byzantium's once extensive landholdings on the peninsula. Ravenna, a Roman and then a Byzantine imperial city, passed into the hands of the Lombards in the mid-eighth century. The Franks came next, and in 784 Ravenna became part of the Papal States. During the early Middle Ages Ravenna functioned as the center for the study of Roman law, and its

15. Becker, *Medieval Italy,* 64.

16. Charles Radding, "Legal Theory and Practice in Eleventh Century Italy," *Law and History Review* 21.2 (2003), 377–81.

school remained so until Bologna surpassed it. Manuscript production was limited in Byzantine territory, but active enough to produce four distinct calligraphic styles. The first bilingual manuscripts date from the eleventh century.[17] With the coming of the Normans manuscript production increased. Arriving in southern Italy in 1017, Normans first engaged the Byzantines in Apulia. By 1029 they received territory for services to the duke of Naples, and by 1046 they ruled territory in northern Apulia. Calabria (host to a profitable silk industry) and all of Apulia was under their control by 1059. The last Byzantine stronghold of Bari fell in 1071. It took the Normans until 1091 to wrestle Sicily away from the Muslims, but by the end of the eleventh century Italy was wholly in Western hands. The Norman conquest of Byzantine lands may have contributed to events leading up to the schism of 1054 between Rome and Constantinople, although an alliance between the pope and the Normans was formed five years after the schism began.

Interest in art began to revive around this time. There were some significant changes in architecture. Built in the ninth century, San Pietro at Agliate was one of the first churches constructed with elements characteristic of a new style we call Romanesque. Abbot Guido of Ravenna oversaw the building of a new abbey church at Pomposa, one of the best examples of Lombard Romanesque architecture. Matilda, countess of Tuscany, was an active patron of the arts in the latter half of the eleventh century and did much to encourage Romanesque architecture throughout her territory. In Milan efforts to rebuild the great Basilica di Sant Ambrogio began with the south tower in the tenth century, while the entire church was rebuilt in 1067. Inside, the crypt of St. Ambrose and the altar canopy date from the tenth century. Sant Ambrogio and the neighboring Sant Michele at Pavia are significant for their solutions to vaulting the naves. San Minniato al Monte, with its unusual interior and raised sanctuary, is one of the earliest (1018–62) surviving churches

17. Andre Guillou, "Production and Profits in the Byzantine Province of Italy (Tenth to Eleventh Centuries): An Expanding Society," *Dumbarton Oaks Papers* 28 (1974), 89–109.

in Florence. The cathedral and baptistery of Pisa were begun in 1063 (the campanile dates from 1174) in celebration of the Pisan defeat of the Saracen fleet near Palermo. St. Mark's in Venice was also begun in 1063. Abbot Desiderius's rebuilding of the abbey church of Monte Cassino has, unfortunately, not survived, but a series of frescos modeled on Monte Cassino's can be found in Sant Angelo in Formis. Likewise, the cathedral of Torcello survives as an excellent example of early eleventh century Italian architecture. In music, Guy of Arezzo promoted the use of the staff, which consequently opened the door to innumerable musical developments.

Politics: *Regnum* and *Sacerdotium*

Eleventh-century Italy was dominated by local lords, German emperors, and popes. Otto I tied the destinies of Germany and Italy, empire and papacy, together for the next nine centuries when he was crowned *imperator augustus romanorum et francorum* by Pope John XII in 962. He swore to protect church and pope, never to "hold court or make laws within papal jurisdiction," to restore all papal lands, and to insure that his successor would likewise be "your helper in defense of the ecclesiastical state."[18] When the politically inept pope fled the city after betraying Otto I, the emperor called for a synod, its goal being the deposition of John XII and the elevation of a new pope, Leo VIII (963–65). This was accomplished on December 1, 963, but it only succeeded in worsening the chaos.

Revolt, reinstatement, murder, imperial appointment, and random excommunication continued for decades. There was no real reform or resolution. By the time Otto II came to power (973–83), two factors of immense political influence were in place, German presence in Italy and the empire's control of ecclesiastical offices by right of appointment. Married to the Byzantine princess Theophano in 982, Otto II tried unsuccessfully to rebuff the Saracens' attack on Byzantine cities in southern Italy, but did successfully introduce Byzantine culture into his German and Italian domains. The mon-

18. MGH, G. H. Pertz (Hanover, 1873), 4:29.

asteries in Reichenau and Echternach gave birth to a new artistic style based on Byzantine models. Monte Cassino and Lucca followed suit. While Otto III (983–1002)—*stupor mundi*—did little to advance German interests in Italy during his short and youthful reign, he did further solidify the bond between crown and church. He appointed his former tutor, Gerbert of Aurillac, to the throne of Peter as Sylvester II (999–1003).[19]

Otto III died in 1002, the year before Sylvester did, and Otto's cousin Henry of Bavaria (1002–24), the last of the Ottonian emperors, was elected. It was during his reign that Damian was born. Admired for his personal piety (he was canonized in 1146), Henry II enjoys a respectable reputation as emperor.[20] He began his reign with a focus on Germany, a strategy not appreciated by German nobles accustomed to ruling without imperial interference.[21] He could not ignore Italy forever, though, if he hoped to receive his imperial crown, so in 1014 Henry and his army proceeded to Rome for his coronation and then promptly left. He returned in 1021 to battle with the Greeks in Apulia; during this trip he stopped at Monte Cassino and became ill. His subsequent miraculous cure there became the stuff of legends, as did his desire to become a monk.[22] His relationship with monasticism went well beyond his short stay at Monte Cassino. He actively supported the Cluniac movement and recognized eighty-five monasteries as royal houses with protection and patronage. His status as canon of numerous cathedrals placed him within the clerical order, and his appointments of clergy to imperial administrative posts, along with his generous endowments of land to the church, further blurred the lines between *regnum* and *sacerdotium*.

19. See Gerbert of Aurillac, *Die abriefsammlung Gerberts vom Reims,* ed. Fritz Weigle, MGH, Briefe der deuschen Kaiserzeit 2 (Weiman: Böhlau, 1966). Even the choice of name indicates Gerbert and Otto's desire to create the Roman world: Sylvester I was pope/advisor during the reign of Constantine.

20. See his vita in AASS, July, v.3, in MGH, SS, 4.

21. This focus can be seen in Henry's dropping Otto III's *renovatio imperii romanorum* for the more limited *renovatio regni francorum.*

22. After vowing obedience to the abbot of Saint-Vanne at Verdun, legend tells us, the abbot commanded him to continue ruling the empire.

Conrad II (1024–39) came next, and with him, the Salian dynasty. He disagreed with Henry II's ecclesiastical policies and turned instead to lay *ministeriales,* low-born men who owed their new positions of power wholly to the emperor. Creation of this class may be Conrad II's greatest political contribution, for it anticipated the rise of the middle class in Italy, a factor at the heart of Western economic and social development. His son Henry III (1039–56) ruled next; these were the prime years of Damian's adult life. Peter had a personal relationship with Henry III, close enough for Peter to remind the emperor of a promise he had made at Sant' Apollinare to honor any petitions for pardon Peter should make.[23] Henry III shared Henry II's reputation for sanctity and devotion to reform, probably surpassing him, despite the fact that Henry III was never canonized.[24] Henry III was the first emperor to denounce simoniac practices, although he did retain the right to invest prelates with staff and ring; in 1046 Damian wrote the emperor to praise him for removing the archbishop of Ravenna, "who was trafficking in the Church."[25] This was also the year Henry called the synod of Sutri to depose three popes and elect a fourth.

The situation was complex yet simple, an almost predictable result of the factors surrounding the pre-reform papacy. After the death of Pope Sylvester II in 1003, a series of obscure popes reigned. In 1012 Gregory of Tusculum gained control of the papacy and placed two sons (Benedict VIII and John XIX) and a fourteen-year-old grandson (Benedict IX) on the throne, consecutively. Benedict IX's life is particularly instructive for any who doubt the extent of corruption visited upon the papacy by Italian families. Total debauchery, attempted assassinations, uprisings, imperial interventions, and the appearance of an anti-pope (Sylvester III) filled the years of Benedict's reign. Eventually he decided to abdicate (as tradition has it, to marry) and thus to sell the throne. Giovanni Gratiano, an

23. Letter 43.4, in L, 2:219–20; B, 2:6.

24. See Damian's comments, Letter 20.1, in L, 1:194; B, 1:199–202, telling of many reports and of the proof in words and deeds of the emperor's "holiness and virtuous gifts."

25. Letter 20.1, in L, 1:195; B, 1:201.

archpriest of St. John at the Latin Gate, was from all reports a sincere and well-intended individual. He was disgusted at the level to which Benedict IX had lowered the papacy, so he supposedly bought the office for fifteen hundred pounds and took the name Gregory VI. When Benedict IX had assumed the throne, Damian had written an enthusiastic letter of congratulations to him after his election; apparently he was unaware at first of a money payment.[26] Soon it was common knowledge, though, and twenty months later, when Gregory failed in his attempt to restore order in Rome, the taint of his simony played into the hands of Benedict IX and Sylvester III, who had both decided to return to Rome and resume their reigns.[27] Three popes ruling at once was more than even the Romans could tolerate, so they appealed to the emperor. On December 20, 1046, Henry III convened the synod at Sutri. Sylvester III was condemned and imprisoned, Gregory VI abdicated and went into exile in Germany (with his chaplain, Hildebrand), Benedict IX was deposed, and the emperor nominated and the synod elected Clement II as pope.[28]

Henry III's intention throughout was clear, "to lift the papacy out of the field of Roman party politics."[29] Furthermore, Henry was not acting out of a desire to control the universal church but rather was "controlled completely by the immediate political interests of the existing empire."[30] Benedict IX did not made it easy for Henry to attain his goal. The pope returned to Rome once more, forcing

26. See Letter 13, esp. n. 2. See R. L. Poole, "Benedict IX and Gregory VI," *Proceedings of the British Academy* 8 (1917–18), 199–235, for a lenient view of the transaction; if payment is made "to remove a scandalous holder . . . I leave to those better versed in canon law than I to decide"(219) whether it is truly simony.

27. Letter 72.63, in L, 3:145; B, 2:363: "Since payment had intervened, he [Gregory VI] who accepted the money was deposed."

28. Hildebrand remained in Germany probably until Gregory's death in December 1047. See Cowdrey, *Pope Gregory*, 29, for reconstruction of Hildebrand's life during exile.

29. G. Tellenbach, *Church, State and Christian Society at the Time of the Investiture Contest,* tr. R. F. Bennett (Toronto: University of Toronto Press, repr.1991), 176. Tellenbach also reminds us that the question of this being religiously or politically motivated is a modern, not medieval, question.

30. Paul Kehr, *Vier Kapitel aus der Geschichte Kaiser Heinrichs III* (1930), 48, cited in ibid., 171. Tellenbach agrees, as does Augustin Fliche, *La réforme grégorienne,* 3 vols. (Paris: Spicilegium sacrum Lovaniense, 1924–27), 1:110.

Henry in July 1048 to chase him out of the city. This time it was permanent; Benedict disappeared into legend. Writing to Pope Nicholas II years later, Peter Damian relates that Benedict appeared to a man once as a huge monster. "I find no mystery behind his vision," Damian declares, "for, since this man [Benedict] lived at the very height of luxury from the beginning of his calamitous pontificate until the end, it is proper that he appear to have the ears and tail of an ass."[31] So ends a tumultuous era in papal history; "there begins a new epoch in the history of western Europe."[32]

The moment may not have been as dramatic and definitive, but surely it played a significant role in future developments. For generations now these events have been considered within the historiographical motif of the Gregorian Reform, the pre-Gregory VII part of the story. Periodically the motif is challenged, but, for better or worse, it remains standing.[33] Whatever we choose to call it, the institution of the papacy underwent changes in the mid-eleventh century, changes that Peter Damian and his contemporaries actively promoted. Clement II and Damasus II died within months of their elections, but by the time Emperor Henry II appointed Bruno of Toul as Pope Leo IX (1049–54), precedent was firmly established. For a few centuries at least, Italian families could no longer treat the papacy as a prize to be won by battle with enemies.[34] It was in a council of bishops at Worms "in the presence of the glorious Henry II" that Bruno "was unanimously chosen ... [and] seeing, therefore, that there was no way in which he could escape the emperor's command," Bruno accepted the office, but only "on the condition that he received

31. Letter 72.22, in L, 3:124–25; B, 2:337.

32. Tellenbach, *Church,* 88.

33. See O. Capitani, "Esiste un' età gregoriana? Considerazione sulle tendenze di' una storiografia medievistica," *Rivista di storia e letteratura religiosa* 1 (1965), 454–81; G. T. Gilchrist, "Was There a Gregorian Reform Movement in the Eleventh Century?" *Canadian Catholic Historical Association Study Sessions* 37 (1970), 1–10; Karl Leyser, "On the Eve of the First European Revolution," in *Communications and Power in Medieval Europe,* ed. T. Reuter, 1–20 (London: Hambledon Press, 1994); and Cushing, *Papacy.*

34. Families once more gained control during the early modern period, although thankfully their struggles were slightly less violent. Their debauchery was probably equal if not worse after their victory.

the general consent of all the Roman clergy and people."[35] The new pope was determined to bring respect back to the office, and he began his reform by calling his first synod at Rome in April 1049. Here "he restored the decisions of the four principal synods ... condemned the heresy of simony ... and deposed certain bishops whom the heresy marked."[36] Throughout his reign he attacked clerical abuses and asserted the right of the pope to legislate for the secular as well as ecclesiastical world.[37] Leo also drew into his circle men who developed the ideas that guided ecclesiastical reform during the next four decades: Humbert of Silva-Candida, Hildebrand, Boniface of Albano, and, of course, Peter Damian.

Peter's reputation was well established by the mid-eleventh century. After gaining a substantial reputation in Ravenna as a scholar and teacher of rhetoric, around 1035 he entered the monastery founded by a disciple of Romuald's, Ludolph, at Fonte Avellana.[38] After a year's novitiate he traveled throughout Italy and in 1040

35. *The Life of Pope Leo IX,* 2:4, in *The Papal Reform of the Eleventh Century: The Lives of Pope Leo IX and Pope Gregory VII,* tr. I. S. Robinson (Manchester: Manchester University Press, 2004), 130–31.

36. Ibid., 2:10, 136.

37. Unfortunately, Leo also promulgated an extremely offensive papal act in his reform. Peter writes: "In plenary synod it was Pope Leo of blessed memory, who decreed that whenever these damnable women, living with priests as their mistresses, were found living within the walls of the city of Rome, they were to be condemned from then on to be slaves of the Lateran palace." Doubly offensive, especially for a self-appointed defender of Damian's social thought like myself, is Damian's reaction to the decree: "I have also decided to publicize this salutary law, so replete with justice and equity, throughout all dioceses, so that ... every bishop may acquire as slaves of his diocese all the women in his territory that he finds living in sacrilegious union with priests. It is clearly a matter of justice, that those who have stolen the ministry of the servants of God at the holy altar, should at least reimburse the bishop with their service." Letter 112.37, in L, 5:278; B, 280–81. I see this as a reminder of how arduous the task is to rise above the mentality and confines of one's society, even for a genius and saint. See Cushing, *Papacy,* 20.

38. See John of Lodi, *Vita B. Petri Damiani,* PL 144, 117. Romualdian monasteries include those founded or reformed by Romuald and by the Hermitage of Fonte Avellana. The Camaldolese Congregation was established as an autonomous union of houses nearly a century after Romuald's death by Pope Paschal II's bulls *Ad hoc nos* (1105) and *Gratias Deo* (1113). The Avellanita Congregation (also known as Congregation of the Dove) received its bull of establishment in 1076 by Gregory VII; it was suppressed in 1569 and its members joined the Camaldolese Congregation. See Peter-Damian Belisle, "Primitive Romuladian/Camaldolese Spirituality," *Cistercian Quarterly* 3 (1996), 413–29.

he was asked by Abbot Guido of Pomposa to teach Scripture to his monks. Next he stayed at St. Vincent's monastery at Petra Pertusa, reformed the house, and began writing the life of Romuald. By 1043 Peter was prior of Fonte Avellana (the community numbered about twenty hermits), and he began founding hermitages and cenobitic houses that he loosely gathered into a congregation. With each accomplishment his reputation increased, aided in large part by his growing literary output. He began casting his net in a wider circle. In 1043 he appealed indirectly to the papacy; two years later he corresponded directly, and in the spring of 1046 he wrote the emperor.[39] That year he also participated in the synod at Sutri. His reputation as a reformer, author, practical politician, scholar, and theologian continued to grow, and in 1059 he found himself elevated (he tells us, "I did not enter the net but was violently ensnared") to the prestigious position of cardinal-bishop of Ostia by Pope Stephen IX (1057–58).[40] Upon Stephen's death months later, yet another election crisis surfaced, one that led to the Papal Election Decree of 1059. Damian tells us that Stephen IX declared that "if he [Stephen] were to die before Hildebrand ... should return from the court of the empress, no one should elect a pope."[41] Count Gregory of Tusculum ignored Stephen's command and on April 5, 1058, six days after Stephen's death, his papal candidate, Cardinal John II of Velletri, was installed as Pope Benedict X (1058–59). As the designated consecrator of popes, Damian went into hiding until Hildebrand returned.[42] In December

39. See letters 4, 11, 13, and 20. His relationship with emperors and popes continued throughout his life. In 1069 he tells us that "I have often spoken with his majesty the emperor, telling him what I thought should be said, and at papal invitation I have participated in councils." Letter 165.81, in L, 7:221; B, 4:223.

40. Letter 57.3, in L, 2:370; B, 2.165. See also Letters 57, 72, and 79. In Letter 75.3, in L, 3:157; B, 2:376, Damian hints that Hildebrand was behind his appointment. He also writes that he "was compelled—however it was done" to accept his election. In Letter 48.2, in L, 2:263; B, 2:53.

41. Letter 58.4, in L, 2:392; B, 2:193–94. Cowdrey, *Pope Gregory,* speculates that this may have been because of negotiations in progress with the empire regarding papal elections, or because he had commissioned Hildebrand to get German approval of his candidate, Gebhard of Florence.

42. If the papal nominee was not already a bishop, it fell to the cardinal-bishop of Ostia to consecrate him.

Damian and his colleagues elected Gebhard of Florence and on January 24, 1059, Gebhard was installed as Pope Nicholas II (1059–61). On April 13 Nicholas convened the Lateran synod that promulgated the election decree. One hundred thirteen bishops attended, nearly all Italian and no powerful imperial bishop.

Scholars have debated who wrote the actual text, but there is little doubt that the decree reflected Damian's major concerns and solutions.[43] Already in the fall of 1057 Damian had addressed a treatise to his fellow cardinals describing his ideal bishop, and it "found its echo" in the decree two years later.[44] Sometime that first year Nicholas II sent Anselm of Baggio, bishop of Lucca, and Peter Damian to Milan as his legates. Damian's report to Hildebrand on his mission includes an exposition of Damian's conception of papal authority and privileges.[45] The 1059 synod also dealt with problems within clerical and canonical religious life, problems that Damian had written about at length in Letter 39, *De communi vita canonicorum* (ca. 1051).

The death of Nicholas II in 1061 brought Damian's friend Anselm of Baggio to the throne as Alexander II and with that, a schism. The Election Decree included a centuries-old custom of first offering the papacy to any available Roman cleric, and only after that, to an outsider.[46] When the Roman clergy elected Anselm, the Lombard bishops balked and petitioned the court of the young Emperor Henry IV (1056–1106) to ignore Anselm's election and endorse their candidate, Cadalus. Damian placed himself in the forefront of the dispute, writing two passionate open letters to Cadalus condemning his

43. Kennerly Woody, "Sagena Piscatoris: Peter Damian and the Papal Election Decree of 1059," *Viator* 1 (1970), 33–54, presents evidence that at minimum Damian wrote the *narratio* of the decree. Cowdrey, *Pope Gregory,* 44, says that it "seems" to be the work of Damian and Humbert. Text is in Dether Jasper, "Das papstwahldekret von 1059," *Beiträge zur Geschichte und Quellenkunde des MA* 12 (1986), 98–119.

44. Blum, intro. to Letter 48, in L, 2:263.

45. See Letter 65.5, in L, 3:27; B, 2:233–34: "The Word ... founded the Roman Church. Clearly, it enjoys privilege and is supported by his authority. And so without doubt, whoever deprives any church of its rights commits an injustice, but if one attempts to deny the Roman Church the privilege granted it by the head of all the churches himself, he doubtless falls into heresy."

46. Jasper, "Papstwahldekret," 104.

actions.[47] One letter is of particular note, for it includes *Disceptatio synodalis,* a report of a fictitious debate between papal and imperial lawyers over the meaning of the Election Decree. Damian concludes his debate with a plea for compromised peace in a statement describing the dual authority of *regnum* and *sacerdotium.*[48]

By then Peter's work in clerical, ecclesiastical, and monastic matters was vast, and to review it is to review the major issues of the day. *Liber Gomorrhianus* (1049) concerned itself with clerical reform, particularly issues of clerical incontinence; *Liber gratissimus* (1052) was a vehement protest against simony.[49] He reshaped the physical and spiritual essence of Fonte Avellana, paying particular attention to its library; he founded hermitages and reformed existing monasteries.[50] Like Romuald, "I traveled extensively with a de-

47. Letters 88 and 89.

48. Letter 89.102, in L, 3:368; B, 2:572: "Thus, as these two, the empire and the priesthood, by divine dispensation are united in the one mediator between God and men, so may these two exalted persons be joined together in such harmony that, by a certain bond of mutual love, we may behold the emperor in the Roman pontiff and the Roman pontiff in the emperor, reserving to the pope, however, the dignity no other may possess. Likewise, ... the pope should be able to use civil law to control offenders, and the emperor with his bishops should be permitted to adjudicate matters where the welfare of souls is involved.... The former, as a father, should always enjoy paramount dignity by reason of his paternal rights; the latter, as his unique and special son, should rest securely in his loving embrace."

49. The latter is addressed to Henry, archbishop of Ravenna, and was criticized by Humbert of Silva Candida who answered with his own treatise, *Libri tres adversus simoniacos* (MGH, Libelli de Lite, ed. F. Thaner [1891], 1:95–253). The issue was still unsettled in 1061, because, Damian writes, "I was unable to elicit from [Henry] even the slightest spark of a solution," and so Damian appended two paragraphs to it and sent the entire corpus this time to Pope Nicholas II, months before his death. See B, 1:385–88, n. 3

50. At Fonte Avellana Damian build the cloister, acquired bells, two silver chalices, a silver cross, coverings for the altar, and vestments. He donated his books to the library and corrected codices. See Letter 18.20–21, in L, 1:169; B, 1:177–78. His "rule" and its exposition are found in Letters 18 and 50, respectively. The hermitages and monasteries were: St. Vincent at Furlo; Holy Trinity near Frontale; St. John the Baptist at Acerata; St. Nicolas near Ocri; Montepregio, St. Barnabas Gamugno, St. Bartholomew, St. Gregory, in Conca; Holy Mary of Sitria and Holy Savior near Perugia; St. Emiliano in Conguintoli; and St. Benedict (location unknown). See Giuseppe Cacciamani, "La fondazioni eremitiche e cenobitichie di S. Pier Damiano: Inizi della congregazione di S. Croce di Fonte Avellana," *Ravennatensia* 5 (1976), 5–33. Peter was also closely aligned to the reform at Monte Cassino; he wrote eight letters to Desiderius (letters 82, 86, 90, 95, 102, 106, 119, 159), three to Alberic (126, 127, 160), and one to the community (161). He also wrote three letters (100, 103, 113; possibly 125) to Cluniacs and the vita of Abbot Odilo (PL 144, 925–44). He visited Monte Cassino in 1061 and Cluny in 1063.

voted purpose throughout various parts of Italy," Damian confesses, preaching and "striving to recall others to an upright life."[51] Popes Nicholas II and Alexander II sent him on legatine missions, to Milan (1059) where he dealt with the social upheavals of the Patarines; to Cluny (1063), to deal with legal privileges and exemptions; to Florence (1066) to mediate quarrels between a new monastic order (Vallombrosa) and a growing city; to Frankfurt (1069) to provide marital counseling to Emperor Henry IV and his wife, Bertha; and to Ravenna (1072) where he addressed the remnants of the Cadalus schism. He died on his return trip from the Ravenna mission on February 22, 1072. Never officially canonized, his sanctity was officially recognized in 1828 when Leo XII declared his feast day universally observed and bestowed upon him the title *Doctor ecclesiae.*

His death occurred the year before Hildebrand, or "Holy Satan," as Damian called him, was elected Pope Gregory VII.[52] Emperor Henry IV was twenty-two and had been ruling in his own right since 1065. Peter had not had a close relationship with this emperor, but he felt comfortable enough to lecture him, on the occasion of his reaching his majority, in matters concerning *sacerdotium* and *imperium.*[53] Damian's ease probably arose naturally from the very close relationship he did have with Henry's mother, Empress Agnes; he was her spiritual director. When her regency obligations lessened she entered religious life. In 1062 she traveled to the monastery at Fruttuaria and began a spiritual friendship with Damian. The following year she made her general confession to him, and they remained in close contact at least until 1067, the date of the last of his six letters to her. We know of no contact between Damian and the imperial court in his final years.

As one can see, little occurred in Italy's mid-eleventh-century

51. Letter 8.4, in L, 1:102; B, 1:119–20. He discusses his ambivalence early in his monastic life toward preaching in Letter 8.3–5, in L, 1:101–5; B, 1:119–21.

52. He first referred to Hildebrand as such in 1058, Letter 57.4, in L, 2:371; B, 2:167. Cowdrey, *Pope Gregory,* 39–43, says Damian is referencing Job 1:6–12; 2:1–7.

53. For example, see Letter 120.8, in L, 5:390; B, 3:382: "Be careful, I repeat, O king, lest while allowing the sacerdotium to be divided, your empire too, which God forbid, should be divided."

politics that Damian did not have knowledge of or influence. One surprise is that he had comparatively little to say about investiture. He was an early and ardent critic of simony, however, and had no patience with anyone who failed to see that lay investiture was simoniac. "The one depends on the other," he wrote Pope Alexander II in 1066, and he advocated that the pope take a moderate approach in resolving the rampant heresy: "God forbid that [anyone] should obtain the spiritual dignity of ecclesiastical prominence, who has fostered the favor of a secular prince in striving for a prelacy."[54] As Owen Blum insightfully comments, "Whether Damian's was the wisest policy is a matter open to discussion, but it is perhaps significant that the tremendous clash of Church and State occurred only after St. Peter Damian's death."[55] Blum made the comment in 1946, decades before revisionists degraded the historical importance of the Investiture Conflict. The cycle continues, though, for recent scholarship has once again placed the conflict center stage and with its revival comes "a need and an opportunity for much new scholarship."[56] Hopefully, it will include a more thorough exploration of Damian's role.

Religion: The New Monasticism

Eleventh-century Italy was spearheading a breach in the monolithic form of monasticism. The century began with microscopic

54. Letter 140.9, in L, 6:107; B, 3:481–82, and Letter 140.18, in L, 6:111; B, 3:487. He offers a definition of heresy (Letter 140.16, in L, 6:110–11; B, 3:487): "It is not error that makes one a heretic, but stubbornness and inflexibility. Nor are all those who hold erroneous opinions to be called heretics, but only those who obstinately and brazenly preach what is false." We also see how exasperating Damian finds the blindness of others: "If after the receipt or the promise of money, the secular prince handed you the pastoral staff, how can you brazenly offer an excuse for putting the episcopal office up for sale?"

55. Blum, "The Monitor of the Popes: St. Peter Damian," *Studi Gregoriani* 2 (1947), 459–76.

56. In a long overdue article, Constance Bouchard ("'Feudalism,' Cluny and the Investiture Controversy," in *Medieval Monks and Their World,* ed. David Blanks, Michael Frasetto, and Amy Livingstone [Leiden: Brill, 2006], 91) argues "that the Investiture Controversy which has recently threatened to retreat into something of a scholarly backwater, is crucial for the understanding of both monasticism and national government in the twelfth century" (91).

fissures in the Benedictine Rule's monopoly and ended with its rupture. A plethora of new orders with new rules challenged Benedictine dominance. The fissures began with hermits, particularly with Romuald, the patriarch of the new medieval monastic orders.[57] No other person influenced Damian more. Damian's *Vita beati Romualdi* and Bruno of Querfurt's *Vitae quinque fratrum* are the chief sources for Romuald's life, and the impact Romuald's ideas had on Damian is evident throughout the vita. His reason for writing Romuald's vita is profound in its implications and serves as a window into Peter's concept of sainthood.

> I am not trying to write a biography of Saint Romuald—this is something beyond my limited skills. All I want to do is to leave behind a written testimony about him, a brief promemoria without any literary pretensions. But first let me inform my readers that I do not intend to fill up these pages with miracles. All I want to do is convey something that people can imitate, that is, the kind of life Saint Romuald lived.[58]

It is Romuald's witness that is of utmost significance, particularly the way he challenged social conventions and tradition. Bruno tells us this was Romuald's "one outstanding characteristic: whatever people would have liked to see him do, he tried at all costs to do exactly the opposite."[59]

Born around 952 to a nobleman named Sergio and his wife, who is not named in the vitae, Romuald's childhood is not mentioned by either Damian or Bruno. Romuald's life took an abrupt turn when his father murdered a relative over a disputed land claim. "Romuald had wounded no one; yet for the simple fact that he had been pres-

57. See C. H. Lawrence, *Medieval Monasticism,* 3rd ed. (London: Longman, 2001), 14, and Henrietta Leyser, *Hermits and the New Monasticism* (New York: St. Martin's Press, 1984), 29.

58. VR, prol. (171). Bruno's religious name was Boniface. Damian refers to him thus; Matus in his commentary uses Bruno-Boniface. I will use Bruno, as most modern scholars do. See *The Life of the Five Brothers by Bruno of Querfurt* [hereafter V5F], in *Mystery of Romuald.* See also Bruno-Boniface di Querfurt, *Vitae quinque fratrum* in MGH SS, vol. 15, cols. 709–38; also in *Monumenta Poloniae Historica,* n.s. 4, 3 (Warsaw: Panstwowe Wydawnictwo Naukowe, 1973).

59. V5F, 4 (96).

ent, he took upon himself the canonical penalty for the crime. Without delay he went to the monastery of Sant' Apollinare in Classe where he remained in penance for forty days, as is the custom for homicides."[60] He was about twenty at the time, and before his penance was fulfilled "he went and threw himself at the feet of the monks and begged them through his tears to clothe him in the monastic robes."[61]

Sant' Apollinare was a Benedictine monastery, as were almost all monasteries at the time. The standardization of monastic life throughout the Carolingian Empire during the reign of Louis the Pious was still basically in force. The imperial edict issued after the synods in Aachen in 816 and 817, under the direction of Benedict of Aniane and known as the Monastic Capitulary, mandated universal and literal observance of the Benedictine Rule, but, as is frequently the case, literal observance included many changes.[62] Regulations were relaxed (for example, bathing), strengthened (the prohibition of eating fowl), or otherwise altered (increase in choir prayer, decrease in manual labor), but in principle the Benedictine ideal remained and was aspired to in France and German lands. Italian monasteries remained unaffected by the Aachen decrees, and Anglo-Saxon monasteries were too busy with Scandinavian invaders to tend to monastic reform. The latter eventually did so, under the Wessex kings and Dunstan in the tenth century. By then the Carolingian Empire had fallen into disarray under the weight of internal weakness and external threats and no longer had the ability to enforce the Monastic Capitulary.

Two monasteries rose to the occasion now, Cluny (founded 909) and Gorze (restored 933), and put new energy into Benedictine monasticism. Historians disagree about their differences and similarities and their dependence upon each other, but two things they do agree on: both promoted Benedictine monasticism, and both implemented

60. VR, 1 (173).

61. Ibid., 2 (176).

62. See J. Semmler, "Die Beschlüsse des Aacherer Konzels im Jahre 816," *Zeitschrift für Kirchengeschichte* 74 (1963), 15–82; also CCCM 1 (Turnhout: Brepols, 1963), 451–68, 471–81.

successful reforms.[63] In a period of political upheaval and little intellectual activity Cluny, Gorze, and other, smaller reform centers such as those in Cambrai, Metz, Toul, Verdun, Cologne, Mainz, Augsburg, Constance, Ratisborn, and Hirsau provided institutional stability and educational opportunities. These monasteries devised a series of rituals, liturgical routines, and jurisdictional relationships that differed from the original Rule only enough to fulfill the needs of their own society. The introduction of longer, more elaborate recitations of Opus Dei gave monastic life a rigid structure that secular life lacked and often needed, while the addition of the Office of the Dead and the creation of All Souls' Day with its emphasis on the transforming power of eschatology gave society a reason to accept change.[64]

As impressive as the reforms and innovations of Cluny and Gorze were, it was not long before restlessness among religious was once again evident. In 971 the chief proponent of the Gorzian program, Wolfgang of Regensburg, began spreading a reinvigorated monasticism in Hungary and Bavaria. As he was so engaged, Abbot Mayeul of Cluny (965–94) was spreading his monastic model throughout western Europe. Yet we know that it was during this same time that Romuald left the Benedictine monastery of Sant' Apollinare and "boarded a ship heading north" to find a hermit named Marino and "ask the man to accept him as a disciple."[65] As this chronology shows, even as the reformation efforts of Gorze and Cluny were in full force another movement to reshape monasticism was afoot. This movement wanted to shape it into eremiticism.

Hermits have a long and revered role in the history of monasti-

63. The debate started in earnest with K. Hallinger, *Gorze-Kluny,* 2 vols. (Rome: Studia Anselmiana, 1950), 22–25, where he argues that Gorze and Cluny had opposite, even antagonistic, goals. Subsequent research has greatly tempered such claims. See historiographical essay in Barbara Rosenwein, *Rhinoceros Bound* (Philadelphia: University of Pennsylvania Press, 1982), 3–29. See also John Nightingale, *Monasteries and Patrons in the Gorze Reform* (Oxford: Clarendon Press, 2001), who ignores the debate.

64. See my "The Maintenance and Transformation of Society through Eschatology: Cluniac Monasticism," *Journal of Religious History* 14 (1987), 246–55.

65. VR, 4 (178). It is interesting to note that Abbot Mayeul had attempted to reform Sant' Apollinare in 972, the year before Romuald arrived, and met with little success.

cism. *Eremos* is Greek for desert, and the earliest hermits were, as the word suggests, ascetics who lived in the Egyptian desert. Anthony (d. 356) is traditionally called the father of Christian monasticism, and he began his life in the desert. "He spent nearly twenty years in this solitary religious life," Athanasius writes in his vita of Anthony, and by his example "he induced many to take up the solitary life. And so from that time there were monasteries in the mountains, and the desert was peopled with monks."[66] From the beginning hermits figured out ways to maintain their solitude yet live in colonies. The paradox is present throughout monastic history, this search for solitude within community. Pachomius (ca. 292–346) addressed the issue by compromising; he organized individual ascetics into large communities with rules. The cenobitic life soon overshadowed the eremitic life. When the Master and Benedict of Nursia (ca. 480–550) wrote their rules they included a common assumption, that eremiticism was superior to cenobitism. Still, it is a rare vocation, suitable only for those who "after a long probation in a monastery, having learned by the help of many brethren how to fight against the devil, go out well armed from the ranks of the community to the solitary combat of the desert."[67] During most of the early Middle Ages Western monasticism was synonymous with cenobitism, but eremiticism did not disappear completely. The Celtic church hosted many eremitic vocations, Cluny had numerous hermitages on its land, and *laurae* (Byzantine monasteries) populated southern Italy.[68] These hermits give no indication that it was dissatisfaction with contemporary monasticism that led them to the hermitage; rather, it was desire for more or different spirituality. Even Romuald became a

66. Athanasius, *Vita S. Antonii,* PG 26, 866.

67. *St. Benedict's Rule for Monasteries,* tr. Leonard Doyle (Collegeville, Minn.: Liturgical Press, 1948), 1, 6. Many of the pivotal figures in monastic history lived as hermits either before or after cenobitic living: Pachomius, Basil, Cassian, Martin of Tours, including Francis of Assisi.

68. See *Catalogus Sanctorum Hiberniae,* in *Councils and Ecclesiastical Documents,* ed. A. W. Hadder and W. Stubbs (Oxford: Clarendon Press, 1869–78), 2:292; and L. Ménager, "La 'byzantinisation' religieuse de l'Italie meridionale (ixe–xii^{e}s) et la politique monastique des Normandi l'Italie," *Revue d'Histoire Ecclesiastique* 53 (1958), 747–74.

hermit not because his fellow monks did not live up to his standards, but because "his heart found no rest."[69]

Why could tenth-century monasticism not satisfy Romuald's heart's desire? Augustine gave us the ultimate response, that "our hearts find no peace until they rest in Thee."[70] I entertain the question on a less profound level. Why was Romuald searching for a new kind of life, outside the boundaries of contemporary monasticism, and why did so many others willingly follow him?[71] Peter Damian's answer to this crucial query gives us insight into the eleventh-century world of religious and is the main thesis in Romuald's vita: "Only by caring for the salvation of others can the hermit love his neighbor as God commanded."[72] Damian's theology of eremiticism contrasts greatly with Bruno's statement that Romuald resigned as abbot of Sant' Apollinare and withdrew "so that with solitude as his friend, he might at least save himself."[73] For Damian the search for personal salvation is a grievous sin. Damian tells us this is also Romuald's conclusion. While founding the monastery of St. Michael in Bagno, Romuald received seven pounds in wages for some labor he performed. When Romuald distributed it to monks other than those in his own community, his monks "beat him up, took the money, and hurling insults at him, drove him out of town." At this point Romuald was severely tempted to forget his social obligations and focus only on self.

> Bruised and depressed, Romuald turned his back on Bagno and started walking. "Never again," he promised himself: "Never again. From

69. VR, 4 (178). See VR, 3 (177) where Damian hints that Romuald's fervor was a bit overbearing; and Matus's commentary, VR, 3, 176–77.

70. Augustine, *Confessions,* tr. R. Pine-Coffin (Harmondsworth: Penguin Books, 1978), 1:1.

71. Jestice, *Wayward,* 7, answers thus: "The most driving force behind reform was some monks' longing for activity in the world outside the monastery's confines." I add the following: the monks' longing arose from their contemplation of witness and the desire to fulfill this mandate to bear witness. One of the chief goals of this book is to persuade the reader to acknowledge this essential key to the whole history of the High Middle Ages.

72. Colin Phipps, "Romuald—Model Hermit: Eremitical Theory in Saint Peter Damian's *Vita Beati Romualdi,* chapters 16–27," in *Monks, Hermits and the Ascetic Tradition,* ed. W. J. Shiels, 65–77 (Oxford: Basil Blackwell, 1985), 77.

73. V5F, 2 (87).

> now on the only thing that matters is the salvation of my soul. I am going to save my own soul and not bother any more about anyone else's." He turned these thoughts over in his mind until, at a certain point, a deathly terror flooded his brain, and he knew he had come close to the edge of damnation. Had he continued obstinately in the direction his thoughts were leading him, he would have fallen into the abyss of God's judgment.[74]

This temptation, to put the salvation of self over others, is ever present in religious life and dresses in various guises. The devil, realizing "he could not prevail against God's servant directly, tried more devious means" to estrange Romuald from God. "He would try to discourage his concern for his neighbor's salvation. Unable to make Romuald surrender, at least the devil might impede his victory in defense of others."[75]

While Damian may have gleaned these thoughts of Romuald through oral sources, more than likely these conclusions are Damian's interpretation of Romuald's life. Yet one must be careful not to withhold from Romuald his just due; why else would Romuald split his life between prayerful solitude and communal reform? Romuald's wanderlust is so extreme—as Bruno exclaims, he was "always a wanderer, now here, now there"—that it is sometimes hard to take seriously his claim to love solitude.[76] Despite the fact that his contemporaries believed him to be "the greatest hermit of our day," the longest he ever stayed in a hermitage was ten years at Cuxá. Mostly he would settle in a place, stay a short time until the spirit moved him, and then "without a moment's delay he abandoned the hermitage where he had been living and set out for the place to which he had been directed."[77] As he did, "many came to join him, and he provided each with a cell." And here is why we should believe in the sincerity of Romuald's professed love of solitude: "Great was the rigor of their life in the hermitage, and their example aroused great admiration among the people."[78] The hermits needed not

74. VR, 18 (198–99).
75. Ibid., 17 (197).
76. V5F, 3 (91).
77. VR, 19 (200).
78. Ibid., 26 (212).

miracles to inspire imitation; their lives bore witness to the Truth, much as the biblical witness of John the Baptist did. As Damian tells us, "The Bible attributes no miracles to Saint John the Baptist, and yet the living Truth itself tells us that none born of woman is greater than he."[79] It was the witness of John's life that brought them to Christ.

Theology: Witness

Witness is the key to understanding Romuald's life and the key to understanding Damian's theory of eremiticism. In fact, witness is the key to understanding the whole of Damian's theology and life and thus needs further exploration than the remarks offered in the introduction. Witness transmits truth to others through human means. Foreseeing the need for human mediation, Scripture mandates that once one learns of God, she or he must bear witness to others. The obligation is first articulated by Yahweh to the Israelites, transmitted to the New Israel through John the Baptist, and reiterated by Jesus at the Ascension. The first Christian community took the mandate to heart, as we can see in a passage that garnered much attention in the eleventh century, particularly by Damian: "The community of believers were of one heart and one mind. None of them ever claimed anything as his own; rather everything was held in common. With power the apostles bore witness to the resurrection of the Lord Jesus, and great respect was paid to them all" (Acts 4:32–33).

The etymology of the word is highly instructive. It comes from the Greek noun *martus,* witness, and verb *marturein,* to bear witness. Derivatives of *martus* fill the New Testament.[80] At the end of the first century the word began a diachronistic semantic change from *witness* to *martyr* in its current connotation.[81] The change apparently

79. Ibid., prol. (171).

80. It is used about 185 times throughout the New Testament. See Trites, *Concept of Witness;* and James Gall, *Layman's English-Greek Concordance* (Grand Rapids, Mich.: William Eerdmans, 1974).

81. James Sherman, *The Nature of Martyrdom* (Paterson, N.J.: St. Anthony's Guild Press, 1942), 3–28, identifies four stages of diachronistic change. Allison Trites, "*Martus*

arose from the reality of Christian witness; by A.D. 96 the *Epistle of Clement* uses *marturein,* to bear witness, to describe the suffering that resulted from witnessing.[82] Around 116 Ignatius of Antioch uses *martus* to refer to one who imitates Christ's suffering.[83] By the time we get to *Martyrdom of Polycarp* (ca.165–70) *martus* has developed beyond the idea of witness or even suffering witness to dying witness. *Martus* becomes martyr. One rightly may ask what then happened to the original scriptural concept of witness. Clement of Alexandria's *Stromata* (ca. early third century) shows an appreciation of Christian witness outside of martyrdom, but basically the original meaning of *martus* as communication through words and deeds is overshadowed by *martus* as communication through suffering and death. Latin, however, kept the original meaning of *martus* alive with *testor* and its derivatives.[84] During the early Middle Ages the obligation of *testor,* to bear witness, is rarely discussed explicitly, the exception being the Rule of St. Augustine. This Rule is unique among early medieval documents for its emphasis on witness and its grasp of the concept as living communication. That the Augustinian Rule was ignored until the eleventh century—that is, until after Romuald and Peter Damian's resurrection of interest in *testimonium,* witness—makes sense. The eremitic movement of Romuald and Damian brought witness center stage for the first generation of monastic reformers; the Rule of St. Augustine offered the second and third generation the instrument needed to insure that the new communities bore proper witness. Hence, we find numerous new orders adopting not the Benedictine but the Augustinian Rule as their own.[85]

and Martyrdom in the Apocalypse: A Semantic Study," *Novum Testamentum* 15 (1973), 72–80, identifies five.

82. Epistle of Clement, 5.4–7, in ANF 1:6.

83. Ignatius of Antioch, *Philadelphians,* 7.2, ibid., 1:83; *Romans,* 6.3, ibid., 1:76; and *Smyrnaeans,* 5.1–2, ibid., 1:88.

84. For a more complete history of the concept and its documentation, see my "The Concept of Witness in Christian Tradition from Its Origin to Its Institutionalization," *Revue bénédictine* 102:1–2 (1992), 9–23.

85. See my "Rule of St. Augustine." See also *La règle de Saint Augustin,* ed, Luc Verheijen,

The reason the scriptural concept of witness is of such historical significance is simple. It is about communication, and all communication is social. For communication to be effective the message must be presented in a language that can be understood by the audience. Consequently, every time a society's language changes, witness must also change. It is the communicator's duty to know when society changes and adjust communication accordingly. This is evident enough when the language is verbal, but when the medium of communication is action or deeds it becomes less apparent. When Romuald turned to contemporary monasticism he did not find the Christian message clearly communicated. His wanderings were but a quest for the best ways to communicate the Christian message.[86] His goal, after all, was to save others through his witness: "Romuald could not bear to remain sterile. He felt a deep anxiety and a longing to bear fruit for souls, and kept searching for a place where he could do so."[87]

Another paradox surfaces here. It was because Romuald knew society so well that he was able to discern that withdrawal from society was a most effective witness. He did not come to this conclusion easily. In Bruno of Querfurt's vita we learn that Romuald and many of his disciples were torn between witness by life or witness by death. Bruno thought the way to perfection was to live both: "Wouldn't it be better to go someplace where we could live as hermits and die for the gospel," he asked when trying to persuade his friend Benedict to "set out for Poland to preach the gospel."[88] In an act that captures the free-flowing intermingling of the political and religious worlds,

2 vols. (Paris: Etudes Augustinennes, 1967); and *Regla tertia,* tr. D. de Bruyne, *Revue bénédictine* 42 (1930), 318–26. At least twelve orders of canons regular, Knights of St. Lazarus, Knights of St. Iago, Teutonic Knights, Trinitarians, Servites, Hieronymites, Austin friars, Hermits of St. Augustine, and Dominicans adopted the Augustinian Rule during the High Middle Ages.

86. It may seem that Bruno's vita does not support my contentions here. In one way he does not; Bruno does not grasp the concept of witness nor see it in Romuald's life as Damian does. Yet, there is in the vita, intentionally or not, much to reinforce the thesis that these hermits were contemplating the meaning of *martus* with intensity.

87. VR, 35 (229).

88. V5F, 5 (98–99).

Otto III was the one who set this mission in motion. After Adalbert, bishop of Prague, was martyred near Gdansk in 997, Otto decided to complete Adalbert's mission and "conceived the following project: he would choose some of the more fervent brothers and send them to Poland; there they would build a monastery in Christian territory but near an area where pagans dwell, secluded and surrounded by woods." Clearly Otto too understood the concept of witness. His missionaries must bear witness through multiple means: "This would offer a threefold advantage [*tripla commoda*]: the community life [*cenobium*], which is what novices wanted; golden solitude, for those who are mature ... and the preaching of the gospel to pagans [*evangelium paganorum*], for those who long to be freed from this life."[89] To head his project Otto recruited two hermits from one of Romuald's nearby hermitages, and soon they were readying themselves for their dual witness. They learned the native language and "wore their hair short and had adopted the sort of clothing worn by the local people," so their witness would be comprehensible and "easier for them to accept the gospel."[90] Bruno explicitly references the two different ways of rendering witness: "We did all this so that we could either preach the gospel or suffer martyrdom for Christ's sake."[91] Bruno also implies that Otto made the same assumption. When he articulates a variation of his threefold good in his "three highest goods" [*tria maxima bona*], he uses different words—the monastic habit, the hermitage, and martyrdom—to express the same realities. The cenobium is the monastic habit; the hermitage is solitude; and *evangelium paganorum* is *martyrium.* Even though modern readers would likely see preaching and martyrdom as two distinct acts, eleventh-century society understood *evangelium* and *martyrium* as expressions of "the same basic idea of witness."[92] For Romuald's

89. Ibid., 4 (95).

90. V5F, 10 (122). V5F, 11 (129), he adds: "we even shaved our heads."

91. V5F, 11 (129).

92. Joseph Wong, "The Threefold Good: Romualdian Charism and Monastic Tradition," in *Privilege of Love,* ed. Peter-Damian Belisle (Collegeville, Minn.: Liturgical Press, 2002), 92.

hermits they were two sides of the same coin. Their witness by life would bring them to witness by death. And it did; while rendering witness in their monastery, they were murdered. As Damian records Bruno saying, since he bore witness with his life as a cleric, "why then should I not also bear witness to Christ with my blood?"[93]

We learn from Peter Damian that Romuald too made these assumptions. Thus, when "word reached Romuald that his disciple the blessed [Bruno-] Boniface had received martyrdom," he decided to offer witness by martyrdom and organized an expedition to Hungary with twenty-four companions; "in the meanwhile, remaining firm in this intention, he founded in a very brief period of time three monasteries." Even as he prepares to offer witness by death he continues his witness by life. Ultimately, Romuald decides the best way for him personally to render witness is through monasticism. After twice getting sick as he journeyed to Hungary he told his fellow missionaries that "I have thought it all through, and now it seems that it is not God's plan that I go any farther." He acknowledges that the type of witness one renders is a personal choice, so he tells his companions, "I leave you free either to continue your journey or to come back with me." He was at peace with his decision, for it was based on his insight that witness by life was indeed as worthy as witness by death: "So he did not return with a sense of failure. In his heart he had already undergone martyrdom and had accomplished his mission of saving souls by bringing people to the monastic life."[94] Romuald's conclusion had monumental impact on Damian. Damian spent his life devoted to witnessing through body and soul and to persuading others to do likewise.

Again, the historical significance of Romuald and Damian's conclusion is key here. They discerned a thirst for witness among their contemporaries and were determined to do something about it. Damian starts by writing Romuald's vita. "Crowds of believers

93. VR, 27 (214). The story of the murder is in V5F, 12 (131–40).

94. VR, 39 (235–36). Damian emphasizes the role free will plays in determining the type of witness one renders elsewhere, when relating the story of the Five Brothers. VR, 28 (217).

from far and near flock to [Romuald's] tomb," Damian tells us as he explains why he is writing *Vita beati Romualdi.* "They come eager to hear the story of his life, and they find nobody there to tell it." This lack of witness (Latin, *testimonium*) frustrates Damian: "No one has come forth to answer the needs of those who believe," he laments, "no one has provided . . . a few words that might be useful for the many."[95] Damian's goal is to testify to Romuald's witness. Both monks knew that communication demanded knowledge of society. If they hoped to encode their message correctly, they had to know how society interpreted symbols, rituals, linguistic nuances, manners, comportment, and sentiments. This is why Romuald's disciples changed their appearance and learned another language, to make sure their attire and speech encoded the intended message. Damian describes how Bruno learned this truism in the field.

> [Bruno-Boniface] finally reached the presence of the king of the [Prussians] and preached to him in strong and ardent words. The king looked at his tattered clothing and bare feet, and concluded that all this talk of religion was just leading up to a pitch for money. So to get him to stop his raving, the king promised to make him a wealthy man. At this Boniface went straight back to his lodgings, changed into his finest pontifical vestments, and returned to court. At the sight of his splendid garb, the king said, "Now I know that it is ignorance of the truth and not material poverty that makes you speak such nonsense. However, if you really want me to believe your teachings, you must submit to this test [an ordeal by fire].[96]

Thus did Bruno learn that regal garb and ordeals were the proper medium for his message. Because Bruno was open to learning the ways of that society, his message was understood and his mission successful. Those seeking baptism were so numerous that he "had to take them to a large lake, in order to find water sufficient to baptize them."[97]

95. VR, prol. (170). We also hear the call for witness in the plea of the bishop of Pula: "'Do not hide your fire under the ashes,' he told [Romuald], 'instead, set your light on a lampstand, to shine on all the people in God's house.'" VR, 33 (225).

96. VR, 27 (215). Damian mistakenly identifies the king as Russian.

97. Ibid. (216).

In telling Romuald's story, Damian realizes that on the surface it hardly seems to bear witness to the eremitic life. Indeed, at times it appears to be a stretch to call him a hermit. Damian takes care, therefore, to persuade his audience how incorrect such a conclusion would be. Romuald's travels bear witness to his guiding principle, that one is saved by saving others. Damian explains: "Now let me warn the reader not to misinterpret Romuald's movement from place to place. In his case, this was no vice but a virtue, as his intention was always to do the Lord's work. Of course, one of the reasons for his continual change of location was the fact that, wherever he lived, vast crowds of men and women would gather. Hence as soon as he had filled one place, he would have them elect a superior, and then he would go off to fill some other place."[98] Romuald's "longing to bear fruit for souls" led him to adjust his individual needs as a hermit to accommodate the needs of the community.[99] One's personal search for salvation must be conducted so as to aid in society's salvation; this was Romuald's witness.

This is not to say that Romuald and his hermits or even Damian did not understand that a certain real withdrawal from aspects of society was essential to their witness. When King Boleslaw of Poland asked Romuald's hermits to bring back his crown from Rome, they refused: "'We are in holy orders,' they said, 'and it is not permitted us to become involved in worldly affairs.'"[100] The hermit's challenge is to discern when involvement in society is necessary, and when it is detrimental. If he judged involvement to be beneficial to the community and not detrimental to the individual, Romuald became involved. Hence Romuald attended the court of Emperor Henry II and "had a great deal to say: about restoring to the churches what was rightfully theirs, about the violence of those endowed with power, about the oppression of the poor, and about many other things."[101]

98. VR, 49 (244–45).

99. VR, 35 (229), and above, n. 88.

100. VR, 28 (218). The hermits were Benedict of Benevento and John (two of the murdered brothers).

101. VR, 65 (261).

At other times and places Romuald petitioned nobility for land, heard confessions, distributed goods to the poor, preached to the masses and to clerics, promoted ecclesiastical reform and the canonical life, ministered to women and built them a monastery, provided spiritual direction, and conducted business transactions.[102] Romuald even acted as a political mediator. When Otto III lay siege to Tivoli after the townspeople killed the imperial commander of the troops and barred the emperor from entering the city, it was Romuald who "obtained an agreement of clemency for the townspeople and thus further bloodshed was avoided."[103]

The eremitic movement Romuald fathered was successful, because its witness was clearly understood by society. A good part of the reason for that rests, however, with Peter Damian. Damian was the movement's first theologian and greatest promoter. It was a movement of utmost significance. It disseminated a theology of witness which in turn became the motive for change within monasticism and then within society. This gave birth to new attitudes toward change. Numerous religious groups were formed in the High Middle Ages in response to the witness mandate. Vallombrosans, Fontevrists, Prèmonstratensians, Carthusians, Tironines, Cistercians, a multitude of canons regular orders, the Templars, the Hospitallers, a host of other military orders, Grandmontines, Gilbertines, Austin Friars, Carmelites, Franciscans, Dominicans, and so many more, all offered their own distinct witness. Each group tailored its witness to a particular aspect of society that the monolithic Benedictine Order was unable to offer. As society continued to change, religious orders continued to multiply in response to these changes, much as the scriptural concept of witness demands. It is to the everlasting credit of eleventh-century monastic leaders, chief among whom are Romuald and Peter Damian, that witness becomes a fundamental goal and controlling criterion in all future forms of Western monasticism.

102. See VR, 35 (229–30); 59 (255); and 26 (212).
103. VR, 23 (206).

Two

ESTABLISHING FUNDAMENTAL PRINCIPLES

Letter 1

After a year's novitiate (ca.1035–36) Damian traveled to different monasteries throughout Italy. At the monastery of S. Vincenzo at Petra Pertusa he began writing Romuald's vita around 1042, but a year or two before he had probably written another work, *Tract against the Jews,* his first lengthy work for public consumption. In Romuald's vita we have our first glimpse of Damian's spiritual principles and outlook; in Letter 1 we have his initial speculative thoughts as he begins his literary and ecclesiastical career. While ostensibly a defense of Christianity against Jewish arguments, and written at the request of a monk from Pomposa, Damian uses the opportunity to summarize his understanding of the basic tenets of Christianity.[1] Significantly, his introduction focuses on the obligation to bear witness to the faith and the role the intellect plays in faith.

I have decided that it is appropriate to comply with your request. Surely it is disgraceful for a man of the Church to hold his tongue out of igno-

1. Letter 1.2 in L, 1:38; B, 1:65–66. Damian tells us the nobleman Honestus, later a monk, "sent word to me, begging that I should write something for you to use in silencing, with reasoned arguments, the Jews." Letter 81, written after 1060 and often called Damian's primer for Catholicism, is similar to Letter 1 but broader and more explicit.

rance when those outside the fold set things in a false light.... One may add that often harmful ineptitude and dangerous simplicity in such matters not only excite boldness in the unbelieving, but also beget error and doubt in the hearts of the faithful.... One must know, however, that a Christian man should not enter this fight for reasons of empty glory or for the love of conflict alone, but rather because he hopes to be able to benefit the soul of his adversary.... He should be advised not to anger his adversary by contentious invective or proud conceit, but with kindly love and most patient seriousness should attract his mind.[2]

This is the premise upon which Damian will conduct his life. He will bear intellectual witness to his faith. It is not the only premise, but it is the dominate one. He will refine, adapt, and cultivate his reasoned witness but never abandon it. Mindful of the rules of communication, he will take the culturally laden language of Scripture and recast it in a form contemporary society will comprehend: "But although almost all the books of the Old Testament bear witness to Christ [*sed cum omnia pene veteris testamenti volummina testimonium Christo perhibeant*], putting aside this abundance of words, I take pains to set before you a few clear statements of the prophets."[3] Most importantly, he is acutely aware that he must know his audience if his witness is to be understood.

And so, dear brother Honestis, notice that as I attempted to take into account your lack of training, I did not try to employ the flowers of rhetorical eloquence nor the sharp arguments of the dialecticians. Given that I did not care to adopt the trappings of worldly wisdom, and that I was aware that you were also involved in secular affairs and were unable to devote yourself to much reading, I did not wish to burden you with wordy and extended proofs. Wherefore, in placing before you almost bare texts from Scripture I have sent you, as it were, a bundle of arrows for your quiver.... I have indeed supplied the weapons.[4]

Throughout the treatise Damian makes conscious efforts to keep himself focused on the needs of his audience and present his testi-

2. Letter 1.2–3, in L, 1:38–39; B, 1:66.

3. Letter 1.4, in L, 1:39; B, 1:67. When deemed helpful for clarification or emphasis, I arbitrarily include Damian's original wording.

4. Letter 1.74, in L, 1:82; B, 1:101–2

mony accordingly. "By a mixture of the statements of the prophets," he confides, "I have purposely tried to avoid tiring my hearer who would grow bored if many proofs from the same author were lumped together." He even tries to anticipate future needs and encourages further investigation: "I am also trying to give the names of prophets associated with each piece of evidence, so that when something is stated, and you would perhaps care to go to the source, you might easily discover it."[5]

His methodology is twofold. First, he presents "evidence of the prophets, that you may view in summary" all the "diffuse and scattered" pronouncements they make concerning "the coming of the humanity of Christ and [proceed] through the passage of time until its end."[6] If, however, this does not communicate to the unbeliever effectively he has another method, rational argumentation: "If so many pieces of evidence from Holy Scripture [*sacrae scripturae testimonia*] do not attract you to faith in Christ, if such clear and obvious sayings of all the prophets do not change you, I would still like to argue with you from reason."[7] He knows the power and role of the intellect in matters of faith and uses it. He assesses the power of his own witness humbly, though, acknowledging that his prayers are more powerful than his preaching. "I have indeed supplied the weapons," but only God and the individual can decide how and when to use them.[8] These are two methodologies employed in the vast majority of Damian's writings.

Damian also discusses the prerequisites for learning, reminding the audience that they too have responsibilities: "Let all your innermost senses be free to understand, let your heart thrust aside the ancient veil of ignorance, let the ears of your mind be carefully attuned. Let your tongue speak, so long as it thinks it has something to say that is likely true."[9] Damian consistently demands that his audience possess these attitudes. He does not endorse blind faith but

5. Letter 1.37, in L, 1:60–61; B, 1:83–84.
6. Letter 1.60, in L, 1:72; B, 1:93.
7. Letter 1.67, in L, 1:79; B, 1:99.
8. Letter 1.74, in L, 1:82; B, 1:101.
9. Letter 1.10, in L, 1:43; B, 1:69–70.

constantly reminds his audience to engage their intellect in matters of belief. The process is simple: "We read, we believe and therefore are convinced."[10] He repeats: "Examine, inspect, and leaf through all the pages of Holy Writ," and when confused or doubtful, "read through the rest of [Scripture] and understand its true meaning."[11]

Damian begins his debate by questioning the Jewish denial of the Trinity. His first argument focuses on grammar, noting the purposeful and frequent scriptural use of the plural and the singular to emphasize the doctrine of the Trinity.[12] Next he focuses on the Incarnation. This exposition forms the largest portion of the treatise. Here the argument is firmly rooted in the power of witness. For Damian, that is the purpose of Scripture, to bear witness to Christ. His list of witnesses is lengthy: "Listen also to the prophet Micah's witnessing [*testimonium*] to Christ"; "but, if all these witnesses [*testes*] to the truth do not yet suffice for you, Jew, listen to what your Jeremiah says"; "let Daniel also take the stand and testify [*accedat ... testimonium*] to Christ"; "further evidence [*testimonium*] about Christ from Isaiah," "Habakkuk also presents evidence [*testimonium*]," "listen also to the testimony [*testimonium*] which the same Isaiah gives"; "of him Zechariah also testified [*testatur*]"; "Jesus son of Sirach ... would you also not wish to testify [*testimonium*]"; "hear still more and more clear evidence [*lucidissima testimonia*]."[13] Witness also comes from creation ("like the moon, which remains forever—a faithful witness [*testis ... fidelis*] in the sky") and from the Creator ("the Father who is speaking gives clear evidence [*testimonium*] of the Son").[14] After "such an array of evident testimony [*evidentissima ... testimonium*]," Damian asks, "Would you also not wish

10. Letter 1.11, L, 1:43; B, 1:70.

11. Letter 1.30, 31, in L, 1:57; B, 1:70.

12. Letter 1.5, in L, 1:40; B, 1:67. He continues, noting similar grammatical testimony in Gn 1:26; 5:1–2; 11:5, 7; 18:1–4; 19:18–19; Ex 26; Is 6:3; and Ps 32:6, noting that "my tongue would probably grow tired before I ran short of texts." Letter 1.10, in L, 1:43; B, 1:69.

13. Letter 1.13, in L, 1:46; B, 1:71; Letter 1.14, 15, in L, 1:46; B, 1:72; Letter 1.19, in L, 1:49; B, 1:74; Letter 1.22, in L, 1:51; B, 1:76; Letter 1.23, in L, 1:52; B, 1:77; Letter 1.28, in L, 1:56; B, 1:80; Letter 1.33, in L, 1:59; B, 1:82; and Letter 1.43, in L, 1:64; B, 1:86.

14. Letter 1.29, in L, 1:57; B, 1:80; and Letter 1.20, in L, 1:50; B, 1:75.

to testify?"[15] He mockingly adds, "Obviously, for anyone who still needs evidence after such enlightening testimony [*post tam per sicuam exemplorum lucem adhuc testimoniis indiget*], it remains for him to request a lighted lamp to view the radiant sun at noontime."[16]

Only through witness is the Incarnation known. Indeed, Christ is the ultimate witness, the one, Damian tells us, of whom Isaiah 55:4 speaks: "I made him a witness to the people, a leader and commander of the nations." Consequently, "it follows that we must accept [the prophecy] as relating undoubtedly to Christ."[17] Habakkuk's witness tells us that "this Word, born of the Father before the ages, at the end of time wished to become man in the womb of the Virgin."[18] Daniel's witness informs us that the Word brings a new law (Dn 9:24–26); Isaiah "clearly points out the humanity of our Redeemer" (Is 45:13–15) and explains Christ's passion (Is 53:1–10, 12). Solomon's testimony tells of Christ death (Ws 2:12–22), while the witness of the Psalmist (Ps 71), Zechariah (Zec 13:2), Jeremiah (Jer 23:5–6), and Isaiah (Is 45) proclaim Christ's role as savior. Damian emphasizes Scripture's witness to the humanity of Christ; he sees Christ's humanity as the ultimate stumbling block for the unbeliever. In the Word Incarnate is "both the weakness of humanity and the power of divinity in the one mediator between God and man."[19] That Damian sees the humanity of Christ so clearly and underscores it at every opportunity situates him historically at the beginning of medieval society's reconceptualization of Christ.[20] "Who is the Most High, who is called both man and the Most High?" he pointedly queries. "Consider thoroughly that the term 'Most High' is used everywhere of God and is never found applying to a mere man. It follows then, that when 'Most High' and 'man' are brought together, we are to understand that God and man are called one person." To stress the Incarnation's union of the divine and the human even more, he marvels at the

15. Letter 1.33, in L, 1:58–59; B, 1:82.

16. Letter 1.45, in L, 1:65; B, 1:88.

17. Letter 1.24, in L, 1:53; B, 1:77,

18. Letter 1.11, in L, 1:44; B, 1:70.

19. Letter 1.21, in L, 1:51; B, 1:76. Christ as mediator is a favorite theme in the sermons. See S, 4:18; 5:95; 6:337; 17:335; 17/2:391; 34:56; 44:114, 198; 46:317; 49:66, 209; 53:87; and 63:87.

20. See Willemien Otten, *From Paradise to Paradigm* (Leiden: Brill, 2004).

fact that Christ was both born in Zion and founded Zion. He ponders, "But who has the power first to build a city and in it later come forth from his mother's womb? Who, I say, but our Redeemer, who deigned to be born in the things which he made?"[21] Unsurprising, then, is Damian's stance that the Incarnation bears witness to society's call to manifest faith both externally and internally: "His tomb, moreover, is glorious since, in addition to the fact that we, redeemed by his death, give glory to him with all our heart, we also observe the place itself."[22]

The third section of the tract continues to emphasize the inclusion of the material in salvation history by discussing rituals and customs. Damian changes the format here to a brief discourse in dialogue form, in the hope that the reader "will be compelled either to agree that you [the Jewish addressee] have lost, or depart in confusion because of your shameful disbelief."[23] The discourse consists of ten questions, all which begin with variations of "if Christ did not come to abolish the Law but to fulfill it, why...?" What the Old Law says about circumcision, food, and celebrations is compared to the New Law, and the same justification is given for all changes: the coming of Christ demands change. While at first glance this section appears to be of little consequence, it contains core principles that have highly significant implications for Damian's thoughts and actions. It reveals a most positive attitude toward change. To change is *imitatio Christi.* If Christ brings change, then change is to be welcomed, embraced, and celebrated. For Damian, though, change is not called "change"; it is the arrival or the return of the intended form. "Today a Christian does not submit himself to circumcision because Christ carried out what had been foretold," Damian argues, because when Christ came "all things that had existed as something temporary ceased to be."[24] Old Law regulations were replaced "for

21. Letter 1.30, in L, 1:57; B, 1:81.

22. Letter 1.32, in L, 1:58; B, 1:93. For lengthy discussions of the Incarnation, see S, 3:191–99; 4:7–40; 18; 39; 48; 61; 63; 64; and 65:1–30.

23. Letter 1.46, in L, 1:66; B, 1:88.

24. Letter 1.47, in L, 1:66; B, 1:88; and Letter 1.58, in L, 1:72; B, 1:93.

the simple reason that what was prefigured was fulfilled in Christ."[25] Even more strongly does Damian state his opinion of outdated remnants of the past. "When the true highpriest had come," Damian exclaims in relief, "the highpriest of the former dispensation is nowhere to be found, nor is there any room for him."[26] This is necessary, because "one who was still a babe ... [might] be carried away by the very sight of these divergent forms." To avoid confusion, then, Christ made sure the Old was "utterly removed."[27]

Damian makes a strong connection between change and eschatology. The world must change so "truth might survive."[28] "After such a cloud of witnesses" [*post tantum testium nubem*] and all "the evidence of the prophets" [*prophetica testimonia*], in the fourth section Damian offers an eschatological peroration, from the Incarnation "through the passage of time until its end."[29] He states the basic premise again, that Christ gives new meaning to change. This is not the change that "is observed happening universally in the human race"; it is a different kind of change.[30] "Since he states that the one whom he first called a child would later be known as Mighty God and Father of the world to come, he certainly and with great clarity shows that he is both God and man."[31] This is change of the profoundest kind; Christ brings us out of "this land of exile" into a new world. "By the love [Christ] gives us he does not allow us to fix our attention on this world" but makes us focus on our final goal, the next world.[32] Malachi prophesied that the angel of God would prepare the way for Christ's Second Coming (Mal 3:1–2); Jews must now prepare for his Second Coming.[33] This is possible because of the changes wrought by the Incarnation: "Through Jeremiah he promises us the law of the New Testament which he would proclaim throughout the world when he says ... 'I will make a new covenant with the house of Israel.'"[34]

25. Letter 1.49, in L, 1:67; B, 1:89.
26. Letter 1.58, in L, 1:71; B, 1:93.
27. Letter 1.59, in L, 1:72, B, 1:93.
28. Ibid.
29. Letter 1.60, in L, 1:72; B, 1:93.
30. Ibid.
31. Letter 1.61, in L, 1:73; B, 1:94.
32. Ibid., in L, 1:74; B, 1:94–95.
33. Letter 1.62–64, in L, 1:74–77; B, 1:95–97.
34. Letter 1.65, in L, 1:77; B, 1:97.

The fifth section is short, occasioned by Damian's desire to concentrate on reason rather than scriptural witness. The arguments, however, are still supported by Scripture, this time with biblical history rather than prophecies. His discussion shows how deeply intertwined he considers faith and reason to be. He raises a question: what was the greatest sin of the Jewish people? Damian considers three—grumbling, idolatry, and fornication—and concludes that, because the prophets "continually interceded for their sins," they suffered only "short-lived vengeance." On the other hand, the bondage and dispersal of the Hebrew people have "lasted for so many centuries," and will continue, because "you have killed Christ" and "refuse to have recourse to the fountain of life."[35] Despite the gravity of this iniquity, they have it in their power to end the punishment: change.

In the treatise's sixth section, he wonders about how best to change, to "put off the garb of your old self and accept the sacrament of new grace." He knows that "I can do more for your soul by praying to God than by preaching to you," so he asks that "the God of your fathers remove the ancient veil of ignorance from your heart, and ... flood you with the new light of his knowledge."[36] In the conclusion, though, Damian admits that ultimate responsibility lies with the individual. The community—in this case, Damian as spokesman—can go only so far in bearing witness before individuals have to work on their own to reach their eschatological goal. "I was unable to instruct you fully," Damian admits, but the tools are there. The individual has only to decide whether, when, and where to put the tools to work. After the work is done, and with God's help, they will come "safely through the battles of this world to [God's] heavenly kingdom."[37]

Letters 2 to 37

Damian's entire corpus is remarkable for its accordance with this first work. This is not to say that his thought does not mature,

35. Letter 1.70–72, in L, 1:80–81; B, 1:100–101.

36. Letter 1.73, in L, 1:82; B, 1:101.

37. Letter 1.74–5, in L, 1:82–83; B, 1:101–2.

only that whilst in the midst of the eremitic movement Damian found his intellectual bearings and did not deviate from them. Years of reflection and experience bring him new insights, widen his horizons, and extend his applications, but he remains faithful to the fundamentals discovered in his early, more secluded years. As the years pass he takes his rather rudimentary understanding of witness expressed in Letter 1 as primarily oral and written testimony and amplifies it into a sophisticated concept of relationship, communication, and communal responsibility. His acknowledgment of the need to work toward change is developed into a theology of work.[38] There are exceptions, of course—personal failures and aging make him more pessimistic, especially about the conditions of his society—but in general his later accomplishments are rooted in ideas born during these more contemplative years. His most original (*Liber Dominus vobiscum*), most unusual (*Liber Gomorrhianus*), and most celebrated (*Liber gratissimus*) works were written between 1048 and 1053. Each is anchored in principles first enunciated in the *Tract against the Jews:* the Incarnation is the central mystery and paradox of life; in the Incarnation creation is fully embraced, so every good Christian must likewise embrace creation; and, Christians are obligated to bear witness to the Incarnation through faith and reason, much as Old Testament witnesses do. To these main tenets Damian adds two corollaries, that Christians maintain a relationship with society in order to communicate that witness effectively and that individuals change the world to ready it for the Second Coming.

This is how he begins and ends his eremitic-monastic life, as a theologian living a life based on these principles, keenly aware of his social obligations. His desire to be separated from the secular world must not be equated with desire to abandon society.[39] Nothing could

38. See my *Theology of Work,* especially 71–76.

39. Phyllis Jestice falls into this error in "Peter Damian against the Reformers," in *The Joy of Learning and the Love of God,* ed. E. Rozanne Elder, 67–94 (Kalamazoo, Mich.: Cistercian Publications, 1995). It is, unfortunately, a significant misunderstanding of Damian's relationship to the world and with other reformers. She tempers her stance somewhat in *Wayward Monks,* published two years later. See discussion below, chapter 3, on Damian's attitudes toward the world and the worldly.

be further from the truth. He lives his life in isolation *because* he loves society; his role in the Body of Christ is to save the community by the witness of his solitary life. His worldview embraces community because of the Romualdian premise, salvation of self comes with salvation of society. In this respect one could label all of Damian's theology as social theology, for the many diverse topics he addresses throughout his life—simony, homosexuality, politics, the Incarnation, Mary, eschatology, writing, work, justice, monastic life, reform, and preaching—find unity in the desire to save society.

His focus on social conditions is evident in things large and small. In the extant letters written during the three years after Letter 1 (all brief messages), Damian touches upon many of the social issues that will dominate his life. In Letter 2 Damian reminds margrave Boniface of Tuscany to view life eschatologically for guidance in social matters, particularly in matters of stewardship in the community: "Using the good sense with which your gifted nature has endowed you, keep heaven in perspective, focus your attention on the termination of this very brief life, and carefully consider who it is to whom you must give an account of your extensive and long-lasting stewardship." He reminds his audience of the relationship between faith and intellectual powers: "Therefore, my dear friend, zealously consider these points, bring them unremittingly before your mind, and carefully ponder not what you are, but what you will be forever."[40] In Letter 3 Damian mentions avarice, a vice he will continually single out for condemnation; for Damian avarice is an individual's desire for more than his or her rightful share of communal goods.[41] He identifies in Letter 4 two specific ways he renders witness to society: "by my tongue" and "by my imagination." Reinforcing his sensibility for individuality and introspection, he adds, "In the repository of my heart, not where my father or mother but where I myself reside [*ubi ipse sum*], I seek to store you away as my other self [*te alterum reconditum*]."[42] Admiration for learning is also

40. Letter 2.2–3, in L, 1:85; B, 1:103–4.

41. Letter 3.2–3, in L, 1:88–89; B, 1:107–8.

42. Letter 4.2, in L, 1:91; B, 1:110. See S, 30:216; 50:30ff; 51:9; 65:185; and 72:298.

evident here in his praise of Lawrence of Amalfi, the addressee, as a man of "such wisdom and erudition of every kind."[43] Eschatology dominates Letter 5, as well as fundamental statements on the relationship between creation, humanity, and God: "God indeed gave all created things for man's use [*usibus*], reserving only souls to himself."[44] Friendship is the reason for Letter 6; Letter 7 is a complaint against a friend's infrequent correspondence (even friendship is cerebral for Damian; upon receiving a letter he keeps "carefully thinking over this matter" and "silently turning over the following words in my mind").[45] Letter 7 is also complaint against a social injustice being perpetrated by Archbishop Widger of Ravenna.

In 1045 Damian starts writing more lengthy epistles, and, again, social issues dominate.[46] In Letter 8 Damian tells us how difficult a process it was to determine his personal vocation: should he be a hermit or a preacher? In his ruminations we find the principles responsible for all his choices. He begins by admitting that he had agreed to go on a preaching tour to Ravenna because he believes himself to be popular and capable of "saving souls." When his mission failed and he had to deal with "the denial of applause," he faces his vanity and considers his life.[47] He is a hermit at heart, a preacher by extension. "I traveled extensively with a devoted purpose throughout various parts of Italy," he confesses, "barely able to avoid the blame of wanderlust." He wanders, because he cannot decide where he can best serve self and society. "Which is more useful for me [*quid mihi utilius sit*]: whether I should live in a place where a harvest of souls can be reaped and where popular respect is shown me; or rather should I live in a place where I must endure a life equally without harvest or the honor? Both seem dangerous to me."[48] This dilemma arises because his starting point is society's salvation, not his own.

43. Letter 4.3, in L, 1:92; B, 1:111. See S, 3:2, 147; 4:154–55; 21:26; 41:345; and 53: 263.

44. Letter 5.2, in L, 1:94; B, 1:112.

45. Letter 7.2, in L, 1:98; B, 1:116.

46. Since many of his letters can only be approximately dated or as before/after a certain date, the chronology is inexact. Still, I present the letters as chronologically as possible to give the reader a general sense of development in Damian's life and thought.

47. Letter 8.2, in L, 1:101; B, 1:119.

48. Letter 8.4, in L, 1:102; B, 1:120.

"Clearly, all the statements of Sacred Scripture were written in its many books for no other reason than for the salvation of souls," and if one were "to neglect the welfare of souls, it is perfectly clear that the intention for which the Scripture should be observed is not being maintained." The community's salvation is the "one end" and "most important objective" of Scripture, so we must always "protect our neighbor" and "assist our comrades." If we do, "we obtain a double reward": self-salvation and salvation of neighbors.[49] To support his contention, Damian turns to Old and New Testament witnesses and the model witness of Christ, "the mediator between God and man." In a statement revealing Damian's astute awareness of the mechanics of witness, he argues that Christ intentionally came "as one revered and admired that he might convert the hearts of his admirers," for unless the preacher "appears somehow worthy of respect to the audience his message ... will be equally held in contempt."[50] When the holy put the welfare of others above their own, "what else are they doing but imitating the example of their head?"[51] Verbal witness, lived witness, utility, *imitatio Christi,* communal obligations, salvation of self and society: these were the considerations foremost in Damian's mind as he decided the shape of his life and thought.

Letter 10 is the first of a kind of letter that is sprinkled throughout his corpus, letters written as an intellectual exercise or outlet. Ostensibly an attack on dependency on wine, Damian uses the opportunity to sharpen his rhetorical skills by writing an extensive prosopopoeian discourse in which water sings its own praises. Throughout the years he writes a bestiary, exhibiting his knowledge of natural history (Letter 86); legal disputations on consanguinity (Letters 19 and 36); an essay on genealogy and numerology (Letter 160); and a historical summation of decadent Roman leaders (Letter 104). In Letter 108 he includes a smattering of history, natural science, astronomy, and philosophy. It is abundantly clear that Damian enjoys using his intellectual muscles, even while cautioning readers

49. Letter 8.5, in L, 1:103–4; B, 1:120–21.

50. Letter 8.8, in L, 1:106–7; B, 1:123.

51. Letter 8.9, in L, 1:108; B, 1:124.

against intellectual overindulgence. This paradoxical tendency of Damian to employ sophisticated rational arguments to criticize excessive cerebral preoccupations can easily lead to the accusation of anti-intellectualism.[52] Already in *Dominus vobiscum* (1048–53), probably his most penetrating speculation outside of Letter 119 (*De divina omnipotentia*), Damian may puzzle the superficial reader with his unabashed (and oft-quoted) denunciation of Greek philosophy.[53] To the contrary, Damian's statements are not anti-intellectual but made to demonstrate "his militant independence, as a theologian, from cultural trends, ideologies, and movements of thought."[54] Damian is explicitly rejecting cultural determinism, not culture. People must use culture as a means to an end, not vice versa; one should "read the poets and the philosophers in order to be more vigorous in penetrating the mystery of the heavenly word."[55] Worldly wisdom is complex, but Truth Itself is simple, so Damian prays, "Let the simplicity of Christ instruct me."[56]

Despite periodic outbursts and occasional confusing statements, Damian remains faithful throughout the years to the principle stated in Letter 1: intellectual activity is essential to salvation. It was Christ himself "who opened his disciples' minds [*qui discipulis aperuit sensum*] that they might understand."[57] One must never "hold his tongue out of ignorance"; indeed, "surely it is disgraceful."[58] He recognizes that the intellectual life "delights a great many laymen almost as much as marital intercourse," but he respects it as long as

52. See Jonathan Sanford, "Peter Damian," in *A Companion to Philosophy in the Middle Ages,* ed. Jorge Gracia and Timothy Noone (Oxford: Blackwell, 2003); Jean Gonsette, *S. Pierre Damien et la culture profane* (Louvain: Publications Universitaires de Louvain, 1956); and Maurice de Wulf, *History of Medieval Philosophy,* tr. Ernest Messenger (New York: Dover, 1952).

53. Letter 28.4, in L, 1:257–58; B, 1:251–52. Damian cites certain philosophers symbolically, not from personal knowledge. See Gonsette, *Pierre Damien,* 24; and Dressler, *Petrus Damiani,* 187.

54. John Saward, *Perfect Fools* (Oxford: Oxford University Press, 1980), 53. See Sanford, "Peter Damian," for appraisal of him as an anti-intellectual.

55. Saward, *Perfect Fools,* 54. Saward cites the source incorrectly; it is from Letter 160.16, in L, 7:130; B: 4.134.

56. Letter 28.4, in L, 1:258; B, 1:252.

57. Letter 1.55, in L, 1:79; B, 1:92.

58. Letter 1.2, in L, 1:38; B, 1:66.

one does not "begin loving it unduly."[59] In a letter to the judge Bonushomo, Damian acknowledges his reputation as an intellectual and knows it leads others to critique his writing for "rhetoric color," "dialectical subtlety," and "hypothetical syllogisms." He accepts their criticism but notes that they will not find "the graces of studied style" in his writing, only the simplicity of the lamb.[60] His goal differs from that of philosophers. "It is absurd and completely improper, moreover, to use the same prudence and the same exactness in human affairs as one might expend on those which are spiritual and divine."[61] Each role in society has its own specific requirements.[62] Since as judge Bonushomo cannot "avoid using the language of the world in your contact with your associates, or at times devoting yourself in some degree to literary studies, you should follow this norm."[63] Society needs it this way. The danger comes when one makes pursuit of secular knowledge into the ultimate activity. It is not. Pursuit of knowledge of God is. "Whoever, therefore, devotes himself to secular learning," Damian argues, "with the intensity one should reserve only for inner scrutiny to please God, deserves to perish because he dissipates the incense, reserved for God alone, on temporal and perishable things."[64] It is a matter of degree. "The study of spiritual wisdom should be of paramount concern [*in summa cordis*]," but secular knowledge is still necessary for the proper functioning of society.[65] He never denigrates those involved in secular affairs. In fact, he respects their expertise: "I leave you with your problems, for I do not presume to possess another official's skill."[66] As the years pass he never abandons this fundamental belief in the inherent goodness of intellectual activity.

59. Letter 23.14, in L, 1:222; B, 1:222–23.

60. Letter 23.2–4, in L, 1:216–17; B, 1:217–18.

61. Letter 23.11, in L, 1:221; B, 1:221.

62. This is an important principle for Damian, and his anger toward the Vallombrosians in 1068 rests in part on their transgression of it. He accuses them of fulfilling roles not proper to monks. See Letter 146.

63. Letter 23.10, in L, 1:220; B, 1:220.

64. Letter 23.12, in L, 1:222; B, 1:220.

65. Letter 23.23, in L, 1:226; B, 1:225.

66. Letter 19.20, in L, 1:185; B, 1:192. See S, 6:73, 206; 38:32ff.

Other dominant concerns surface before mid-century. As a hermit-monk, Damian devotes much literary energy to cajoling religious to reform, encouraging lay people to join monasteries, explaining monastic practices to members, criticizing misconduct, and recommending new practices.[67] His respect for the laity is firmly established in these writings. His high opinion of their spiritual status is evident in a letter to a Ravenna nobleman in which he argues that the riches of the Office are for "all Christian faithful," not merely a spiritually elite group.[68] This attitude is consistent with his belief in the spiritual equality of all individuals. Because clerics and monks are not superior to nobles, or nobles to peasants, the laity has the right to criticize the hierarchy. He even advises them to do so.[69] All share the same obligations and opportunities: "If you can attend the office in church, or when chanted by a priest, all is well; otherwise, if you are riding horseback, or perhaps are engaged in work in the fields or in any other enterprise, while you work, in your travel, pay in kind your dues to the Lord with that commodity which is at hand. Thus, if there are psalms to say, say them."[70]

Damian's abhorrence of luxurious clothing also surfaces early. Given Damian's insistence on witness, his awareness of the power clothes have to communicate is unsurprising. Still, his grasp of the connection is unusually strong; Damian himself always tried "to appear in your presence in ordinary garb and thus practiced what I preached."[71] Clothing is his primary focus in a letter to Abbot Mainard of Pomposa, who rejoices "in the useless splendor of bodily attire."[72] John the Baptist, whose "vesture bristled with camel's hair,"

67. For example, Letters 9 (explanation), 10 (encourages laymen to join), 14 (reform), 17 (explanation), 18 (introduces own rule), 24 (criticism of clothes), 25 (encourages laity), and 27 (criticism of food).

68. Letter 17.2, in L, 1:145; B, 1:156; and Letter 17.19, in L, 1:154–55; B, 1:164–65. Damian discusses the Little Office in 17.23, in L, 1:146–47; B, 1:156–57.

69. See Letter 20 to Emperor Henry III. He promotes this right throughout his life. See Letter 51 to Beatrice, Duchess of Tuscany; and Letter 74.

70. Letter 17.19, in L, 1:155; B, 1:164.

71. Letter 24.2, in L, 1:228; B, 1:227. See S, 4:61; 5:109ff; and 6:300–302.

72. Letter 24.9, in L, 1:234; B, 1.231.

and Christ, born "wrapped in common swaddling clothes," are humanity's models.[73] Only on the Last Day will splendid clothes be warranted "because the whole choir of the elect is freed from the mournful squalor of the sadness of time and is clothed in a robe of immortality in the splendor of everlasting happiness."[74] Eschatology provides the motive: "Appear now in gloomy attire so that later you may exchange your rough garb for one of unfailing brightness."[75]

By mid-century Damian's flexibility and moderation are well known. He conscientiously avoids rigidity, praying that God will reconcile him to Pope Leo IX "lest I remain inflexible."[76] While his personal goals are often immoderate, he does not demand the same from others. He argues that ideally this world should "not [flourish] in our heart" but he realistically recognizes that "since these conditions are impossible for some, especially for laymen, who find themselves totally unable to excel in the affairs of both worlds, they should be admonished to attempt at least to subordinate those things which they cannot completely despise."[77] When his interpretation of the laws on consanguinity are questioned, he readily submits to judgment, asking others to "tell me whether in calculating the degrees of relationship I should continue in the opinion I first described" or change his mind.[78] The reason why he is willing to change is twofold: rereading the sources led him to conclude that his method "could be changed"; and, second, others pointed out that his conclusion "had in it a cruel and inhuman rigidity."[79] In general, he also approaches law with moderation. He has great respect for the law and recognizes its utility. "Through circuitous routes of legal intricacies" it forms a wall that restrains bad decisions and forces you "even against you own will [to] return to the right path."[80] He

73. Letter 24.3, in L, 1:229; B, 1:228. For John the Baptist, see S, 24 and 25; 17/2:148; 19:18; 37:109ff; 51:177; 64:34ff; and 67:34ff. Second quote: Letter 24.8, in L, 1:233; B, 1:231.

74. Letter 24.11, in L, 1:235; B, 1:233.

75. Letter 24.9, in L, 1:234; B, 1:232. See S, 4:61; 5; and 6:300–302.

76. Letter 33.5, in L, 2:58; B, 1:334.

77. Letter 23.13, in L, 1:222; B, 1:222.

78. Letter 36.11, in L, 2:70; B, 1:345.

79. Letter 36.3, in L, 2:65; B, 1:340.

80. Letter 25.13, in L, 1:242; B, 1:238. In the ecclesiastical discussions of the late 1050s

is not legalistic. In *Gomorrhianus* he assiduously examines the canons to determine their authenticity and calls those who blindly accept laws "so stupid [*tam hebes*]" and "so irrational [*tam insanus*]."[81] He desires rational investigation, not blind acceptance, because Scripture teaches "that human ignorance should not believe what it hears without investigation [*sine experimentis*]."[82] He is, at heart, a man of the spirit: "Away, then, with the written letter that brings death; let the life-giving Spirit attend us."[83]

Damian also has profound respect for authority. "I will not delay in saying what I think about this question," he declares in *Dominus vobiscum,* "so that your authority may correct what I have said badly."[84] He is likewise humble enough to realize that his arguments do not persuade everyone: "Just as Truth Itself testified, not everyone in this world can accept what I have said."[85] When disagreements arise, they should "be resolved by the rational mediation of the attentive heart," a statement that captures his understanding of the dual nature of proper decision making: mind and heart.[86] His personal humility is often hard to separate from the rhetorical humility he employs. To modern sensibilities its use may serve to render him vain, but however confident of his powers and determined to bear witness, he still bows to those in authority. Even his *Dominus vobiscum,* he claims, "is not a definitive statement but a dissertation airing its reasons," and he declares that he has no intention of "usurping the authority of the master [Leo]."[87] When writing to Bishop Ubertus, Damian encourages charitable actions but adds in a note of sincerity, "But why do I teach the master?"[88]

---

and early 1060s Damian is acknowledged to hold a moderate view. Blum, "Monitor of the Popes St. Peter Damian," 476, calls him "cautious but hopeful."

81. Letter 31.28, in L, 2:21; B, 1:301.

82. Letter 33.4, in L, 2:57; B, 1:333. See also Letter 34.3, in L, 2:69; B, 1:335–36; Letter 31.76, in L, 2:53; B, 1:329 [*diligenter inspectis*]; Letter 19.3, in L, 1:173; B, 1:181 [*ulterus inquirendum*]; and Letter 31.73, in L, 2:51; B, 1:328.

83. Letter 28.5, in L, 1:258; B, 1:252.

84. Letter 28.6, in L, 1:259; B, 1:253. See S, 49:32ff. Secular authority is discussed at length below in chapter 6.

85. Letter 31.70, in L, 2:48–49; B, 1:325.

86. Letter 19.18, in L, 1:183; B, 1:190.

87. Letter 28.56, in L, 1:288; B, 1:250.

88. Letter 32.2, in L, 2:54; B, 1:331.

Because introspection is a gift from God it must be utilized.[89] Calls to "examine your life with great subtleness," judge "your own deeds," "go back within your conscience," let one's "conscience bear witness"—these flow throughout even his earliest writings.[90] Moreover, Damian lives what he preaches and never hesitates to "consult my conscience [and] review the secrets of my soul."[91] Often introspection results "in crisis over any matter of conscience."[92] This demands courage, as when he challenges the papal establishment to look squarely into the growing sexual situation among clergy. Damian knows that he will be accused "of being an informer and a delator of my brother's crime," but he has "no fear of the hatred of evil men nor of the tongues of detractors." He bravely publicizes the issue "to prevent the departure of members," and because if he did not, "I should become responsible for another's crime."[93] His courage comes from the purity of his motive: "I seek not to dishonor, but rather to promote the advantage of my brother's well-being."[94] His courage includes stout defenses against his attackers, strongly suggesting—but not accusing—that Leo IX believes Damian's foes "without investigation."[95] In all things he practices what he preaches: "Shake off this ignoble cowardice, this deep-seated listlessness, take up arms like a man, and with the shield of deep introspection ward off the javelins launched by your opponents."[96]

The same keen sense of justice that leads him to unpopular issues makes him champion the poor. He supports the education of a "poor little man," the future bishop Henry of Sarsina and is particularly sensitive to avarice, because it affects the poor.[97] "Kill avarice," he lectures Archbishop Gebhard of Ravenna, and "lift up the fallen."[98] The wealthy and powerful must not aspire to more for them-

89. Letter 30.3, in L, 1:295; B, 1:283.

90. Letter 21.16, in L, 1:207; B, 1:210–11; Letter 12.3, in L, B, 1:141 [*intra conscienciam tuam revertere*]; and Letter 34.2, in L, 2:59; B, 1:335, respectively. See also S, 30:216; 50:30ff; 51:9; 65:185; and 78:298.

91. Letter 33.4, in L, 2:57; B, 1:333.

92. Letter 28.2, in L, 1:256; B, 1:250.

93. Letter 31.71, in L, 2:49–50; B, 1:326.

94. Letter 31.74, in L, 2:52; B, 1:328.

95. Letter 33.4, in L, 2:57; B, 1:333.

96. Letter 27.10, in L, 1:253; B, 1:247.

97. Letter 32.2, in L, 2:54; B, 1:331.

98. Letter 3.3, in L, 1:89; B, 1:108.

selves but judiciously care for those with less. He warns margrave Boniface of the account he must give in the next world "of your extensive and long-lasting stewardship"; he repeats the same warning to a bishop named John.[99] His repulsion of avarice is undeniable in his exegesis on the parable of the rich man and Lazarus. "There are two sins committed by the rich man," Damian explains. The first is not sharing his clothes, the second, not sharing his food. "In both cases he was clearly shown to be insensitive and inhumane," Damian heatedly proclaims. "This is an important matter and one need not wonder that it had extensive antecedents."[100] His compassion is, of course, not limited to material matters or status; his letter to Senator Amelric and his wife, Ermilina, at the death of their infant child reveals Damian as a very emotional, sensitive man. Upon hearing of the child's death, "I was overcome with instant sorrow, and bitter pangs of compassion pierced my heart." Frustrated in his desire to assuage their pain, Damian puts the death in eschatological perspective. "[God] has brought a child of your flesh to the kingdom of heaven, placed him among the angels," he writes. "He has gathered him into his own arms, kissed him like a loving father, and as his own son took him with joy into his own eternally restful bedchamber."[101] At his optimistic best, Damian encourages the parents to "put aside all signs of sorrow and bereavement, restore to your home the accustomed gayness," while Damian prays that God will "grant you many children to replace this child."[102]

It may be hard to persuade the reader who knows Peter only through quotes from *De contemptu mundi* (Letter 165) that at mid-century he had an intense love of the world. I ask the reader to consider the modern English connotations for the words *world* and *worldly*. He loves the world; he hates the worldly. Most critics fail to see this distinction. God created the world in love, and the Word Incarnate embraced that world. Damian would do no less. In *Dominus*

99. Letter 2.2, in L, 1:85; B, 1:103; and Letter 12.3, in L, 1:128; B, 1:141.

100. Letter 9.3, in L, 1:110; B, 1:126.

101. Letter 15.2, in L, 1:140–41; B, 1:151.

102. Letter 15.7, in L, 1:142; B, 1:152.

vobiscum and again later in Letter 49, he bears witness to his love of the world and expands on the ancient microcosm-macrocosm analogy: "Just as in Greek man is called microcosm, that is to say, a little world [*minor mundus*], because in his physical composition he consists of the same four elements that are found in the whole earth; so also each of the faithful seems to be, as it were, a little Church."[103] What Damian does hate is "the worldly," humanity's reduction of the world into a godless, loveless state. He hates the blurring of lines between the temporal and the eternal, the elevation of the mundane into the celestial, the corruption of creation's goodness by human vice. Similarly, Damian loves society as part of the created world and when it acts as the rightful possessor of "a certain sovereignty over all the living things of the earth [*inter omnia terrae*] ... and a kind of preeminence of greater excellence."[104] He hates society when it abandons its sovereignty and preeminence and lets "the flame of love, deprived, as it were, of its kindling, [grow] cold as the result of human depravity."[105] This is the world Damian has contempt for, not a properly behaved world. For example, his respect for secular authority, when exercised as intended, is intense; his contempt for it when misused is likewise intense.[106] He has contempt for that part of creation corrupted by humanity's depravity.[107] This distinction is clearly articulated later in life, but is already part of his worldview prior to mid-century.[108] It is present in Letter 21 (before 1047), where he juxtaposes the splendor of what God intended with the damage humanity inflicted.[109] It is there in Letter 5 (1043) when he writes that God "gave all created things for man's use [*cunta nimirum*

103. Letter 28.25, in L, 1:270; B, 1:262.

104. Letter 49.12, in L, 2:278; B, 2:69.

105. Letter 19.8, in L, 1:176; B, 1:184.

106. See Letter 20 for admiration of the proper use of authority, and Letter 14 for its misuse.

107. Letter 86, written in 1061, is a glowing tribute to the wonders of the created natural world and is prefaced by a ringing denunciation of the distortions humanity has made in the social world.

108. Letter 165 is discussed at length below, in chapter 5. The letter was written at age 62, three years prior to his death.

109. See, for example, Letter 21.15, in L, 1:205–6; B, 1:209–10.

condita omnibus Deus usibus hominum tradidit]" so that "eternal benefits may be acquired," and warns against fashioning an evil society through misuse of the world.[110]

Taken as a whole, his views on the created world are overwhelmingly positive. Just as "the star carries out its assigned function," so too does the individual, and "while both proceed toward their goals by different paths, the very elements of the world seem in their subservient way to be in harmony with the servant of God."[111] His letter to a hermit (before June 1045) in which he personifies water provides an indisputable example of the deep respect and even pleasure he takes in creation, particularly in its utility and "majestic powers."

> I wash your body, your clothes, and everything else that you use; I continuously water your fields so they might bring forth crops; I furnish routes for your ships. I refresh all life on earth, and produce an abundance of fruit and vegetables which you eat. I will say nothing about the birds and the fish that are daily begotten in my realm . . . the mighty earth itself, where all visible things come into being, in association with the air, rests on my support as its very foundation, and by my power is kept in existence.[112]

The power of water is awesome in all respects. It affects humanity's spiritual well-being: "Finding you soiled and filthy, I did not hesitate to wash your body and soul."[113] It contributes to humanity's intellectual maturity. "When the geometrician or the astronomer strives to construct a clock to determine the interval of hours," water boasts, "they at once have recourse to me."[114] It contributes

110. Letter 5.2, in L, 1:93–94; B, 1:112–13. Camaldolese historian Peter-Damian Belisle, "Overview of Camaldolese History and Spirituality," in *Privilege of Love,* ed. P-D. Belisle (Collegeville, Minn.: Liturgical Press, 2002), 12, tells us that this is the heart of Romuald's theology: "Romualdian monasticism is also most definite about its rejection of the world and its ways—but not engulfed by it; grounded in that world, but not buried by it."

111. Letter 28.50, in L, 1:284; B, 1:275. The basic harmony between the world and humanity is also seen in Damian's description of Romuald's "stopping now and then to sit under a tree and sing twenty psalms, then moving to another tree to sing thirty more." VR, 41 (178–79).

112. Letter 10.5–6, in L, 1:115–16; B, 1:130; citation for "majestic powers" is Letter 10.9, in L, 1:116; B, 1:131.

113. Letter 10.4, in L, 1:115; B, 1:129–30.

114. Letter 10.9, in L, 1:117–18; B, 1:.131–32.

to culture; music's "very name is dependent on my laws ... since in the Greek language *musa* means *water*."[115] In brief, creation of water makes human life more enjoyable and easier. "If my strength were not at your service, who, I ask, would turn the great mill wheels that grind your grain?"[116] In light of the overwhelming goodness and power of creation, humanity has only one option, Damian's standard instruction: "You should diligently investigate these matters." Creation, however, is beyond the grasp of rationality, so humanity must humbly bow to its superiority: "When you are unable to explain them with certainty, you must conclude that the innermost forces of my [water's] nature are unfathomable."[117]

Damian also writes of another element in creation, God's love. In Letter 19 (1046), Damian reminds his audience not to "marvel that love be brought into discussion of begetting men, since at creation God, the maker of all things, seems to have provided for this."[118] He created several kinds of every other living thing, except man, from whom he generated woman. He did this "to demonstrate the value of love and to join them in the bond of mutual love."[119] Likewise, when God created the Church he "divided [it] into the great number of persons involved" but then "the love of God has been poured into our hearts" and fused the many into one.[120] God's love is found in the creation of manna, "this food of life-giving nourishment" boiled "in the pot of fervent love."[121] Damian's underlying attitude regarding creation as created for man's use is based on the postulate that God is love and Christ is the new creation.[122] Creation's utility, granted in love, gives him unquestioned pleasure: "While not seeing the eye

115. Letter 10.10, in L, 1:118; B, 1:132.

116. Letter 10.7, in L, 1:116; B, 1:131. Of course, Damian's grasp of natural science is premodern, so we also hear him make some naïve claims.

117. Letter 10.8, in L, 1:117; B, 1:131.

118. Letter 19.7, in L, 1:176; B, 1:184.

119. Letter 19.8, in L, 1:176; B, 1:184.

120. Letter 28.14, in L, 1:263; B, 1:256.

121. Letter 27.6, in L, 1:250; B, 1:245.

122. Letter 5.2, in L, 1:94; B, 1:112; and Letter 1.53, in L, 1:69; B, 1:91. Some say this is the underlying attitude of Judaic-Christianity. See Lynn White, "The Historical Roots of Our Ecological Controversy and the Old Testament," *Bulletin of the John Rylands Library* 55 (1972–73), 9–32.

that grants me sight, I still enjoy its service."[123] Finally, Damian sees creation, both earthy matter and humanity, as one. Humanity "consists of the same four elements that are found in the whole earth," and Damian uses the ancient macrocosm/microcosm metaphor to express this belief.[124]

Already in Romuald's vita and in Letter 1 Damian has well-defined concepts of self and community.[125] "The tabernacle of God is the community of Christian people," Damian writes.[126] Thus every person is responsible for the welfare of the tabernacle: "The salvation of my neighbor is of such concern for me that I do not consider it wasteful to light a mighty bonfire to kill even a tiny venomous lizard if that were necessary for the people's safety."[127] This is an extremely personal conviction of Damian's, one that he manifests in his behavior. He responds to the needs of everyone. He cares deeply about the community's problems and directs his action and contemplation to solving these problems, be they personal (the death of a child), canonical (regulations for marriage), proprietary (land dispute), ecclesiastical (clerical scandal), or social (care for the poor).[128] For example, in Letter 12 (ca. 1045) we see Damian's awareness of individuality in his call to examine one's conscience, and his perception of community in his call to fulfill the obligations of stewardship (*villicacione tua*). His own sense of individuality and community is evident in his Rule for Fonte Avellana (Letter 18). He gives thanks to God for "this office of unworthy service in a community small in number," where "I lead the way for such men in returning to our fatherland, but only to rejoice if I am able to keep up with the footsteps

123. Letter 11.2, in L, 1:125; B, 1:138.

124. Letter 28.25, in L, 1:270; B, 1:262. See also Letter 17.7, in L, 1:148; B, 1:158.

125. Colin Morris, *The Discovery of the Individual* (London: Camelot Press, 1972), favored the term "individual" in his influential study; Carolyn Walker Bynum, "Did the Twelfth Century Discover the Individual?" *Journal of Ecclesiastical History* 31.1 (1980), 1–17, argues that "self" is more accurate. The literature is extensive, and both arguments for terminology are sound. Rather than take sides I will use the terms interchangeably.

126. Letter 1.55, in L 1:69; B, 1:91.

127. Letter 19.31, in L, 1:192; B, 1:198.

128. See, respectively, Letters 15, 19, 34, 31, 35, 2 and 12.

of my brethren."[129] As always, he sees individual salvation as a communal affair. Most importantly, he sees the individual's love for others as the basis for community: "One item that seems to exceed all the rest, one thing that may be said to surpass all the virtues of those who live here in holiness, is that there is such love among the brethren such unanimity of will forged by the fire of mutual charity, that everyone considers himself born to serve all and not himself."[130]

He also has a deep sense of the individual's debt to posterity. All actions should be done with both the present individual and the future community in mind. He writes his Rule "for the welfare of my brethren" but also for "those who will come after you." We see a sense of history, optimism for future community members: "I am no less solicitous for the future religious life of this hermitage than I am concerned for those who live here now."[131] This love of community present and future translates into action for Damian. It is the reason why he tries to become a traveling preacher; he is "anxious about where I might reap a more plentiful harvest of souls, and compelled by zeal for my neighbor."[132] It is for both that he acquires property, collects books for a library, corrects codices, has a cloister built, and procures numerous liturgical items. As always, Damian places this love in an eschatological setting. "Whoever you may be who succeed me in living in this holy place, I implore you," he concludes, "that in loving exchange you also assist me with your prayers after I am dead; and as I prepared for you a place suited to religious life, may you supply me with the means of obtaining generous forgiveness."[133]

Awareness of this relationship between persons and community does not hinder his strong sense of self. Perception of himself as writer is particularly individualistic. Eleventh-century epistolary style demanded certain rhetorical formulas, but early on we see that despite these societal requirements Damian still managed to imprint his own individual mark on works. In Romuald's vita he imposes him-

129. Letter 18.3, in L, 1:161; B, 1:170.

130. Letter 18.15, in L, 1:166; B, 1:175.

131. Letter 18.17, in L, 1:167; B, 1:174–75.

132. Letter 8.4, in L, 1:102; B, 1:119–20.

133. Letter 18.22, in L, 1:170; B, 1:179.

self full force on the story in the prologue; it is his testimony that he deems important. Twice he tells "my readers" what "I want to do."[134] The conclusion of Letter 2 is filled with strong "I" statements, well beyond the norm. Letter 8 contains lengthy autobiographical material.[135] In his defense for writing *Gomorrhianus* we see a strong individual, independent and capable of withstanding social pressure. The calls for introspection *(oculos cordis),* self-awareness, reflection, and examination of conscience that fill his early letters tell us that Damian is already cognizant of the individuality that historians document in twelfth-century literature. These scholars argue that emphasis on friendship, intention, and a new piety are indicative of the medieval discovery of the self; all are found in Damian's early writings.[136]

Damian's perception of the individual and community is keen enough for him to recognize an inherent conflict between them. When faced with a shortage of priests because of a church discipline forbidding fornicating clergy to celebrate mass, some argued that "in the face of practical necessity," the ban should be lifted. Damian pondered: "Shall we wipe out a rigorous judgment to benefit an individual, but retain it unchanged even to the deprivation of an entire people? If we do not sacrifice a principle to benefit a vast multitude, shall we violate it to promote one man's advantage?"[137] His answer is clear. If one cares for the well-being of the community, one must first attend to the welfare of the individual. A sinful individual is "paving the way to error ... for those who follow him," because all

134. VR, prol. (170–71).

135. Letter 8.2–4, in L 1:100–102; B, 1:118–20.

136. For friendship, see Letter 12; intention: Letter 33.4, in L, 2:57; B, 1:333; piety: Letter 1.42, in L, 1:63; B, 1:86; Letter 14.5, in L, 1:137; B, 1:152, and Letter 17. Damian's close friendship with Desiderius and the monks at Monte Cassino is evident in his many letters to them (Letters 82, 86, 90, 95, 102, 106, 119, 126, 127, 159, 160, and 161). Letters 54, 55, and 117 are to close friends Ariprandus and Rodulfus; letters to Empress Agnes (104, 124, 130, 144, and 149; he wrote 71 in the name of others) also reveal a deep friendship. Numerous other letters (for example, Letters 14 and 72) indicate strong friendships with others. Given the accusation of Little, "Personal Development," 336, that Damian was friendless, and Christopher Brooke's statement (*Age of the Cloister* [Mahwah, N.J.: Hidden Springs, 2003], 89) that "he disliked his fellow monk," it is important to document the opposite.

137. Letter 31.13, in L, 2:10; B, 1:291.

behavior bears witness to something. Thus, the errant priest must be disciplined regardless of the immediate effect it has on the community, because the long-term effect is much more devastating: "By the example of his own presumption he has invited others to emulate his sin."[138]

To avoid damage to the community the individual must constantly be aware of the dual impact thoughts and actions have on self and others. It is this awareness that leads Damian to place extraordinary emphasis on witness. For Damian there is no such thing as an insular act. In later years he writes a commentary on Acts 4:32–35, the classic description of the primitive community and model for the vita apostolica. He argues that verse 33, "with power the apostles bore witness," is the key to the passage and the primitive community. Accordingly, those wishing to live the vita apostolica must bear witness to their society. Their lives must communicate the message of Christianity "with power."[139] Canons must live a life of poverty and community, because both bear witness to Christian values.[140] Again, clothes are of major concern, because they bear immediate and visible witness. The temptation to wear clothes that bear false witness must be resisted. Everyone "wishes to shine in his brilliant clothes so that smartly attired he might delight the eye of his admirers and indulge the visual pleasure of others," but the temptation should be withstood. Rather, one should follow the example of John the Baptist whose clothes "clearly stated that those who affect the adornment of fastidious dress ... are judged worthy of serving earthly kings and not the King of heaven."[141] In fact, the whole of John's witness incites in Damian the deepest admiration and desire to imitate.

138. Letter 31.14, in L, 2:12; B, 1:291–92.

139. Letter 98.27–28, ibid, 5.101–2; B, 3.96–97.

140. See Letters 39 (ca. 1051) and 98 (1063); they are foundational documents for the canons regular. Both have Damian's witness theology at the center.

141. Letter 24.2–3, in L, 1:229; B, 1:228. These themes concerning the witness of John the Baptist are developed more fully in S, 24 and 25. See also S, 17/2:148; 19:18; 37:109ff; 151:177; 64:34ff; and 67:34ff. In Letter 27 to Honestus, Damian criticizes him for his excessive love of food and "the vain desire for precious clothes." He advises him to read Letter 24 on the issue of clothes and witness.

The concept of witness is essential to Damian on a personal level, for it gives meaning to the hermit's life. He knows that its communal value is not always or easily grasped, for a solitary, invisible life hardly appears communal. This is the reason why he includes history in *Dominus vobiscum,* to help fellow hermits see how the witness of their solitary life binds them to the community: "I will briefly explain. It is possible that in their simplicity some of the brothers might be tempted while living alone to think that they are somehow separated from the community of the faithful." The Hebrews bear witness to the opposite. The tribes "testify to the communal bond of Israel."[142] *Dominus vobiscum* is a celebration of the power of witness to bind the individual to the community. In 1045 Damian rejected the preacher's life, not because he thought it inferior, but because he would bear better witness as a writer.[143]

Finally, the reason for labor becomes clearer in light of the witness mandate. Bearing witness to others involves activity, oftentimes in the city of man. Be it spiritual, intellectual, or manual, labor is needed in order to prepare for the eschaton. Indeed, the only way to reach the city of God is to attend to one's obligations here and now. "Do not in your preoccupation with any of the affairs of this world pass up this certain remedy for your soul," Damian instructs a nobleman, for "the whole life of the virtuous man may reasonably be called a prayer," the prayer of witness. One always has the ability to offer one's work as a prayerful witness.[144] Only when "various duties are performed in harmony" will the community have a city worthy of the eschaton.[145] As the tribes at Shiloh "meant their work to be witness for their children," so too must Christians mean their work to bear witness.[146]

142. Letter 28.27, in L, 1:271; B, 1:263.
143. See Letter 8.
144. Letter 17.18–19; in L, 1:154–55; B, 1:164.
145. Letter 28.54, in L, 1:287; B, 1:277.
146. Letter 28.27, in L, 1:271; B, 1:263.

Three

THE MATURE THEOLOGIAN

Each in its own way, the two *opuscula Liber "Dominus vobiscum"* and *Liber Gomorrhianus,* written mid-century, are essential to any study of Peter Damian's life, thought, and influence.[1] Given their significance, readers needs to be well acquainted with their content before judging Damian for themselves.

Letter 28: *Liber "Dominus vobiscum"*

Because the eremitic movement was young, limited in number and location, and isolated by definition, members were not always sure of proper protocol. When Romuald's first mentor, Marino, started his quest for solitude, "no one had trained him in the hermit life; he had simply taken it on by himself, moved by his own good will." His routine reflected the experimental nature of his life: "He would wander aimlessly, stopping now and then to sit under a tree and sing twenty psalms, then moving to another tree to sing thirty more, and so on."[2] Romuald too looked for guidance. When he read that St. Sylvester "introduced fasting on Saturday," he followed suit.[3]

1. *Dominus vobiscum* was written 1048–53; *Gomorrhianus* in 1049.

2. VR, 4 (178–79). Gregorio Penco, "Eremitismo irregolare in Italia nei secoli XI–XII," *Benedictina* 32 (1985), does remind us, though, that thirty-four Italian hermits from the eleventh and twelfth centuries were revered as saints.

3. VR, 9 (187).

When he read in the *Lives of the Desert Elders* that they had a common meal on Saturday and Sunday, "from then on, for fifteen years or so, Romuald followed this practice."[4] Some confused hermits "sent messengers to Romuald, asking him how to organize their life in the hermitage."[5] In *The Life of the Five Brothers* we see how much was established by trial and error; Bruno tells us that Benedict of Benevento could not decide what form his life should take.[6] At this early stage of the eremitic movement there was little agreement about practices or organization, for the hermits "were all accustomed to privacy and the freedom to do as they wished."[7]

Introduction Often these pioneering hermits, Damian included, were puzzled over theological matters. He admits that "one anxiety still bothers me," the question of which life is more theologically advantageous, martyr or monk. He cites conflicting scriptural passages, lays out arguments for both sides, and then frustratingly implores his advisor to "either intimate another point of view, or confirm what I have said with the authority of your sound judgment."[8] So it is quite within the norm when Damian writes his spiritual father, the hermit Leo of Sitria, to critique his judgment concerning a theological matter. The matter is one of grammar, but as happened so frequently in the High Middle Ages, it was a grammatical question that encased profound theological and philosophical issues. As Damian reports, he had been asked by numerous hermits "whether, since they live alone in their cells, they are allowed to say, 'The Lord be with you' [*vobiscum,* pl], and 'Pray, sir, your blessing,' and whether, since they are alone, they should reply to themselves according to the practice of the Church."[9] To answer these queries Damian makes his own inquiry, and the result of that investigation forms the first and longer part of the treatise. The second part is a laudatory discourse on the eremitic life.

4. VR, 8 (185).
5. VR, 32 (224).
6. V5F, 2 (87–88).
7. VR, 34 (228).
8. Letter 8.4 and 10, in L, 1:102 and 108; B, 1:120 and 124.
9. Letter 28.3, in L, 1:256; B, 1:251.

Damian's introductory remarks establish the nature of his relationship with Leo and, while doing so, he tells us much about his interior life and about the practice of spiritual direction among eleventh-century hermits.

> I regard you, not as just some colleague or friend, but as a father, a teacher, a master, and lord.... Since I have regarded you as my guardian angel from whose mouth has come advice whenever doubtful matters made me hesitate and inquire, I have readily and unquestioningly accepted your word as if it were the voice of an angel speaking to me from heaven. So, whenever I am in crisis over any matter of conscience, before coming to consult you I first privately beg the Lord in his goodness to make up as it were an instrument of his Will, that from your lips He might command the course I am to take in the doubtful matter that lies before me. Now, too, following my usual custom, I ask you to teach me what I should reply to those many inquirers who have often demanded an answer of me.[10]

Here is the decision-making process Damian employs when faced with questions. He finds someone he believes is his spiritual superior and seeks his advice. Given Damian's admissions about the frequency of his requests for Leo's direction, we can surmise that Damian's examination of conscience is likewise frequent. One also notes that private prayer precedes any conference with a spiritual director. These are the simple steps Damian took to attain spiritual direction: examination of conscience, identification of a director, prayer for divine oversight, and discussion of issues.[11] Even here Damian is innovative, for the process describes the return of individualized guidance. Early desert spirituality focused on revelation of inner thoughts and the surrender of one's will to a single spiritual director. When monasticism took root in the West, personal direction was diminished in importance as cenobitism replaced eremiticism and formal written rules replaced individual guidance. As Jean Leclercq

10. Letter 28.2, in L, 1:256; B, 1:250.

11. See my "A Key to Counter Reformation Women's Activism: The Confessor-Spiritual Director," *Journal of Feminist Studies in Religion* 10.2 (1994), 7–26; and *A Woman's Way: The Forgotten History of Women Spiritual Directors* (New York: Palgrave, 2000), 49–66.

observes, because the primary duty of the Rule was "the collective guidance of the community," and because the Rule dominated Western monasticism in the early eleventh century, "personal guidance had lost something of the importance it enjoyed."[12] As eremiticism returns to the West, Damian reports that personal spiritual direction also returns.[13] Because Damian writes for a relatively large public, this report spreads beyond the world of monasticism into the (only slightly) larger world of literacy.

If we ponder the introduction to Letter 28 further, though, we discover innovations that distinguish Damian's spiritual direction from ancient spiritual guidance. Damian is writing his spiritual director for advice on how to become a proper spiritual director to others. He seeks Leo's guidance, because he is concerned about the rigor of his argument. Damian is not asking Leo to critique his spirituality as a desert abba would do, but to judge the logic of his solution. "And so, dear father, prudently analyze what is here set forth," so that "it will be of no further use for anyone to discuss this question."[14] The direction Damian seeks is guidance to Truth Itself.

The focus of this introduction is significant. Damian is asking his mentor to assess an answer to a specific question regarding the use of plurals by an individual while praying. The question is complex and demands the full use of one's rational powers. Indeed, one must go beyond human abilities and access divine sources. Answers that rely solely on reason are human answers, hence restricted by the capability of the intellect. Answers which come from faith are divine answers, hence unrestricted. When read outside this context, Damian's explanation of his approach in constructing his argument appears to be anti-intellectual and disdainful of past human intellectual accomplishments. Within its proper context it becomes a boast.

12. Jean Leclercq, "Traditions of Spiritual Guidance: Spiritual Direction in the Benedictine Tradition," *The Way* 27 ((1987), 54–57; and Leclercq, "Spiritual Guidance and Counseling according to the Rule of St. Benedict," in *Abba,* ed. John Sommerfeldt (Kalamazoo, Mich.: Cistercian Publications, 1982), 64.

13. Damian also reports Romuald's use of it in VR, 4 (178–79).

14. Letter 28.5, in L, 1:258; B, 1:252.

Damian will not be limited by past human endeavors. He will surpass them. He will approach the divine for the wisdom that is Itself. He forswears literal interpretation and the confines of previously established rules for intellectual inquiries. "Away, then, with the written letter that brings death," he demands, "and do not permit the long-winded schools of the proud philosophers to circumvent the disciple of the humble Christ." Damian wants to push beyond past human limits and seek wisdom at its source. Since he perceives the divine primarily as Truth Itself, Damian uses his reasoning powers to logically conclude that the spirit must likewise join in the search for wisdom. This is why Damian submits his answer to his spiritual director, for assurance that he is following the path beyond "the fount of Ciceronian eloquence, but rather to the source of divine wisdom." Damian wants more than either the past or philosophy can give. "Tell me that of which all the naïve dialecticians are ignorant," he begs of Leo. "For I seek from you the highest Truth," he explains, that which "has been made manifest to all the world and reigns in everlasting majesty in heaven." It is this desire for more that evokes the strong protests. "I reject Plato," "I count [Pythagoras] for little," "I reject" Nicomachis, Euclid "I disdain," "I pass by [*praetereo*] all the rhetors," Damian proclaims, because they do not provide the full answer. He does not believe any of the ancients can answer this question (*omnes dialecticos cum suis silogismis et sophisticis cavillationibus indigros hac questione decerno*), because it lies beyond the realm of secular knowledge. The highest truth (*summam veritatem*) resides solely in "the simplicity of Christ."[15]

It is most important, however, to acknowledge this caveat: Damian is not condemning secular knowledge; he is underlining its limitations. The use of secular knowledge in the pursuit of divine knowledge is consistent with his worldview. I have already documented in those works written prior to *Dominus vobiscum* his profound respect for human intelligence and his insistence that it be

15. Letter 28.3–5, in L, 1:257–58; B, 1:251–52.

utilized to its full potential. Nothing in this treatise belies his previous statements. To the contrary, they are entirely compatible. Hence it is quite natural that immediately following his protestations on the limits of secular masters he announces that his methodology here will be "after the fashion of the masters in the schools." As in the schools he will say "what I think about this question" and then wait for his teachers to "correct what I have said badly." Concerning the usage of *"Dominus vobiscum,"* he will "first attempt to show for what purpose these practices became customary in the churches, and then ... explain my position on the points that have been raised."[16] We see, therefore, Damian embrace all that secular wisdom has to offer not as a final goal but as an intermediate one that will propel him onward to the ultimate goal of divine wisdom. Only then will there be "no further use of anyone to discuss this question."[17]

Part One As promised, Damian starts his dissertation with a probe into the Church's customary use of the phrase. After citing the Old and New Testaments he makes two claims: first, "this greeting is not some recent human innovation but is ... based on the ancient authority of Sacred Scripture"; and, second, "it is often found both in the singular and in the plural."[18] The priests' greeting, "The Lord be with you," and the people's response, "and with your spirit," as well as the bishop's greeting, "peace to you," apply to "the house of God in which all should be children of peace."[19] Because it has "the authority of divine Scripture," it is always "to be observed according to the Church's tradition ... even if only one is present."[20] Once he has established the purpose of the custom, to observe the biblical practice, he explains his opinion of the custom. It is here that Damian makes his most impressive contributions.

At the heart of the issue over the use of the first person plural by a single individual are the realities of self and community. Can

16. Letter 28.6, in L, 1:259; B, 1:253.

17. Letter 28.5, in L, 1:258; B, 1:254.

18. Letter 28.7, in L, 1:260; B, 1:254.

19. Letter 28.8, 9, in L, 1:260, 261; B, 1:254, 255.

20. Letter 28.10, in L, 1:261; B, 1:255.

a single individual consider oneself in the plural? Is there a difference between the individual and the community, and if so, what is it? Damian sees the complexity of both in ways which few if any of his contemporaries do, and his articulation of that insight is masterful. Both appear complex because both are simple, and simplicity is the hardest truth for humans to perceive. Simplicity rests solely in the divine. It cannot be fully grasped by rational powers. Only the irrational power of faith can appreciate the simplicity of Truth Itself. To say that the Church "is both one in all and complete in each" is an irrational statement.[21] It occurs, therefore, "by reason of the sacramental mystery."[22] Rationally the individual and community are separate and distinct entities, but, irrationally, "we believe ... by the mystery of baptism" that each individual is the whole Church and the whole Church is the individual. "And although, because of the great number of people, the Church seems to be of many parts," Damian admits, "it is still one and simple [*una tamen et simplex est*] in the mystical federation of one faith."[23] The basis for this oneness is likewise simple: "The church of Christ is so joined together by the bond of love."[24] It is "by the power of the Holy Spirit ... [that] our solitude is at once plural and our community is singular."[25]

This truth he repeats and repeats. The Church "is divided into the great number of persons" but "fused into one by the fire of the Holy Spirit"; it is divided in "physical circumstances" but has a "mystic integrity of her inmost unity."[26] The Church is "simple in many by reason of the unity of faith, and multiple in each through the bond of love and various charismatic gifts."[27] In this the communal and individual realities of the Church imitate the Trinity, where "this same spirit who is undoubtedly both single and multiple ... grants his charism to holy Church which he fills, so that she is both one in her

21. Letter 28.13, in L, 1:262; B, 1:256.

22. Letter 28.15, in L, 1:263; B, 1:256–57. Damian also reminds us of the gift of intellect: "In mind and spirit rational man was created in the image and likeness of God, and in these faculties is capable of receiving divine grace and enlightenment."

23. Letter 28.12, in L, 1:262; B, 1:256.

24. Letter 28.11, in L, 1:262; B, 1:255.

25. Letter 28.15, in L, 1:264; B, 1;257.

26. Letter 28.14, in L, 1:263; B, 1:256.

27. Letter 28.13, in L, 1:262–63; B, 1:256.

totality and whole in all her parts." It is not through reason that Damian perceives this but rather through God: "Truth Itself affirmed the secret of this indivisible unity."[28] This has practical implications in grammar, "since in the one case being alone does not prejudice the use of the plural, so too in the other a group of the faithful does not cause disharmony by using the singular." In summary, "our solitude is at once plural and our community is singular."[29]

After establishing the veracity of his thesis in the irrational realm of faith, Damian returns to the rational and applies the laws of logic to identify other implications of the simultaneous singularity and plurality of the individual and the community. If normal grammatical rules apply to reciting *"Dominus vobiscum,"* then they must apply to other customs "too numerous to mention." Therefore, "you should therefore think carefully about these things," for if the individual and community were not one and many, then the doctors of the Church would have "thought it expedient" to give "one form for those who perform the Church's offices alone, and another for a group." Instead, they were "satisfied to establish one form without distinction."[30]

Damian's next corollary is highly significant. If all prayers, regardless of whether they originate with an individual or a group, are "offered by all the faithful," then that means "not only by men but also by women, even though it appears to be offered only by the priest in particular." This is particularly evident at mass "when we say, 'Remember, Lord, your servants and handmaids,' and again, when the priest prays, 'We therefore beg you, Lord, that at your pleasure you accept this offering of our service and that of your whole household.' By these words it becomes clearer still that the sacrifice placed upon the altar by the priest is offered in common by all the family of God [*sed et cunctae familiae tuae*]."[31] This specific inclusion of women in the household and family of God places Damian firmly within "a strong and enduring tradition of women's spiritual equality."[32] It is a

28. Letter 28.14, in L, 1:263; B, 1:256.
29. Letter 28.15, in L, 1:264; B, 1:257.
30. Letter 28.19, in L, 1:265; B, 1:258.
31. Letter 28.20, in L, 1:266; B, 1:259.
32. See my *Women and Spiritual Equality in Christian Tradition* (New York: St. Martin's

tradition not all are aware of, but one of utmost, pivotal importance in the history of women. Damian's open insistence that women are full and complete members of God's household does much to prepare the way for the new opportunities and respect in religious life women were afforded as the monastic renewal movement unfolded during the next two centuries.[33] Later letters also reveal Damian's implementation of this principle in his spiritual direction of women.[34]

The next discussion may be Damian's most penetrating and compelling; I believe it is surely his most exquisitely written. It is relatively brief (seventy-nine lines in *Briefe*), but it contains the essence of Damian's social theology. The focus is on the Body of Christ and the effects the scriptural concept has on our understanding of self and community. When Damian writes this passage the Berengarian controversy over the Eucharist was stirring. In 1047 Berengar circulated his doubts concerning the Real Presence in the Eucharist, and his former schoolmate Adelman of Liège wrote him, urging him to abandon his "new and false path."[35] Berengar responded scornfully that he would proceed undeterred, and thus the debate began. Between 1048 and 1059 it was waged with benign vigor.[36] In 1059, after the Roman synod, it turned permanently acrimonious when Hum-

Press, 1998), 231. For Damian's contributions, see 133–38. I am not claiming that Damian was not as misogynistic as the culture that surrounded him; he was. See his discussion on priests' wives, Letter 112, where he allows his hatred for the sin to be transferred to the sinner. See also Letters 114 and 162.

33. For documentation, see my *Women and Religious Life in Premodern Europe* (New York: St. Martin's Press, 1996). Not only were there new orders founded for women, but new types of religious life became readily available.

34. In particular, see Letter 51.3–4, in L, 1:336; B, 1:133.

35. Adelman of Liège, *Epistola ad Berengarium,* in R. B. C. Huygens, "Textes latins du XIe au XIIIe siècle," *Studi medievali,* 3rd ser., 8 (1967), 476–89. Also cited in Jaegar, *Envy,* 219–20.

36. Lanfranc, Hugh of Langres, Ascelin of Chartres, Wolphelm of Brauweiler, Theodium of Liège, Anastasius of Cluny, and Duran of Troarn wrote in opposition. Bruno of Angers, Eusebius, and Geoffrey Martel wrote in support. Berengar claimed Damian supported him; see Charles Radding and Francis Newton, *Theology, Rhetoric and Politics in the Eucharistic Controversy, 1078–79* (New York: Columbia University Press, 2003), 19 and ch. 4. Synods in Vercelli and Paris condemned Berengar's theology, and in 1054 Hildebrand as papal legate accepted a compromise statement from Berengar, which ultimately failed to please either side.

bert of Silva Candida drafted an astringent profession of faith and the council demanded Berengar submit to it. Nevertheless, during the next twenty years Berengar continued to argue his point, ending only in 1079 when he signed a new profession of faith written in Aristotelian language. Although he lost the war one may argue that he did win at least one battle, for the controversy necessitated the inclusion of logic and dialectics in all future Eucharistic discussions, an implicit demand in Berengar's arguments.[37] The war that he lost, nevertheless, also embodied high stakes. It was a war over the identification of the human body of Christ with the body in the Eucharist, and the whole sacramental nature of Christianity was at stake. Damian was not an active participant in the debate (although in later years he did let his opinion be known), but he was keenly aware of the controversy and was a key member of the Roman synod that condemned Berengar.[38] In *Dominus vobiscum* Damian emphasized aspects other than those the debate focused on; he was more interested in the effect the doctrine had on humanity's understanding of self and community. Emile Mersch writes that during the Middle Ages "it was a common and emphatic teaching" that the Eucharist's objective "is to incorporate us in Christ and with one another."[39] I believe Damian's sermonette here contributed greatly to that teaching, its dissemination, and acceptance. It also is partially responsible for the semantic transition of the term *corpus mysticum* from Christ's Eucharistic body to the Church community.[40] As in so many matters Damian's concern was primarily pastoral. His interest was on

37. See Gary Macy, "The Theological Fate of Berengar's Oath of 1059: Interpreting a Blunder Becomes a Tradition," in *Interpreting Tradition,* ed. Jane Kopas (Chico, Calif.: Scholars Press, 1984), 27–38.

38. In Letter 102, ca.1063–64, he writes to the community at Monte Cassino (which was very involved in the debate) and regales them with tales concerning Eucharistic miracles. The host is "at once the very 'bread that came down from heaven' and at the same time the very flesh that proceeded from the substance of the Virgin's womb." Letter 102.3, in L, 5:124; B, 3:119–20.

39. Emile Mersch, *The Whole Christ: The Historical Development of the Doctrine of the Mystical Body in Scripture and Tradition,* tr. John Kelly (London: Dennis Dobson, 1962), 442.

40. See Pius XII's encyclical *Mystici Corporis,* para. 58, for modern definition. Accessed through www.vatican.va/holy_father/pius_xii/encyclicals/docum.

the effect belief in the Mystical Body of Christ had on the person and society. To that end he investigates, examines, scrutinizes, and theorizes about the doctrine, as is the duty of all intelligent beings, but he never forgets the goal of the investigation, to bear witness to the social realities of Christianity.

For Damian the doctrine of the Mystical Body of Christ holds the answers to individuation. Expanding on Paul's body metaphor to explain society's diversification (1 Cor 12) Damian proclaims that since "the part functions for the whole and the whole for its parts ... whatever a single member performs is rightly deemed to be the function of the body; and on the other hand, whatever the body does, to that all the parts consent by their cooperation." As the eyes, tongue, feet, and hands have their own specific function to perform, so too does each member of the community. Functions may vary but membership is equally complete for all. All benefit and suffer together: "Whatever function is assigned by nature to a particular member can be said to be performed by the body which is its whole, so that one may quite properly say that the part functions for the whole and the whole for its parts."[41]

Given this premise one can only conclude logically that "where there is unity of faith, it allows neither for solitude in one, nor for a schism of diversity in many."[42] To be sure he is understood he repeats the premise: "The whole Church is the one body of Christ, and we are the Church's members." Then he applies the premise to the real-life question before him: "What is to hinder us as individuals from using the language of our body, namely, the Church, since we are truly one with her? For if, while we are many, we are one in Christ, as individuals we possess our totality in him; and hence, even though in our bodily solitude we appear to be far removed from the Church, still by the incorruptible mystery of unity we are always most intimately present in her." Clearly Damian sees solitary life as solitary only in one aspect, physicality. Otherwise it is as "most in-

41. Letter 28.22, in L, 1:268; B, 1:260–61.
42. Letter 28.23, in L, 1:268; B, 1:261.

timately present" in the community as all other lives are. Damian sees the community as essential to the individual. This communion is so important that Christians bear witness to it in the Creed: "For right after saying: I believe in the Holy Spirit, the holy Church, we immediately add: 'the communion of the saints'; and as we witness to our faith in God, at the same time we testify to the community of the Church." At all times, though, he counters his insistence on community with an emphasis on self: "What belongs to all is the right of each; and what is singularly special to each is, in the wholeness of faith and love, common to all."[43] Damian turns to an ancient metaphor to help describe this relationship between self and community: "Just as in Greek man is called a microcosm, that is to say, a little world, because in his physical composition he consists of the same four elements that are found in the whole earth; so also each of the faithful seems to be, as it were, a little Church, since with all due respect to the mystery of hidden unity, each person also receives all the sacraments of human redemption that God provided for the universal Church."[44]

For those who are still not convinced, in the next section Damian alternates new evidence and restatements of his thesis. He offers examples from history and canons and then returns to the initial grammatical question. He explains again why one may flout "the rules of grammar" in expressing the relationship of the individual to the community; "ecclesiastical custom possesses such authority."[45] He reinforces his thesis: "For we are not here concerned with the number of persons but rather with the mystery of the Church's unity. Here, indeed, unity does not exclude multiplicity, nor does multiplicity violate unity, for one body is at once divided among many members, and from the various members one body is made complete." He concludes this argument with a strong reminder that

43. Letter 28.24, in L, 1:269–70; B, 1:261–62.

44. Letter 28.25, in L, 1:270; B, 1:262. Damian employs it in Letter 49.7, in L, 2:275; B, 2:66. See also Letter 17.7, in L, 1:48; B, 1:158; and Letter 108.10, in L, 5:201; B, 3:195.

45. Letter 28.32, in L, 1:274; B, 1:265.

neither individuals nor the community lose their separate identity because of their relationship: "Nor are many members lost in the unity of the body, nor is the wholeness of the body minimized in the multitude of its members."[46] Damian continues with another argument, this time from Israelite history and the Church calendar, and then "return[s] to what we were saying above"; given their unity in Christ, it is proper that "individuals use the language of many, and that many speak as individuals."[47] He defends his use of liturgical evidence, arguing that even though they "on the surface seem frivolous and trivial [*in superficie quidem frivola videntur*]" within things like feast days, priests' vestments, and arrangements of the tabernacle, "mystery lies hidden," in this instance, the mystery of the one and the many.[48] A short epilogue follows so he can "briefly sum up what I set out to explain." Although physically absent, the hermit is intimately united to the community and should "demonstrate it externally in public rite" by proclaiming *"Dominus vobiscum."*[49]

Part Two Damian does not end the treatise here but includes a second section on the value of the hermits' lives. Early manuscripts separate this portion from the body of *Dominus vobiscum,* and in a superficial reading a division may appear warranted.[50] The inherent relationship of the two, nevertheless, is clear when one considers Damian's pastoral purpose. It is to offer hermits guidance concern-

46. Letter 28.33, in L, 1:274; B, 1:266.

47. Letter 28.39, in L, 1:277; B, 1:268.

48. Letter 28.41–42, in L, 1:278–79; B, 1:272–73.

49. Letter 28.43–44, in L, 1:279–80; B, 1:271–72.

50. Blum notes that some thirty manuscripts separated it. See L, 1:281, n. 98. There is a vital connection between the body of the treatise and the appendage that is often overlooked. See, for example, Little, "Personal Development," 334–36, where Little once again uses (bad) pop psychology instead of theological analysis. He claims that Damian wrote this section out of boredom, "for therapeutic value," "let loose with a sudden bust of emotion" and "lost all sense of proportion." He does not consider its theological and logical significance to Damian's main thesis. Interpretations like this make it most upsetting to see Little's unscholarly article still cited so frequently. In "The Priest's Wife: Female Erasure and the Gregorian Reform," in *Medieval Religion: New Approaches,* ed. Constance Berman, 123–55 (New York: Routledge, 2005), Dyan Elliott's use of Little's article as the basis for his own interpretation nullifies his thesis.

ing the intangible realities of their isolated lives. In the first section Damian establishes the relationship the solitary monk has with the community. In this second section he identifies the function that monk fulfills in the community. Although this issue was not explicitly raised, Damian intuits the hermits' insecurity concerning their role in society and their need to appreciate that function. Thus he starts this section by telling them that, while he is at it, "I should like to include a few ideas on the value of the solitary life." He reasons that by understanding the value of eremiticism they will best appreciate the worth their individual lives have to the community. He begins by defining eremiticism as a life in search of meaning. "The solitary life is indeed the school of heavenly learning," Damian writes. It is "where one learns where life is heading [*illic Deus est ubi describitur, vita quo tenditur*]."[51] The eremitic life helps in this search by providing a place of liminality where "earthly possessions are stripped away."[52] Here "the soul that hungers for God . . . separates itself from the affairs of this world, and soars to the heights." Once the hermit is "set apart from the troubles and vexations of this life" the hermitage will "open the way to heavenly life."[53] What Damian is describing here is a rite of passage. The eremitic life helps persons change: "You bring it about that man at the summit of contemplation [*in mentis arce*] sees all the things of earth passing beneath him, and beholds himself also passing away in that very stream of change."[54]

The change is radical. In the cell, "the wondrous workshop of spiritual effort" and locus of transition, "earthly wares are bartered for heavenly ones, passing things for those that are eternal." It is here that "the human soul restores within itself the image of its

51. Letter 28.45, in L, 1:281; B, 1:272.

52. Letter 28.47, in L, 1:282; B, 1:273.

53. Letter 28.51, in L, 1:285; B, 1:275.

54. Letter 28.47, in L, 1:283; B, 1:273. See Arnold van Gennap, *The Rites of Passage*, tr. Gabrielle Caffee and Monika Vizedon (repr. London: Routledge and Kegan Paul, 1960); Victor and Edith Turner, *Image and Pilgrimage in Christian Tradition* (New York: Columbia University Press, 1978); Carolyn Walker Bynum, "Women's Stories, Women's Symbols: A Critique of Victor Turner's Theory of Liminality," in *Fragmentation and Redemption* (New York: Zone Books, 1991), 27–51; and P. Cricco, "Monasticism and Its Role as a Liminal Community in Medieval Society" (Ph.D. diss., West Virginia University, 1981).

creator and regains its original purity." Damian also sees this change as extremely personal and self-revealing, for the solitary life allows "dull senses [to] recover their subtle sharpness," whereas before the hermit "wrapped up in his own darkness, he did not know even himself."[55] When the hermit engaged "in looking upon Him who is above all, man rises above himself" and discovers the true meaning of life "to live again for God."[56] Thus it makes "gluttons sober, cruel men kind, angry men mild, and hateful men fervent."[57] Just as the subject in a rite of passage enters liminality to ease transition into another state, so too does the hermit enter the hermitage to ease the transition into heaven, the ultimate destiny of the individual. The cell is "the meeting place of God and men, the crossroad where those in the flesh encounter heavenly spirits."[58] Here one readies oneself for life's intended end: "Whoever, for the love of God, observes the solitary life to the end of his days, after departing his fleshly dwelling will arrive at an eternal edifice."[59]

The hermit's search is communal as well as personal. Thanks to the Renaissance claim to discover the individual, much attention has been given to medieval individualism in order to set the record straight, but one must not forget that medieval society also altered the concept of community it had inherited from antiquity. Damian contributed to this alteration by emphasizing the limits of individualism outside the context of community. He demands changes in grammar to reflect this reality: "Our solitude is at once plural and our community is singular [*his solitudo pluralis et illic multitudo intelligitur singularis*]."[60] Accordingly, the community and the individual are ultimately paradoxes, as is the Incarnation. The Body of Christ is physically singular but spiritually plural, "and even though we seem to be physically distinct we cannot be separated from another in spirit."[61] After employing a series of flower metaphors de-

55. Letter 28.47, in L, 1:282; B, 1:273.

56. Letter 28.51, in L, 1:285; B, 1:275.

57. Letter 28.52, in L, 1:285; B, 1:276.

58. Letter 28.49, in L, 1:284; B, 1:274.

59. Letter 28.55, in L, 1:288; B, 1:278.

60. Letter 28.15, in L, 1:264; B, 1:257.

61. Letter 28.21, in L, 1:267; B, 1:260.

scribing certain virtues of eremiticism, Damian admits that even talking about individual virtues is limited. "Why do I speak of each of these individually?" he asks, when the life encompasses all virtues, all "holy souls."[62] Damian underscores this by referring to Old Testament figures and to John the Baptist, the Christian witness par excellence. John's life in the desert did not merely save himself. He bore witness to the whole community and contributed to the salvation of all. So too does the hermit's solitary life bear witness to the community. "Once, at the very beginning of the world's redemption, the Savior of the world made his herald a dweller in the desert, so that with the dawn of the new age the morning star might come forth from you, after whom would come the rising of the full sun to illumine a dark world with its radiant splendor," Damian reminds his audience. The hermit's witness is "Jacob's ladder that lead[s] men to heaven"; it is "the golden road on which man returns to his fatherland; you are the course that leads to their crown."[63] Because of the witness of the solitary life, Elijah "recognized the manifestation of the Lord as he passed by." Moses and Elisha were likewise indebted.[64] The cell offers the community knowledge and gives it access "to the secret deliberation of God with men [*Cella denique conscio est secreti consilii, quod habet cum hominibus Deus*]."[65] The solitary life is an incomparable witness and judge of humanity's search for God and meaning: "The cell, moreover, witnesses how much the heart is aflame with the love of God and whether one seeks his presence with the urgency of perfect devotion [*Cella denique testis est, quanto divini amoris igne cor ferveat et utrum perfectae devotionis instantia quis Dei faciem quaerat*]."[66]

The search is intense and demands arduous labor, therefore Damian frequently employs work metaphors. The hermit works hard in his search. "He watches the course of the stars"; "he performs his service"; he recites the psalms "as the stars, early and late." The her-

62. Letter 28.46, in L, 1:281; B, 1:272–73.
63. Letter 28.49, in L, 1:283; B, 1:274.
64. Letter 28.48, in L, 1:283; B, 1:274.
65. Letter 28.49, in L, 1:284; B, 1:274.
66. Letter 28.50, in L, 1:284; B, 1:275.

mit's cell is "the workshop where precious stones are polished."[67] It is "a resort of quiet for those who labor."[68] Damian's perception of all of the hermit's efforts as work has an important corollary in the history of the concept. With this corollary the stratification of class by function begins to weaken. It is a long journey before the tasks of the warrior, the worker, and the one who prays are considered of equal dignity and worth, but the first steps are taken here by Damian.[69] He sees all work as contributing to the good of the whole. No longer is it punitive or demeaning. Quite the opposite, it is sanctifying, for when an individual works, "he now walks in [Christ's] footsteps."[70]

> And when in these cells various duties are performed in harmony, where here one is chanting, there one is praying, in another one is writing, and in still others various kinds of manual labor are performed, who will not recognize how well suited to the hermitage are the words of God which say: "How fair are your tents, O Jacob!"[71]

After asking Leo to "carefully inspect" his treatise for false assumptions and "erase them with a sharp knife," Damian ends the treatise.[72] He has accomplished his primary task, to unravel the theology behind a grammatical dilemma over the hermit's use of the plural. The hermits are fully entitled to evoke the plural, because they are members of Christ's body with an assigned task to perform for that body. The witness of their lives lights the way to God and inspires others to follow their path.

Damian accomplished other tasks as well. His eloquent, persuasive analysis provided encouragement and rational justification

67. Ibid.

68. Letter 28.53, in L, 1:286; B, 1:277.

69. See my *Theology of Work;* and "Franciscan Work Theology in Historical Perspective," *Franciscan Studies* 71 (2009), 41–70.

70. Letter 28.55, in L, 1:288; B, 1:278.

71. Letter 28.54, in L, 1:287; B, 1:277. Damian develops these ideas about differentiation of labor and class distinctions in Letter 67 (ca.1059–63), written to Duke Godfrey of Tuscany. See, for example, 67.6, in L, 3:72; B, 2:282: "All the members of the Church are not assigned the same office, for one duty is proper to a priest, another to a judge."

72. Letter 28.57, in L, 1:288; B, 1:273.

for specifically Western concepts of community and self and their relationship. He reinforced Pauline social theology and recognized its implication for class and function in society. He reminded readers of humanity's similarity to the rest of creation by recalling the ancient microcosm/macrocosm analogy. He advocated intellectual investigation, acknowledged its limitations, reminded us that divine wisdom completes human knowledge, and defended the superiority of divine over secular knowledge. Finally, by revealing the liminal nature of the hermit's experience, Damian provided new appreciation for eremiticism. This last was personally important to him. We saw in Romuald's vita how deeply he believed that self-salvation is attained only when one focuses on others; here he establishes a theoretical basis for that tenet.

Letter 31: *Liber Gomorrhianus*

Damian addressed *Gomorrhianus* to Pope Leo IX, and in most manuscripts Leo's note to Damian acknowledging its receipt is included as a preface. "It is proper that we intervene, according to your wishes, with our apostolic authority," Leo writes, "so let it be certain and evident to all that we are in agreement with everything your book contains." Having said that, he then admits that he disagrees about disciplining the guilty. "Acting more humanely, and relying on divine mercy, it is our wish and also our command," Leo declares, that punishment not be as severe as Damian advocated.[73] Damian wanted clerics guilty of sodomy removed from office. Leo would remove only the hard-core practitioner, while those who "curbed their desires and have atoned" could "be admitted to the same grades." Apparently Damian did not persuade bishops, either, for the hierarchy did not address the problem in any councils. This is particularly telling since so many other canons issued mid-century reflected Peter's reform platform.[74] As John Boswell concludes, "Peter in fact had no luck in convincing anyone that gay sexuality de-

73. Letter 31.3–4, in L, 2:4–5; B, 1:285–86.
74. See Mansi, 19:897–99.

served hostile attention," and he is probably correct.[75] I do not agree, however, that lack of support leads to the conclusion that Peter perceived a problem where there was none, or that Damian's interest in the subject was personal, to fill "some needs of his own," as Little claims.[76]

I believe that a more likely reason is one that Little mentions and then summarily dismisses: "Perhaps what we are really witnessing here was a newly awakened awareness."[77] This would be consistent with the main thrust of Damian's work. He had a keen eye for observing his world. He saw things years, even decades, before others did. He was an avant garde critical thinker in so many areas; why is it not probable that here too he identified a problem that contemporaries failed to see as early as he did? Damian himself hints at his prophetic powers, telling those "who are furious with me and sneer at heeding my writing, should at least listen to the prophetic voice [his own] that speaks to you."[78] If one is hesitant to subscribe prescient powers to Damian, there are other possibilities. C. Colt Anderson maintains that Damian believed "publicly revealing the [Church's] worst sins was the means to preserve the credibility of the church."[79] His contemporaries may have thought differently. Damian certainly assumed they did, and he braced himself for wide

75. John Boswell, *Christianity, Social Tolerance and Homosexuality* (Chicago: University of Chicago Press, 1980), 213. Boswell adheres to Alfonso Capecelatro's theory, *Storia de San Pier Damiano e del suo tiempo* (Florence, 1862), 166, that in 1069 Pope Alexander II stole *Libri Gomorrhianus* and "locked it in his office." Little, "Personal Development," 334, also agrees, but as Blum says (L, 2:4, n. 4), "this opinion has received little support." For a bibliography of the debate, see Reindel, B, 4:75, n. 4.

76. Little, "Personal Development." Little presents no evidence to support his interpretation. Indeed, statements such as "Peter appears to have been a lonely man, lacking close friends" (336), are easily disproven and reveal a limited knowledge of Damian's corpus. See Mark Jordan, *Invention of Sodomy in Christian Theology* (Chicago: University of Chicago Press, 1997), 53, for a contrary interpretation.

77. Little, "Personal Development," 333.

78. Letter 31.52, in L, 2:39; B, 1:317. Examples come to mind: Damian decried the custom of sex offenders "confessing to one another" (31.21, in L, 2:16–17; B, 1:297). It takes two centuries before another reformer, Caesar of Heisterback, acknowledges this problem. It takes a half century (1102) before the hierarchy anywhere acknowledged the problem of sodomy among clergy.

79. C. Colt Anderson, *The Great Catholic Reformers* (New York: Paulist Press, 2007), 54.

criticism. Repeatedly and with courage Damian refers to the unfavorable reception his call for reform had and would continue to have.[80] He expected it: "If we see the command of God's voice belittled by gross-hearted reprobates, why should we marvel that we who are of earth are not believed?"[81] The whole tone of his letter is one of a solitary voice crying in the desert. One need only reference the current American Catholic clergy scandal to consider how opposed the hierarchy can be to public disclosure of clerical misconduct. Moreover, many report pressure exerted to silence those who attempted to publicly reveal the incontinence.[82] Why, with such a modern example glaring at us, would we think it improbable that Damian experienced the same treatment?

Another possible explanation is that Leo thought dealing with clerical homosexual behavior would divert his attention from myriad problems he had already identified. At his first synod at Easter 1049, and again at Mainz in October and Lucca in 1051, Leo addressed the "the detestable marriage of priests."[83] Leo, though, was preoccupied with simony, heretical Eucharistic teaching, practical abuses, political interference in papal territory, a growing rift with the Byzantine Church, episcopal challenges to papal authority, and a "startling reshaping of the papacy."[84] Is it any wonder that he was unwilling to take on yet another problem?

Gender studies offer an interpretation that muddles the issue of the treatise's reception, for if true it makes us wonder why Damian's call for action against homosexual incontinence did not elicit a re-

80. See Letter 31.52, in L, 2:39; B, 1:317; Letter 31.71–72, in L, 2:49–51; B, 1:326; and Letter 31.74, in L, 2:52; B, 1:328.

81. Letter 31.56, in L, 2:40; B, 1:318.

82. Publications documenting this abound. Even though the vast majority of cases (claims range from 80 percent to 95 percent) involved priests and younger men or boys, public discussion of this aspect of the scandal is still stifled. See Leon Podles, *Sacrilege* (Baltimore: Crossland Press, 2008); Philip Lawler, *The Faithful Departed* (New York: Encounter, 2000); N. Cafardi, *Before Dallas* (New York: Paulist Press, 2008); and the John Jay College report to the U.S. Conference of Catholic Bishops, May 2011.

83. Bonizo of Sutri, 5, *Liber ad amicum,* 1.588–89; in *Papal Reform,* 198.

84. Eamon Duffy, *Saints and Sinners,* 2nd ed. (New Haven, Conn.: Yale University Press, 2001), 114–16.

sponse from at least some reformers. The Gregorian Reform was a turning point in the Western Church's attitude toward clerical marriage.[85] Between the pontificates of Leo IX (1049) and Innocent II (d. 1143), clerical marriage went from being tolerated to being condemned. Who and what was responsible for this historic change is still debated. Joanne McNamara argues that all clerical action is aimed at denying women power and sees the demand to end clerical marriages as but another "superficial" ruse to deny women participation in church affairs by "the ungendering of the public man."[86] Maureen Miller, however, offers a better-documented thesis. In the eleventh century a variety of conditions emerged that led to popular hostility toward married priests. Land clearance, incastellaments, new communities, and restructuring of old communities "led to new social tensions." In particular, there was a need for an independent local leader capable of resolving new tensions, an arbitrator "unfettered by familial and seigneurial bonds."[87] Reformers responded to this need by trying to create a clergy that was radically independent of laymen. Miller argues that while the reform was about men, it was specifically "about what kind of men should exercise authority." Consequently, "the real struggle in the reform movement was not men against women, but clerical men against lay men."[88] In this

85. H. E. J. Cowdrey, "Pope Gregory VII and the Chastity of the Clergy," in *Medieval Purity and Piety,* ed. Michael Frassetto (New York: Palgrave, 1998), 269–302. He says, though, that to claim that Gregory played "an epoch-making role" in enforcing celibacy is "to be excessive."

86. Joanne McNamara, "Canossa and the Ungendering of the Public Man," in *Render Unto Caesar,* ed. Sabrina Ramet and Donald Treadgold, 131–50 (Washington, D.C.: American University Press, 1995). She concludes that "the men who headed the hierarchies of religion and politics cooperated and supported one another.... They were at one in legitimating the gender system that allotted public space solely to men." This interpretation inflates the importance of the actual meeting at Canossa, ignores issues arising from property rights and community structures, downgrades the political interests involved, denies Canossa's role in Western conception of church-state relations, and allows no room for the individual personalities who dictated much of the action.

87. Maureen Miller, "Masculinity, Reform and Clerical Culture: Narratives of Episcopal Holiness in the Gregorian Era," *Church History* 72.1 (2003), accessed through Ebsco Host Research Databases, 11. Miller is citing R. I. Moore, *The First European Revolution c. 970–1215* (Oxford: Blackwell, 2000).

88. Miller, "Masculinity, Reform and Clerical Culture," 1, 10.

struggle the goal of each group was to appear the most masculine and thus more deserving of power. The clergy decided that this "extreme masculinity" could best be achieved by distancing themselves completely from "female impurity" and "familial entanglements."[89] If Miller is correct, then Damian's claim that homosexuality makes "a mistress of a cleric, or a woman of man" is quite threatening to the construction of extreme masculinity and deserving of reformers' attention.[90] Yet, his warning went unheeded. That Damian wanted independent, distinctly masculine clergy is demonstrated throughout the letter; that contemporaries did not adopt this plank of his reform platform is also clear. I believe that the reformers missed an opportunity.

How complex the situation was becomes clearer when one considers Damian's attitude toward lay criticism of the clergy. He was an ardent advocate of the laity's right to censure the priesthood, in direct contrast to papal initiatives to silence them. Already in 1046 Damian had praised Emperor Henry III for depriving Bishop Widger of his see in Ravenna. In 1047 Damian did not hesitate to reproach Pope Clement II for not heeding Henry III's demand that the pope address the "complete disarray because of evil bishops and abbots ... in the churches of our region."[91] In later years Damian became even more insistent of the laity's right, even obligation, to correct the clergy; he urged Duchess Adelaide of Turin to "correct the situation" regarding "the incontinency of clerics"; he praised Duchess Beatrice of Tuscany when she "violently threatened" an errant cleric; and he had no problem per se with the Patarines' criticism of Milanese clergy.[92] That a pope trying to silence lay criticism of

89. Ibid., 2.

90. Letter 31.19, in L, 2:15; B, 1:294.

91. Letter 26.2–3, in L, 1:244–45; B, 1:240–41. See also Letter 20. See summary of scholars' opinions on this matter in Anderson, *Great Catholic Reformers,* 233, n. 50. Damian, of course, also champions clerical criticism of lay authority in secular matters (see Letter 67) and believes a priest's criticism of a bishop are justified: Letter 38.5, in L, 2:75; B, 1:350.

92. Letter 114.2, in L, 5:295; Letter 141.5, in L, 6:114; B, 3:490; and Letter 65. For Patarines, see Richard Gyug, "The Milanese Church and the Gregorian Reform," *Scintilla* 2–3 (1985–86), 29–65.

ecclesiastical affairs should ignore a complaint made by someone who claims that "what all the people are complaining about should not be hushed up in council by the leaders of the church" is hardly surprising.[93] One final possibility to explain the treatise's lack of influence: Damian was hardly gracious in his admonitions. One could surely appreciate why some bishops chose to ignore a demand made so aggressively: "Listen, you do-nothings, superiors of clerics and priests. Listen, and even though you feel sure of yourselves, tremble at the thought that you are partners in the guilt of others.... Listen, I say, and be shrewd enough to understand that all of you alike 'are deserving of death.'"[94]

Given the lack of pertinent documentation, we will never know with certainty how widespread or problematic clerical homosexual behavior was. If, however, we let discussion about the historical realities of clerical homosexuality be the sole focus of treatise's analysis we will be all the poorer, for it also tells us much about Damian's attitudes toward public accountability, discipline, justice, relationships, logic, eschatology, witness, change, laity, and natural law. It is easy to overlook these aspects of the treatise when focusing so intensely on sodomy. True, Damian's "lurid details" disturb many scholars and do demand attention.[95] But we should remember Charles Wood's wise observation that "it would be difficult to think of any other age in which the facts of life came closer to being no more than just that."[96] When Damian describes the four va-

93. Letter 61.3, in L, 3:4; B, 2:207–8. This comment is made later, in 1059, to Nicholas II, but reveals Damian's same concerns: "The genuine custom of the Roman church seems to be observed in this way ... a proper investigation is held, but a prudent silence is maintained concerning clerical sexuality for fear of insults from laymen."

94. Letter 31.18, in L, 2:15; B, 1:294.

95. Boswell, *Christianity,* 211. Leclercq, *S. Pierre,* 70, is almost alone in his declaration that Damian discusses sodomy "avec précision et clarité, aucune vulgarité." I agree; Jordan, *Invention,* 45, stridently disagrees. Some scholars' description of *Gomorrhianus* is so extreme that I am often left concluding that they never read the work but are just repeating previous summaries. See, for example, Seward, *Perfect Fools,* 51; and Lawrence, *Medieval Monasticism,* 152.

96. Charles Wood, *The Quest for Eternity* (Hanover, N.H.: University Press of New England, 1983), 38.

rieties of sodomy, one wonders whether his contemporaries deemed these lurid details or facts of life. There is every indication that they viewed them as facts, for Damian's source was Burchard of Worms's *Decretum.* Burchard evoked no criticism or indignation then or now (rightly so) for his descriptions, yet he is much more provocative, even salacious, than Damian.[97] Eleventh-century society had its own sensibilities and rhetorical expectations.[98] Once we see beyond our own hypersensitivity and view Damian's descriptions as his contemporaries did, as facts, we are better able to appreciate the varied treasures hidden within the treatise without distraction.

Damian begins by acknowledging the Church as the appointed arbitrator of Truth Itself. This is the basis of his appeal. Damian implores the pope, as the head of ecclesiastical discipline, to address "a certain abominable and most shameful vice [that] has developed." The vice is "the befouling cancer of sodomy," and it is "spreading so through the clergy or rather, like a savage beast, is raging with such shameful abandon." As Damian sees it, "unless immediate effort be exerted by the Apostolic See, there is little doubt that, even if one wished to curb this unbridled evil, he could not check the momentum of its progress."[99] The types of sodomy are not equally serious: "Those who sin with others" are guiltier than "those who masturbate alone."[100] What concerns Damian most, however, is not sodomy,

97. A comparison is revealing. Damian's most detailed description is Letter 31.9 in L, 2:7: "Some who pollute themselves, ... others who befoul one another by mutually handling their genitals, others still who fornicate between thighs, and other who do so from the rear." The following are the questions Burchard of Worms, *Decretum libri xx,* Book 19.5, PL 140, 967–68, directs confessors to ask: "Did you ... take the shameful part of another in your hand, and he yours in his, and thus alternately moving the shameful parts with your hand, so that by pleasure you eject seed from yourself? ... that you yourself took your manly member in your hand and so slide your foreskin [*praeputium*] and move [it] with your own hand so as to delight to eject seed from yourself?" Translated in Jordan, *Invention,* 52. Jordan (53) mentions other sources which so discuss sodomy, concluding that "Peter need not have gone far to find a dozen texts." For citations from other sources see Pierre Payer, *Sex and the Penitentials* (Toronto: University of Toronto Press, 1984), 135–39.

98. I. S. Robinson, "The 'Colores Rhetorici' in the Investiture Contest," *Traditio* 32 (1976), 226, reminds us that Damian was an early and "formative influence in the development of the medieval *ars dictandi;* and his works came to be regarded as stylistic models of rhetorical denunciation."

99. Letter 31.7, in L, 2:6; B, 1:286–87.

100. Letter 31.8, in L, 2:6–7; B, 1:287–88.

whatever its type, but the Church's response to sodomy. He accuses it of "permissive indulgence" that "only stimulates its growth."[101] Damian believes this leniency "is clearly contrary to reason and opposed to the canonical decrees of the Fathers," and so he proceeds "to make my own position clear" on the need for stricter discipline.[102] It is straightforward. The demands of ritual purity differ from those for forgiveness, so even when the sodomizer's repentance is sincere and total "it is perfectly clear that when a capital crime has degraded a man, no subsequent holy life will reform him to the point where he might receive orders and ecclesiastical status." To do so is "in total opposition to the norms of Holy Scripture and in complete disregard of the regulations ordained by God."[103]

Ritual purity is a prime concern of Damian's, and its importance should not be dismissed too quickly or its significance misunderstood. "This is the meaning of ritual purification," Mircea Eliade instructs us: "The sins and faults of the individual and of the community as a whole are annulled."[104] Once again we see Damian's dual concern for the one and the many. Because medieval claims of ritual impurity often centered on sexual contact, it is easy to forget that ritual impurity is not about sex per se. The demands for ritual purity are rooted in *homo religioso*'s understanding of the sacred and the profane and in the belief that the profane must be purified of its profanity before touching the sacred. What is often forgotten is that "this impurity is not to be understood as a physical or moral defilement" any more than ritual purity is to be equated to forgiveness or holiness; "they are rather 'states' or 'conditions' from which men must emerge in order to re-enter normal life."[105] To the medieval mind ritual purity was essential for contact with the sacred. A priest's ritual purity insured the community of his ability to enter the sacred realm and then return to their profane world. R. I. Moore adds further insights into eleventh-

101. Letter 31.9, in L, 2:8; B, 1:288.

102. Letter 31.10, in L, 2:8; B, 1:287.

103. Letter 31.12, in L, 2:10; B, 1:290.

104. Mircea Eliade, *The Sacred and the Profane,* tr. Willard Trask (New York: Harper and Row, 1959), 78. It is an underlying concern in letters 61, 65, 112, 114, 141, and 162.

105. Roland de Vaux, *Ancient Israel,* vol. 2 (New York: McGraw-Hill, 1965), 460.

century concerns for ritual impurity. "Fear of pollution was the fear of manipulation" of the power allotted to priests. Sexual pollution was a particularly dangerous pollution, for it subjected the priest to pressure from a specific family and community. Thus, ritual impurity "deprived him of his holy freedom, his ability to act as the perfect representative of community before God."[106]

Damian's ability to distinguish between the community's requirements for ritual purity and an individual's holy life is part of his genius. Concerning the ritually impure priest, Damian's rule is clear: "Such a man can indeed receive full forgiveness of his guilt, but nowise can he be permitted to aspire to ecclesiastical orders."[107] As Anderson rightly notes, though, he moved "beyond ritual concerns to seeing inherent abuse of power" involved in clerical sexual relationships, because he believed injustice more troubling than transgressions against ritual impurities.[108] While still essential, ritual demands are rooted in the Old Law; in the New Law they are superseded by moral demands. Damian's positioning of clerical incontinence within moral as well as ritual dimensions is innovative. In later years he applies this criteria to the whole of the priesthood.[109]

His concern for justice manifests itself in a variety of ways. He notes that "some prelates, acting perhaps more leniently than they should" do not discipline offenders properly. This is unjust, particularly to the offenders who are left to wallow in their sin.[110] He sees the inappropriateness of any regulation "which, as justice required, was at first appropriately severe, is now softened in the face of practical necessity." He bases his conclusion on principle. When "we wipe out a rigorous judgment to benefit an individual," it is unjust.[111] Likewise is injustice rampant when illogical criteria for disciplining clergy are imposed.

106. Moore, "Family, Community and Cult," 67–68. [previously cited]

107. Letter 31.12, in L, 2:10; B, 1:290.

108. Anderson, *Great Catholic Reformers,* 31. Cowdrey, *Pope Gregory,* 291, says Gregory also moved beyond cultic concerns to moral ones.

109. See Letter 59.

110. Letter 31.9, in L, 2:7–8; B, 1:288.

111. Letter 31.13, in L, 2:10; B, 1:291.

> If a man sins with a man only by femoral intercourse, he is certainly in need of penance, but from motives of human compassion he should not unalterably be denied sacred orders. But I ask you: If a monk should have relations with a nun, in your judgment, should he remain in the order? There is hardly any doubt that you would agree that he should be dismissed from the order. It follows, therefore, that what you admit as reasonable for a nun, you should also logically allow as applicable to the monk.[112]

Damian is not finished. He offers another example, emphasizing again that justice must be blind to gender. Sins with a man or a woman should be subject to the same standard of justice. If a priest sins with a woman confessee, everyone would agree that he be degraded. However, if he sins with a male cleric, "shall he not in justice be deprived of the benefice attached to his status?" If one follows his argument closely, "it will become perfectly obvious that both he who seduces his own daughter or his daughter by baptism, and he who sins shamefully with his son begotten in sacramental penance, are guilty of the same crime. And just as it is proper in law that he, who sinned with a woman whom he had begotten, or to whom he is godfather, or to whom he had administered sacramental penance" should be degraded, "so too should he be treated who commits unclear acts with his son by the same sacrament."[113] It matters not at all who the partner is, male or female. If the act was performed by "the free decisions of the sinner," then judgment must be consistent. "Because the same law obtains for monks of both sexes, we must conclude that since one who violates a nun is rightly deposed," and one who violates a goddaughter or a female confessee is deposed, "so also one who corrupts a monk must absolutely be prevented from exercising his office."[114] Justice demands that one see past gender and judge only intention and act.

When addressing the issue of "a certain amount of nonsense ... mixed in with the sacred canons," he uses the criterion of justice to

112. Letter 31.24, in L, 2:18; B, 1:298.

113. Letter 31.25, in L, 2:19–20; B, 1:299.

114. Letter 31.24, in L, 2:18–19; B, 1:294–95.

"clearly prove that these and similar documents, wherever they turn up, are false and completely apocryphal."[115] He cites examples from apocryphal canons that "the sodomites rely [and] place their trust in" and proceeds to test them against other "canonical authority and demonstrate textually and in real life whether they should be accepted or rejected."[116] The examination leaves him apoplectic. "Who is there so stupid or so irrational as to think that a penance of two years is a fitting penalty for a priest convicted of fornication" with a girl or a prostitute; the penance is "too light, not only for priests, but even for laymen."[117] As the canon continues, however, it embraces injustice. Five years of penance is imposed on a priest sinning with a nun and two years on a deacon or a monk. Who, Damian impetuously asks, "would be so insanely foolish" as to think this just? Who is "so resourceful in the subtle art of dialectic" as to prescribe three years of penance for a layman "while deciding that a cleric is to do penance for six months?" It flies in the face of justice and is "so deserving of contempt."[118] In another canon two different sentences are given for the same act of sodomy: "With which canons or decrees of the Fathers do these ridiculous ordinances agree, in that they are so self-contradictory?" Damian taunts. "By such variety of forms they cause a person to laugh rather than feel penitential compunction."[119]

Sarcasm aside, Damian sees the inconsistent application of justice to be outrageous. He turns to canons regulating bestiality: how can it be just that the laity is punished with ten years of penance for the sin, while priests get five years, deacons three, and clerics two? It is "so obviously self-contradictory" that it is equally obvious the texts were "falsely inserted into the sacred canons" by forgers.[120] In revealing their spurious nature Damian has "eliminated from the

115. Letter 31.26, in L, 2:20; B, 1:300.

116. Letter 31.27, in L, 2:20–21; B, 1:300–301.

117. Letter 31.28, in L, 2:21; B, 1:301.

118. Letter 31.29, in L, 2:22; B, 1:301–2.

119. Letter 31.30, in L, 2:23; B, 1:302–3.

120. Letter 31.31, in L, 2:23–24; B, 1:303. It should be noted that there was no definitive process for determining the validity of canons, hence the presence of spurious canons was common.

canons this dramatic nonsense on which the sodomites have relied, and ha[s] clearly convicted them with reasonable arguments."[121]

Now he is ready to discuss the authentic canons. He cites a canon from the Council of Ancyra, and again asks the audience to focus on the injustice born of unequal treatment of sinners. "If laymen guilty of the crime, who after performing twenty-five years of penance are to be admitted to common prayer but not as yet to the reception of communion, how can a priest be judged worthy, not merely of receiving but of offering and consecrating these sacred mysteries? If the former is scarcely permitted to enter a church and pray with others, how can the latter be allowed to approach the altar of the Lord to intercede for others?" His examples and rhetorical questions continue, all emphasizing the need to look at the situation logically so the injustice of applying two different standards to the same sin is clear. Here we also find admiration for the laity. If indulgence be had, it should be directed at the layman "who has sinned less grievously, in that his life is spent on the broader paths of the world"; his journey is more arduous and thus he deserves more tolerance.[122]

Damian expresses another insight here, that self-identity is discovered within the community. "Hence, if sodomites of themselves are unable to discern their own identity, they may at least be enlightened by those with whom they are assigned to a common confinement for prayer."[123] He also considers the sodomites' rift with the community a devastating consequence of the sin. "Once one has fallen into the depths of utter degradation he becomes an outcast from his heavenly home, is severed from the Body of Christ," Damian laments, "is despised among men on earth, and is rejected from the company of the citizens of heaven."[124] Despite the gravity of the sin, Damian grieves for the sinner's loss of community. "I mourn for the noble soul made in the image and likeness of God," now fallen. He also grieves for the community "because a soul that had been the daughter of Holy Church has been cruelly wounded by the enemy

121. Letter 31:32, in L, 2:25; B, 1:305.

122. Letter 31.35, in L, 2:27; B, 1:306.

123. Letter 31.36, in L, 2:28; B, 1:307.

124. Letter 31.43, in L, 2:32; B, 1:311.

of the human race."[125] Whether the individual realizes it or not, one sin affects all. Fortunately, it can be redeemed by the community. "I weep for you with unrelenting grief," he explains, "because I do not see you weeping." In addition, "you need the grief of others because you do not grieve over your perilous calamity. And since you appear to be undisturbed by any personal sad feeling of regret, you need all the more the bitter tears and compassion of your brothers."[126]

Compassion is what Damian offers. Because it is expressed within a paradigm that assumes the inherent perverseness of homosexual activity, modern readers finding that presupposition offensive may miss it, but it is there. "Poor unhappy soul, why do you not reflect on the exalted dignity from which you have been cast down?" he sympathetically asks.[127] He seems to understand the frustration of homosexual attraction in a heterosexual world. He hopes his lecture, again using rational arguments, helps end the attraction. "Male virility, I say, should terrify you, and you should shudder at the sight of manly limbs. For it is the function of the natural appetite that each should seek outside himself what he cannot find within his own capacity. Therefore, if the touch of masculine flesh delights you, lay your hands upon yourself and be assured that whatever you do not find in yourself, you seek in vain in the body of another."[128] He warns the sodomites of David's curse, "this disease called gonorrhea" and naïvely asks, "why not stop heaping up vengeance for yourself" and stop the activity.[129] His compassion is also apparent a bit later in the treatise when he talks about any "poor hermit who sinned through ignorance and fell through simple inexperience, thinking this was allowed him as a ordinary natural function." Regarding these, Damian merely advises the Church to "let these miserable souls learn to inhibit this detestable vice."[130] After all, "it is not sinners, but the wicked who should despair; it is not the magnitude of one's crime,

125. Letter 31.44, in L, 2:33; B, 1:312.

126. Letter 31.47, in L, 2:35–36; B, 1:314.

127. Letter 31.45, in L, 2:34; B, 1:312.

128. Letter 31.46, in L, 2:35; B, 1:313.

129. Letter 31.47, in L, 2:36; B, 1:314.

130. Letter 31.60, in L, 2:42; B, 1:320. Damian's compassion may have been enhanced by his awareness of false accusations regarding Romuald. See VR, 49 (244–45).

but contempt of God that dashes one's hopes." He urges the sinner to "beware of drowning in the depths of despondency" by remembering that "your heart should beat with confidence in God's love."[131]

Damian's compassion is for the individual's personal plight. It does not extend to individuals who jeopardize the community by exposing others to the sin. "To what purpose are you so eager to ensnare the people of God in the meshes of your own perdition? Is it not enough that you yourselves are plunging headlong into the depths of sin? Must you expose others to the danger of your fall?" For the sodomite priest this is a pivotal problem, because a priest is the community's intercessor before God: "How can one ask [God] to pardon others if he does not know if God is well disposed toward him?"[132] To avoid this dilemma, potential candidates for the priesthood must take an honest look at their sexual state. "Everyone, in fact, should discreetly judge himself and not dare to accept the office of the priesthood if accursed vice still has power over him," Damian preaches, for "if you are willing to accept your own destruction, beware of being responsible for the damnation of others."[133] Besides failing as intercessor, the offending cleric is also unable to meet the community's needs concerning ritual purity, because "God himself refuses to accept sacrifices from your hands."[134]

Damian now changes the thrust of his argument. He has presented reasons from councils, the Fathers, canons, and Scripture. To these he adds eschatological and psychological reasons. Those who have remained unmoved by previous evidence should "conjure up before him the day of his death" and desist.[135] Sodomites must "repress the lascivious urging of the flesh, and fear in their bones the terrible judgment of divine anger."[136] They must remember "that they who are now addicted to the vice of impurity will be condemned to eternal punishment." While the line is still deeply drawn—"whoever shall have soiled himself with the filth of shameful sodomy ... unless

131. Letter 31.64, in L, 2:45; B, 1:322.
132. Letter 31.50, in L, 2:38; B, 1:316.
133. Letter 31.51, in L, 2:38; B, 1:316–17.
134. Letter 31.52, in L, 2:39; B, 1:317.
135. Letter 31.57, in L, 2:41; B, 1:318.
136. Letter 31.60, in L, 2:42; B, 1:320.

he has purged himself through effective penance, he can never obtain the grace of God"—Damian's compassion and comprehension of the psychological dimensions of sodomy rise to the forefront in this section.[137] "If your impure flesh has deceived you with homosexual persuasion [*mollia suadendo*]," he more gently cautions, "do not be depressed and utterly despair. Once again collect your forces, bestir yourself like a man, dare to perform great deeds, and by so acting you will have the strength, through the mercy of God, to triumph over your enemies."[138] The urge arises in the body and mind, and so too will its suppression. Consequently, Damian's prescription addresses both body and mind. "Think again" of the eschatological ramifications ("momentary pleasure" in exchange for punishment "for thousands of years"), use "the impenetrable shield of thoughts like these," and then discipline both body and mind: "Break the pride of your flesh by fasting; nourish your soul at the banquet of constant prayer. Thus, by disciplining firmness the dominant spirit takes the lead in compelling its subject flesh."[139] He offers other approaches to ease conversion. "Keep in mind the promised rewards of chastity" for motivation.[140] If the temptation is too great, physically relocate: "Move out when the heat of the fire nearby becomes intense." As insistent as he is that the temptation be resisted, he is still sympathetic to the hardships involved. He offers encouragement. "If you should be unable to reach port with your ship unharmed, it is enough to have endured the storm and escaped shipwreck," he cajoles, suggesting that those who do reach shore just "lie out of danger on the beach" and sing.[141]

In the final section Damian defends his attack on clerical misconduct. He is not afraid of being accused "of being an informer or a

137. Letter 31.62, in L, 2:44; B, 1:321.

138. Letter 31.65, in L, 2:45; B, 1:322. Patrick Vandermeersch, "Sodomites, Gays, and Biblical Scholars: A Gathering Organized by Peter Damian?" in *Sodom's Sin,* ed. Ed Noort and Eibert Tegchelaar (Leiden: Brill, 2004), 169, first questioned but now agrees with Blum's translation of *mollia suadendo* as homosexual persuasions.

139. Letter 31.67, in L, 2:47; B, 1:324.

140. Letter 31.68, in L, 2:47; B, 1:324.

141. Letter 31.70, in L, 2:49; B, 1:325.

delator" nor "of the hatred of evil men nor of the tongues of detractors." That he expects the assault indicates he had knowledge presaging the hostile reception of his letter. He knew it would ruffle feathers. Still, because of his strong sense of communal obligation to bear witness to the truth regardless of personal cost, he did not hesitate to write. His belief in the individual's responsibility for the salvation of the community is immutable: "Who am I, when I see this pestilential practice flourishing in the priesthood to become the murderer of another's crime in which I was in no way involved," he exclaims in horror. "How, indeed, am I to love my neighbor as myself if I negligently allow the wound, of which I am sure he will brutally die, to fester in his heart; if, moreover, I am aware of these wounds of the spirit and fail to cure them by the surgery of my words."[142] He reminds the audience that in this he is following the witness borne by Jerome, Ambrose, and Augustine but admits there is a difference. They opposed heretics; he attacks Christians. His reply reflects his concern for continuity. It is "my purpose to prevent the departure of members."[143] In his parting words he once again addresses Leo and summarizes his request for the pope to scrutinize the canons to see if Damian is correct. After such investigation Damian asks him to issue "by solemn decree" a decision on how guilty clerics are to be disciplined.[144]

By focusing attention on other aspects of the treatise I do not intend to diminish its significance in the history of Western homosexuality. Its importance is apparent when placed within its historical context. Homosexuality as identity, inclination, or desire is a modern concept. Until recently it was assumed that all medieval society thought of homosexuality in terms of acts. The *what* was primary, the *who* secondary. If this be so, then Damian's treatise marks a tran-

142. Letter 31.71, in L, 2:49–50; B, 1:326.

143. Letter 31.73, in L, 2:52; B, 1:328.

144. Much could be written here regarding the Donatist debate over the validity of errant priests' mass. Jean Leclercq, *Saint Pierre,* 68–69, claims Damian never changed positions; Anderson, *Great Catholic Reformers,* 39, says he did. See Letter 31.50, in L, 2:38; B, 1:316; and Letter 65.

sition of sorts. As Patrick Vandermeersch points out, Damian does not consider merely the *what.* He places sodomy within a relational framework and is, therefore, in the forefront of cultural developments that culminate in a new psychology. This is a "remarkable" event, "a turning point in the history of Western homosexuality."[145] I have previously mentioned the relational framework Damian employs; it is that of father-child. Vandermeersch calls this a "paternal metaphor," but I suggest it is more. To Damian it is a reality. The priest is the actual spiritual father of his flock, "whom he has spiritually begotten."[146] The priest is not "like" a father; he is one. This belief runs deep. Damian supports it with Scripture: "It is a common expression to call [a penitent] a 'son by penance,' just as we also say 'son by baptism.' Thus we read of blessed Mark the Evangelist," and in 1 Corinthians, 1 Thessalonians, and Galatians, that the sacramental minister goes "through the pain of giving birth to you . . . until Christ is formed in you." Because of this reality, "he is properly called a son who receives penance, and a father who administers it."[147]

This spiritual relationship carries with it the same relational demands as physical relationships. Since it is incestuous for a physical father to have intercourse with his physical children, so it is incestuous for a spiritual father. His conclusion follows logically from these tenets.

> It follows, therefore, that the same sentence is rightly inflicted on him who assaults his own daughter, or who by sacrilegious intercourse abuses his spiritual daughter, and on him also who in his foul lust defiles a cleric whom he has ordained. Perhaps we should distinguish here the quality of both crimes: in the two prior cases, even though he practices incest, he is sinning naturally, because he sinned with a woman; in the latter case by his shameful action with a cleric he commits a

145. Vandermeersch, "Sodomites," 162–71, quote 171. While I basically agree with Vandermeersch, there is still much evidence to argue that Damian sees sodomy as an act, for example, in his discussion of the four varieties of sodomy. I consider Damian's thoughts transitional.

146. Letter 31.19, in L, 2:15; B, 1:295.

147. Letter 31.25, in L, 2:19; B, 1:299. See Letter 61.11, in L, 3:10; B, 2:214: "All the children of the Church are undoubtedly your children."

sacrilege on a son, is guilty of the crime of incest on a man, and violates the law of nature.[148]

Because "it is written that 'spiritual begetting is greater than physical,'" sodomy among clergy is deserving of more punishment than sodomy among laity, for it involves a greater abuse of power and betrayal of trust.[149] One must remember Damian's crusade is not against sodomy per se but specifically against it "spreading so through the clergy." He even suggests that "for many of [these clerics] it would be more salutary to be burdened with service in the world" as laymen than to be priests.[150] Furthermore, if a bishop knows of clerics who are so abusing their power and trust and does nothing, he shares in the guilt. "By "wink[ing] at the sins of their subjects," superiors are failing the individual and hurting the community.[151]

One senses that Damian's outrage originates in his perception of the relationship between self and community. It is every individual's obligation to protect the community; the community protects the individual. Physical incest upsets this relationship; spiritual incest upsets this relationship. His overwhelming concern is for the individual and community. The revulsion is there, but the unnaturalness of the act is not the chief basis for his attack. Thus when he wants "to make my own position clear" concerning "those who habituated to the filth of this festering disease," he does not mention any perversion of nature but instead turns to reason and canon law.[152]

One canon he cites reveals an aspect of the situation not immediately evident in the rest of the treatise and is consistent with a concern for community. The scandal involves the sexual abuse of minors: "Any cleric or monk who seduces young men or boys, or who is apprehended in kissing or in any shameful situation, shall be pub-

148. Letter 31.20, in L, 2:16; B, 1:296. Damian uses the same argument against heterosexual misconduct.

149. Letter 31.19, in L, 2:15; B, 1:295. Reindel attributes the citation to Walafridus Strabo.

150. Letter 31.7, in L, 2:6; B, 1:287.

151. Letter 31.18, in L, 2:15; B, 1:294.

152. Letter 31.10, in L, 2:8; B, 1:289. He does acknowledge it, though. See Letter 31.37, in L, 2:28; B, 1:307; and Letter 31.46, in L, 2:35; B, 1:313.

licly flogged . . . never again allowed to associate with young men for the purpose of improper conversation or advice."[153] Damian's discussion of the canon leaves the impression that he was talking about homosexual behavior with children all along. This does not elicit any special concern for Damian; he treats it in a matter-of-fact manner. The modern reader, I assume, reacts differently and sees the introduction of children as victims adding an entirely new dimension to the scandal.[154] If, indeed, Damian's focus from the beginning was on sex between children and clerics then we can better understand why Damian framed his attack within the individual/community paradigm. It is the duty of the community to protect the most vulnerable, and children are among the most vulnerable. It provides further insight into why Damian perceived the relational aspects of sodomy and why he condemned it as spiritually incestuous. It also explains Damian's adamant insistence on public penance; the act damaged the community, so restitution must be to the community.[155] Finally, if Damian's concern is pedophilia, it helps elucidate why he maintains that this vice "surpasses the enormity of all others."[156] Many today might agree.

To repeat, the whole of Damian's corpus must be studied before correct generalizations can be made concerning single works. By examining the totality of works written before mid-century and identifying Damian's basic tenets, we gain a better perspective on the content of these two influential treatises—and vice versa. In application Damian's later works are innovative and creative, but his basic principles are neither new nor unexpected. They are present in his earliest works, sometimes in unsophisticated form, but, nevertheless, there. Together *Dominus vobiscum* and *Gomorrhianus* form a

153. Letter 31.38, in L, 2:29; B, 1:301–2.

154. This appears to be the reverse of the medieval situation. Whereas Damian saw homosexual behavior as the primary focus of the scandal and the children as secondary (or even inconsequential), Americans seem scandalized about the children, not the behavior.

155. Letter 31.40, in L, 2:30; B, 1:309; Letter 31.36, in L, 2:28; B, 1:307; and Letter 31.39, in L, 2:29; B, 1:308.

156. Letter 31.41, in L, 2:30; B, 1:309

sort of compendium of his theology at mid-century and provide his model for practical application. They bring his social theology to the forefront. Once this is acknowledged, it is easier to recognize other insights of Damian's that were previously overlooked or ignored. This is particularly true of *Gomorrhianus,* where scholarly focus on Damian's portrait of homosexuality has left his concern for social issues—gender and disciplinary inequality, abuse of power, compassion, and relationships—all but unnoticed. *Dominus vobiscum* has fared better, but even here his contributions to the formation of social concepts have been neglected or misunderstood. Hopefully these commentaries help readers recognize the depth and breadth of Damian's legacy. His social theology is of utmost significance in the history not only of Christianity but also of Western culture, for it comes at a time when society is ready and able to break forth in new and astounding ways. During the next two centuries Western society adopted much of what Damian offered. The reform of the institutional Church, the renewal of religious life, and the creation of different kinds of religious orders are areas where Damian's influence has already been noted, but there are so many more.

Four

STANDARDS FOR CHURCH REFORM

It is clear that Damian was a force to be reckoned with when he wrote *Liber Gomorrhianus*. Even Leo IX tells Damian he will act "according to your wishes" and offers him a shield against those who "dare to criticize or attack" him.[1] Leo's closing remarks in the prelude reinforce the power of Damian's witness, for the pope praises Damian not for his writing but for the testimony of his life: "I rejoice indescribably that you promote by the example of your life whatever you have taught by your eloquence," Leo proclaims, adding that it is this witness that ultimately "attain[s] the palm of victory."[2] Damian's emphasis on witness obviously made an impact on Leo and his contemporaries. Thus, even if his reforms concerning sodomy were ignored, the central plank of his social theology was not. The purity of his witness and its message is the primary basis of his authority in society and the reason why he becomes more influential at mid-century. The light of his witness shone too brightly to ignore.

Damian's increased public presence during the 1050s coincides

1. Letter 31.3–4, in L, 2:4–5; B, 1:285.
2. Letter 31.5, in L, 2:5; B, 1:286.

with the overall growth of reform movements. Blum tells us that prior to 1049 Damian "was almost alone" in the call for action.[3] With the accession of Leo IX the movement gained momentum. Another friend of reform, Hugh of Cluny, became abbot the same year, and he may have met Bruno on the eve of their elections at the court of Emperor Henry III, a third advocate of reform. The three voices of authority in eleventh-century society—papal, monastic, and imperial—were in agreement: the papacy must be reformed. To that end Leo embarked on a whirlwind of activity. He insisted that the clergy and people of Rome ratify his imperial appointment and meet canonical conditions before he accept the throne.[4] Next, he looked for reforming advisors and found several: Humbert of Moyenmoutier (later cardinal-bishop of Silva Candida), Abbot Hugh, Hildebrand, and Peter Damian.[5]

Simony

Within months of Leo's accession, papal reform officially commenced when Leo convened a synod in Reims.[6] Here the pope "condemned the heresy of simony which had already invaded some regions of the world and in the same council he deposed certain bishops whom the heresy had marked."[7] When Leo thus "asserted papal authority as it had never been asserted before," the whole clerical structure of the Church was "earth-shakingly challenged."[8] The following

3. Blum, *St. Peter Damian,* 20. Of the thirty-seven letters written before 1051, fifteen of them (2, 3, 4, 7, 11, 13, 14, 16, 18, 19, 20, 26, 30, 31, and 35) advocate reform.

4. Tellenbach, *Church,* 100, notes that canonical election then "consisted of the usual applause of the people as he entered the papal city." See Bruno of Segni, *Concerning Simoniacs,* 2, in *Papal Reform of the Eleventh Century*, tr. I. S. Robinson (Manchester: Manchester University Press, 2004), 380, which describes Bruno's election: "Bruno was elected to the papacy by the clergy and people according to Roman custom with great applause; then he was raised to the throne of the blessed apostle Peter."

5. Strangely, Tellenbach, *Church,* 98, does not include Damian among Leo's advisors, yet notes his leadership role in simoniacal debates.

6. See Noreen Hunt, *Cluny Under Saint Hugh: 1049–1109* (Notre Dame, Ind.: University of Notre Dame Press, 1967), 140–42, for a succinct discussion of these events. The first canon from Reims mandated canonical elections. See ibid., 100.

7. *Life of Pope Leo IX,* 10, in *Papal Reform,* 136.

8. Duffy, *Saints and Sinners,* 115. Henry I of France anticipated Leo's demands and for-

Easter Leo "held a council in Siponto and deposed two archbishops who had acquired the holy ministry in return for payment."[9] At the Roman Easter synod in 1051 Leo sought the advice of his bishops concerning the question of reordination of simoniac clerics. This was the opportunity Damian had been waiting for. He was hoping "to receive permission" from the pope "to solve such a knotty problem": now he had it.[10] He wrote *Liber gratissimus* (Letter 40) in summer 1052.

The word *simony* refers to Simon Magnus's sin, that of trying to purchase grace from the Spirit (Acts 8:18–21). The earliest legislation (300) against it was relatively mild. In 451 at Chalcedon, canon 2 indicated increased but still minor concern. Over the years various councils, popes (notably Gregory I), and theologians condemned it, but the infrequency and mildness of the discussions suggests that payment for spiritual office was not perceived as a significant problem. There is no evidence that simony increased in the eleventh century, only that people now saw the ancient custom as a major evil. Gregory of Tours had described "offering many gifts" for a bishopric without condemnation, and his contemporaries considered it "decent gift-exchange."[11] By mid-eleventh century, however, perception had changed enough for Leo IX to condemn buying and selling of "holy Orders or ecclesiastical offices or altars" and charging for sacraments.[12] Emperor Henry IV supported this attack on simony and refused to engage in it.[13] We can trace the beginning of the transition in perception to the turn of the century and Romuald. Ac-

bade his bishops to attend, so only twenty bishops were present. Leo's actions were made all the more dramatic when later that year the archbishop of Besançon was struck dumb while defending simony. See *Life of Pope Leo,* 10, in *Papal Reform,* 137. Hugh of Cluny supported Leo's attempts, however, in the keynote sermon of the synod. For summary of the Reims council, see Richard Southern, *The Making of the Middle Ages* (New Haven, Conn.: Yale University Press, 1975), 125–27.

9. *Life of Pope Leo,* 14, in *Papal Reform,* 141.

10. Letter 40.2, in L, 2:113–14; B, 1:391–93.

11. Gregory of Tours, *Historia Francorum,* ed. B. Krusch and W. Levisa, MGH, *Scriptores rerum Merovingicarum,* 1 editio altera (1937–51), iii, 2, x. 26; and ibid., 293 and 854.

12. Anselm, *Historia dedicationis ecclesiae S. Remigii,* PL 142, 1436–37; ibid., 827.

13. See Fuhrmann, *Germany,* 39. He adds that "Henry made up the deficit" to the royal coffers by confiscating the laity's lands (40).

cording to Damian, Romuald considered it his mission to instill in his contemporaries a new awareness of simony's dangers.

> In his sermons Romuald frequently lashed out against secular priests who had gotten their ordination for money.... Some of them, considering him a revolutionary, plotted to kill him. Others were hardly aware that simony—buying and selling ordination and church offices—was in anyway a sin, since up to Romuald's time, the practice had been the common custom throughout the region. Speaking to a group of priests, Romuald asked them to bring him all their books of church law. He showed them the canons that condemn simony. "Now you know that what I have been telling you is true," he said. When they had read the texts for themselves, they acknowledged their crime and shed tears of repentance. St. Romuald had them live in community as canons; no more were they to dwell alone or with wives and children, but they were to submit to a superior and live together as brothers.[14]

We see in Damian's report the presence of several pertinent facts concerning Romuald's crusade against simony. Romuald turns to church law, not Scripture, to justify his demands; he links simony and incontinence; and he advocates community as an alternative to simony. After so recording Romuald's stance, however, Damian records his own opinion about the success of Romuald's preaching, thus providing the motive for his own crusade against simony. Romuald had failed: "But I doubt whether St. Romuald, as long as he lived, ever succeeded in converting a single bishop. The commerce in ecclesiastical honors, especially if it is a question of bishop's orders, is so pernicious and hard to stamp out, that no bishop has ever kept his promise to resign." In a conclusion, Damian's substitution of *thievery* for *simony* reveals how his perception of the vice's evil surpassed Romuald's view: "It is easier to convert a Jew to the faith, than to get a bishop to give up his thievery and his trading in church offices."[15] From the vita we see a timeline: Damian has Romuald preach-

14. VR, 35 (229–30). Jestice, *Wayward,* 151–52, interprets this as Damian's belief "that Romuald was the first anti-simony crusader in Italy."

15. Again, the line between Damian and Romuald's thoughts is thin. VR, 35 (230).

ing against simony from Val di Castro, which Romuald founded in 1005. Leo's condemnations began in 1049, and *Liber gratissimus* was written in 1052. In the latter two the perception of the vice is more extreme than Romuald's. What accounts for this increase?[16]

There are numerous possible answers. Simony is a transgression against the freedom of the Spirit that injures the dignity of the Church as Body of Christ, and Christ's body imagery was prominent at mid-century.[17] There was growing awareness of changes within the class structure. Simony was a vehicle of social mobility that gave access to ecclesiastical office to those not traditionally judged acceptable. It aligned the priest with *milites* elite against the *populus* by negating *milites* ability to perform their "most important duty and function ... that of mediator and peacemaker, representative of the united and ordered community."[18] The breakup of large demesnes led to increased prominence of local churches as foci for social activity and to their need as neutral mediators. A simoniacal priest was not seen as neutral. As more simoniacal transactions were conducted in cash the contrast between the sacred and profane became more pronounced.[19] Moreover, the increased power of priests led to increased fear of ritual pollution and fear of manipulation by the anticommunal forces of the nobility.[20] There was heightened awareness among the laity of its rights and duties, particularly its right to judge the clergy. The Church's lack of independence in a society aware of its right to control property put simony in a bad light. Just as mar-

16. Becker, *Medieval Italy,* 77: "Only with the eleventh century did such practices as simony assume menacing form.... What had gone almost unnoticed, and therefore seldom recorded, now became a major occupation."

17. Tellenbach, *Church,* 128–31.

18. A. Murray, *Reason and Society in the Middle Ages* (Oxford: Oxford University Press, 1978), 72.

19. An interesting exchange between Bruno of Segni and the clergy concerning his vita of Leo IX allows us to see how the relationship between money and priests' labor was still in flux. "When I returned home ... and told this vision to our clergy ... they said, 'We think that the blessed Leo required from you no money, but only that you write something that will be a fitting memorial to him. For your wealth is in your writing; and he himself seems to be in need of no other money.'" *Sermon,* 9, in *Papal Reform,* 389.

20. Moore, "Family, Community and Cult," 65.

ried clergy placed the parish under family control, simony placed it under seigneurial control. Simoniacal and married priests alike challenged customary social arrangements and blood ties. Simony was a way to keep blood ties narrow and thwart movements among the *populus* in Milan and Florence to loosen the hold the few had on the many. Finally, the passing of the gift culture made simony outdated.[21]

Damian's writings support many of these interpretations. We find nearly all these concerns and perceptions even in his writings prior to *Liber gratissimus.* Discussions about the individual's role in community, the Spirit's freedom in assigning those roles, and the imagery of the Body of Christ are major components of *Dominus vobiscum.* He talks at length in *Gomorrhianus* about the errant priest's inability to function effectively as mediator to the community.[22] He worries constantly over the status of church property. Before the end of 1044 Damian is troubled about one monastery's cash income and properties.[23] He worries over episcopal jurisdiction of property and tells one bishop to defend "this tiny piece of property," and talks about a person's "free will to dispose of his property [*liberam facultatem*]" as a basic right.[24] The preceding year he referred to the ritual impurity of simony as "foul contagion."[25] We saw in Letters 20 (1046) and 26 (1047) Damian encourage lay criticism of the clergy.[26] In 1050 he condemns the "rape of the Church's patrimony" and those who "steal Church properties."[27] He shares society's preoccupation with blood ties by writing a rambling treatise on consanguinity in 1046 (Letter 19) and revises it some four years later (Letter 36).

21. Becker, *Medieval Italy,* 75–77. Moore, "Family, Community and Cult," 66, and Lester K. Little, *Religious Poverty and the Profit Economy in Medieval Europe* (Ithaca, N.Y.: Cornell University Press, 1978), 31, note this factor but do not place the same emphasis on it.

22. Letter 31.50, in L, 2:38; B, 1:316.

23. Letter 7. In Letter 48.10, in L, 2:269; B, 2:59, written 1057, Damian makes it clear that it is much harder to ignore simony "payed in sparkling coins" than simony paid in service.

24. Letter 34.4., in L, 2:60; B, 1:336. Letter 38.7, in L, 2:77; B, 1:352.

25. Letter 3.2, in L, 1:88; B, 1:107.

26. The layman is Emperor Henry III.

27. Letter 35.2 and 3, in L, 2:61 and 63; B, 1:337–38.

Liber gratissimus

It is, of course, in *Liber gratissimus* that we find the fullest expression of Damian's perception of simony. The book is among his longest. While it is "one of the finest theological works of the century and a classic criticism of the rigorist approach to the problem of simony," it lacks the eloquence of *Dominus vobiscum* and the breadth of *Gomorrhianus.*[28] It is also narrower in scope and a bit redundant. Nevertheless, in the society of his day, *Liber gratissimus* exerted more influence than *Dominus vobiscum* and *Gomorrhianus,* and, despite Humbert of Silva Candida's attack in *Libri iii adversus simoniacos,* its argument won the day.[29] Damian's reputation and status as a major theologian and reformer grew accordingly. His is the voice of moderation. The sometimes virulent rhetoric serves only to support lenient conclusions. In addition, we see here how Damian interacted with his world. He identifies a problem and applies his principles in logical fashion. He draws rational, practical conclusions from his beliefs. He recognizes the change society was undergoing and knows how the Church must change if it wished to communicate to society—as the obligation to bear witness demands.

For three years the Church had struggled to find the proper way to deal with simonists, so Damian's contemporaries begged him "to be of some help and at least to write some short treatise explaining my point of view."[30] The "knotty problem" he sets out to solve is a corollary to simony: whether the ordination of "those who were consecrated gratis by simonists" is valid or whether they must be reordained. To answer this question Damian constructs a sacramental theology. The treatise in this sense is quite narrow. He stays focused on sacramental theology, reiterates his premises, and applies them

28. Colin Morris, *The Papal Monarchy* (Oxford: Clarendon Press, 1989), 90.

29. In MGH, Libelli de lite imperatorum et pontificum, ed. I. Thaner (Hanover, 1891), I, 95–253.

30. Letter 40.2, in L, 2:113; B, 1:391. The three years Damian refers to probably mark Leo IX's first synod in 1049 where the problem of simony was discussed. Discussion continued at synods in 1050 and 1051.

logically in every section.[31] Sacraments are gifts. Christ is the source of these gifts. Priests administer them. "It is clear that from the very beginning of man's redemption Christ Jesus, the mediator between God and man, organized his Church in such fashion that, on the one hand, he distributed his spiritual gifts through ministers of his word, and still as their source retained within himself the fullness of all graces."[32] That Christ is "the mediator between God and man" is key to his sacramental theology and reflects his understanding of the Incarnation. It makes mediation between the human and divine possible. He repeats this epithet for Christ two other times in the treatise.[33] Christ is the person who mediates; sacraments are how he mediates. It is Christ "who distributes his gifts" and the Spirit "is imparted through [priests'] instrumentality."[34] Because Christ is "he who produces the sacrament with its profound effect," it is of "no matter who may exercise the ministry."[35] Twice in the treatise Damian tells us when the actions of the priestly instrument produce a sacrament: it is when "a word is added to the element, and at the descent of the Spirit it becomes a sacrament."[36] The ritual is the essence of a sacrament. It "does not depend upon the merits of the minister or the recipient, but upon the rite ordained within the Church."[37]

Again and again he emphasizes the freedom of the Spirit which "'breathes wherever he wishes' so that actually spiritual grace, which flows from the liturgical practices of the Church, derives from the will of God rather than from the deserts of men."[38] As for why the issue of reordination among simonists was now pressing, Damian's answer is simple. Regarding the three principal sacraments (baptism, Eucharist, and ordination), the question of whether bap-

31. This is the only major treatise to have this context. His social theology takes a backseat here.

32. Letter 40.3, in L, 2:114; B, 1:393–94.

33. Letter 40.10 and 54; in L, 2:121 and 162; B, 1:401 and 447.

34. Letter 10.4, 6, in L, 2:116, 117; B, 1:395, 398.

35. Letter 40.5, in L, 2:117; B, 1:396.

36. Letter 40.6, in L, 2:117; B, 1:398; and Letter 40.40, in L, 2:150; B, 1:435.

37. Letter 40.13, in L, 2:124; B, 1:404.

38. Letter 40.17, in L, 2:128; B, 1:409.

tism and Eucharist "become better when effected by good priests [or] worse by bad priests" has already been asked and answered. "On the ordination of clerics, however, there has not been much discussion," because until recently everyone applied the conclusion concerning baptism and Eucharist to ordination. "Now, however, by acting immoderately, human curiosity propounds a new question" and "imposes darkness onto the clear light."[39] We see Damian's frustration. The answer is so evident to him that he has a difficult time understanding what the confusion is about. "It is obvious, therefore, that like the two sacraments [baptism and Eucharist] ... neither better results are produced by the good nor less worthy outcomes from the evil, so too it is with the ordination of clerics."[40] Likewise, Damian appears frustrated by those who think merit is relevant to the office of priest. He cites Jerome's statement that priestly orders are titles of office, not merit, and as such "God's blessing is attached to the dignity of the office and not to the value of the man." He reiterates the principle with variations: "In a blessing the favor is not from man but from God"; and, "The Spirit does not follow the person, or the dignity, but ordination."[41]

Damian establishes these tenets in the first fifth of the treatise. In the remaining four-fifths he supports his conclusions with scriptural, canonical, historical, and patristic references. Christ is the true priest whose Spirit ordains certain humans as instruments for conducting gifts to others. Humans can do nothing to merit their instrumentality nor can they do anything to hinder it. The priest, good or bad, exists for God's use. "It is God alone who uses evil man for good purposes, and he alone who disposes his gifts either by the hand of good men or even by the wicked."[42] Rather than contradict Damian's theology of witness, his sacramental theology reinforces it,

39. Letter 40.19; in L, 2:129–30; B, 1:410–11. Damian cites, ibid., "Augustine in the *Explanation of John the Evangelist* and Pascasius in his book *On the Eucharist of the Body of the Lord.*"

40. Letter 40.23, in L, 2:133–34; B, 1:415.

41. Letter 40.22; in L, 2:132; B, 1:414; repeated in 40.23, in L, 2:133; B, 1:415.

42. Letter 40.32, in L, 2:143; B, 1:425.

for the simonist's office serves as witness beyond his personal defects: "As I might put it, the light was handed to a blind man, not that he might see, but that he might be at the service of others."[43] He continues his candle metaphor. "The light, which to the candle causes destruction, becomes for us the instrument for seeing in the dark. Of what concern is it to me that the candle is reduced to ashes, so long as the light that I borrow from it unfailingly burns for me? Let the simonist burn and burn, the one from whom the Catholic is enlightened; and by the same light by which he is of service to others may he proceed to the darkness of his own eclipse."[44] Rather than a harsh disregard for the sinner, Damian looks with compassion upon the offender, reminding his audience that "it is one thing to sin against the faith and quite another to fall away from the faith." Justice demands compassion, and it demands that discipline correspond to the sin: "A soldier, for example, who loses his nerve and flees from battle should be charged quite differently from one who ... [goes] over to the enemy camp and surrender[s]."[45] He castigates those who ignore the relationship between justice and compassion: "Some men, indeed, wishing to appear more holy than they are, go to such pains to excise corruption that they proceed to mutilate what is authentic; and that they might seem in public opinion to be staunch defenders of justice, are not ashamed to deviate harshly from the path of human compassion."[46] He cites Pope Anastasius II's decisions on these matters so opponents might "hear of the Apostolic See's compassion and soften the severity of their own position."[47] Compassion and justice shape Damian's judgment as much as canons, especially when canons ignore intention: "This is certainly a cruel decision and a totally inhuman sentence based on an unwise investigation, that punishment should convict as guilty those whose conscience renders them innocent." Most significantly, Damian intuits a connection between compassion and moderation. "I do not, as if I were defending heretics, write

43. Letter 40.25, in L, 2:135; B, 1:417.
44. Letter 40.60, in L, 2:168; B, 1:454.
45. Letter 40.61, in L, 2:169; B, 1:455–56.
46. Letter 40.70, in L, 2:177; B, 1:466.
47. Letter 40.71, in L, 2:178; B, 1:467.

out these points to destroy the other more severe statements of the holy fathers," Damian explains. Instead, he advocates their "moderate discretions [*moderatio discretionis*]" so contemporaries will not act "through intemperate justice [*per inmoderatem iustitiam*]."[48]

Damian's reference to sacramental grace as *donum* pervades the treatise and supports modern theses concerning eleventh-century society's reassessment of the gift/countergift culture. Things that were once acceptable in a gift culture began to look differently when cash was involved. Perhaps it is harder to deny sins against the Spirit's freedom when a simonist tangibly "purchases God's gift" with money.[49] Damian wants to make sure the reader actually sees the crassness of the transaction: "The gift of heavenly grace is not handed out from the purse of the external paymaster, but is granted from the treasury of him who invisibly presides over the ordination."[50] He wants people to realize how contagious the desire for money can be: "Following the example of [the Roman See], in other churches everywhere forged money began to be struck."[51] For Damian, though, the introduction of money into the spiritual life distorts one's spiritual vision, making us think that spiritual victories come from cash instead of "from the generosity of divine grace."[52] Furthermore, "the love of money … restrains one from generosity in showing mercy and loving compassion."[53] In other words, it damages the relationship between individual and community.

Predictably, community and individual are a primary focus in Damian's arguments against reordination. He cites 1 Corinthians 12:12–13 in full and offers another commentary on the implications of the Incarnation.[54] The community must function properly. If the priest's merit is the criterion for the priesthood, then the community has no unity, for its unity "is established on this principle,

48. Letter 40.72, in L, 2:179; B, 1:468. Damian was criticized throughout his life for his moderate treatment of offenders. See Letters 140 and 146.

49. Letter 40.66, in L, 2:173; B, 1:461; and 40.61, in L, 2:169; B, 1:456.

50. Letter 40.53, in L, 2:161; B, 1:446–47.

51. Letter 40.78, in L, 2:185; B, 1:476.

52. Letter 40.112, in L, 2:208; B, 1:503.

53. Letter 40.109, in L, 2:206; B, 1:501.

54. Letter 40.35–37, in L, 2:146–47; B, 1:429–31. See Letter 28.

that Christ retained as his own the power of ordaining."[55] Because the power rests in Christ and is not dependent on one's merit, "it is of hardly any importance whether members of the Church be deformed or comely" and "seems to make little difference what these members are like." All that matters is "the office of the grade assigned to him."[56] Damian is most insistent that this not be the basis for a spiritual hierarchy. Even if the office assigned is superior, the priest functions only to "serve the utility of all [*simul utilitate*].... Thus it follows that what clerics have specifically as a class they owe not so much to themselves but rather to the common utility of the whole church [*non magis sibi quam usui totius aecclesiae communiter debent*]."[57] For emphasis, Damian then applies the theology of the Mystical Body developed in *Dominus vobiscum* to the issues surrounding reordination. Damian also includes a summary of events at Leo IX's 1049 synod. When he voided all simoniacal ordinations, "immediately the Roman bishops broke forth in a great seditious uproar, so that it was claimed, not only by them, but by many other bishops, that nearly all major churches would be without episcopal services, and especially that all celebration of mass would have to be stopped." Consequently, Leo "ordered that for the future all should continue in the orders to which they had been advanced, subject to the aforesaid penance." Damian agreed; the community's welfare trumps all else.[58]

Damian's regard for the individual is not as obvious. One could argue that his insistence on the priest's instrumentality and absence of merit diminishes the individual. Damian, I believe, would not let such an appraisal go unchallenged. Certainly, his arguments against the individual's merit as the controlling factor in sacraments would not be necessary if he did not already acknowledge individual potential. Believing that "man does not give what is divine" places no limits on the individual's power in human matters.[59] Damian speci-

55. Letter 40.29, in L, 2:140; B, 1:422.
56. Letter 40.36, in L, 2:147; B, 1:430.
57. Letter 40.37, in L, 2:147–48; B, 1:431.
58. Letter 40.107, in L, 2:204–5; B, 1:499–500.
59. Letter 40.32, in L, 2:143; B, 1:425.

fies precisely when the individual's worth is inconsequential; it is "in conferring the sacrament of spiritual grace."[60] On the other hand, his compassion is always for the individual: "Where there is no guilt, why should an innocent person be exposed as guilty?" Likewise, "to the upright man his integrity will be credited, and to the wicked his wickedness."[61] He calls upon his readers to subject his treatise to their own individual intellectual scrutiny: "I put off pursuing these ideas any farther, so that I might leave to the judgment of a rational mind the things which when heard should at least be feared, understood rather than read."[62] Damian's use of logic, Scripture, and history testifies to his faith in each person's rational capacities. He heralds the accomplishments of individual laymen.[63] Holiness is individual "and cannot be conveyed to another."[64] Most evident, however, is Damian's own individualism. His unique shadow stretches across the entire treatise. The reader is not allowed to forget for even a moment that Damian is a distinct personality who dances to his own tune. Phrases like "in my view," "I remembered," "I would be free" pepper the work. He has realistic confidence in his abilities, telling us that he will "communicate with gestures and nods where I do not know how to speak."[65] He personalizes the debate: "I lodge complaint," "I have defended your interests," "I condemn you," and similar phrases are found in every section.[66] He confesses his own connection to simony.[67] His numerous comments on his writing style, abilities, and shortcomings leave no doubt that Damian considered his writing unique to himself.[68] Finally, Damian proudly takes sole responsibility for his very personal beliefs: "I do not blush in freely confessing what I believe."[69]

60. Letter 40.36, in L, 2:147; B, 1:430.

61. Letter 40.72, in L, 2:179–80; B, 1:468–69.

62. Letter 40.83, in L, 2:190, B, 1:481.

63. His praise of Henry III's crusade against simony is extraordinary, comparing him to David and Constantine. See Letter 40.109–14, in L, 2:206–8; B, 1:501–3.

64. Letter 40.26, in L, 2:136; B, 1:418.

65. Letter 40.2, in L, 2:114; B, 1:392.

66. Letter 40.115, in L, 2:209; B, 1:504.

67. Letter 40.78, in L, 2:186; B, 1:476.

68. See, for example, Letter 40.119–22, in L, 2:212–14; B, 1:506–9.

69. Letter 40.121, in L, 2:213; B, 1:508.

The Hierarchy and the People

Extant letters are sparse after *Liber gratissimus,* until 1057. In the intervening five years we have only six letters.[70] In the first half of 1057 we find Damian writing boldly to Victor II (Letter 46); obviously Damian realized his new position in the Church.[71] Without flinching Damian declares that Christ Himself "is disadvantaged in the course of your pontificate."[72] It is a short letter, but it contains a synopsis of Damian's understanding of the communal nature of the papacy and of its relationship with secular authority. One cannot help but note Damian's concern for social justice, not doctrine. He records Christ's disappointment with the pope.

> I [Christ] selected you from the common group of clerics and, from among the ministers of the bishop, promoted you to the powers of the episcopal office. I made you, as it were, the father of the emperor and caused him to show favor to you in preference to almost all mortal men. Into your hands I entrusted the keys of the Universal Church and placed you as my Vicar over the Church which I redeemed by the shedding of my own blood. And if that were not enough, I added principality, and after the king was dead allowed you to exercise the rights of the whole Roman Empire then vacant. Having granted you these great favors, I am now unable to find law or justice in your proceedings.[73]

Damian's solution is straightforward: regain a zeal for practicing justice and discipline and "restore Christ's rights." To justify his criticism of a pope Damian ends the letter by reminding Victor II that he is but a man and "a man should not disdain another man's humble suggestions."[74]

Around the same time Damian writes to a bishop (Letter 47) about the need for local church reform. We see how disturbed Damian was, again, not by doctrinal ignorance but by the lack of basic

70. There is one fragment, a short one to a bishop over a property dispute (42), a brief note to Emperor Henry III (43), a sizeable letter about flagellation (44), a treatise on eremiticism (45), and a pastoral letter (47).

71. Blum long ago dubbed him "the monitor of popes."

72. Letter 46.2, in L, 2:250; B, 2:41.

73. Letter 46.3, in L, 2:250–51; B, 2:41.

74. Letter 46.5, in L, 2:251; B, 2:42.

knowledge. "There are priests who are now so deficient in education that not only do they not understand what they read, but can hardly stammer syllable by syllable through the parts of the clause," Damian laments. "How can service be rational when he who offers sacrifice has no idea what he is offering? [*quomodo illic raconabile erit obsequium, ubi es, qui offert, oblacionis suae non concipit intellectum?*]"[75] He begins by championing the superiority of intention and the use of common sense.[76] Damian asks in frustration, "Since Almighty God pays more attention to the desires of the mind in those who offer sacrifice than to the sound of their voice, what can he hope to obtain by his prayers if he does not know what he is asking for?"[77] He is upset, because he knows how such ignorance affects society. When individuals function without comprehending the meaning of that function, and that function is teaching, the ramifications are disturbing. Priests' lives bear false witness: "They simulate faith by their words, but go right on practicing godlessness by their deeds."[78] They also bear errant witness when "they associate with laymen by living amid the citizens of a region, many of them are no different from their neighbors."[79] Damian offers practical solutions to these local problems. First, "bishops must be advised to suspend from administering their office those who are unworthy." Second, "they should appoint qualified men as their representatives, whose duty it will be to visit and supervise them at frequent intervals." Lastly, they must find someone "who will be able to instruct the others in the requirements of the priestly office."[80]

Letter 48 has long been recognized as historically significant in the establishment of the identity and role of the college of cardinals.

75. Letter 47.2, in L, 2:252–53; B, 2:44.

76. In this Damian was again in the forefront of the movement to eradicate false penance and focus on intention, generations before the penitential theology of Abelard and the Victorines emphasized intention. See Sarah Hamilton, "Penance in the Age of Gregorian Reform," in *Retribution, Repentance, and Reconciliation*, ed. Kate Cooper and Jeremy Gregory, 47–73 (Rochester, N.Y.: Boydell Press, 2004).

77. Letter 47.2, in L, 2:253; B, 2:44.

78. Letter 47.4, in L, 2:254; B, 2:44–45. He also cites Titus 1:16: "They profess to acknowledge God, but deny Him by their actions."

79. Letter 47.6, in L, 2:254; B, 2:45.

80. Letter 47.15, in L, 2:260–61; B, 2:50–51.

Many scholars also see in this letter corroborating evidence of Damian's coauthorship of the 1059 Papal Election Decree.[81] Written soon after his own elevation to the cardinalate (latter part of 1057) supposedly "to arouse myself" from "listless inactivity," the letter is an obvious attempt to rally his fellow cardinals to join in his reform work. He begins by painting a bleak scenario in order to heighten the goodness of "the one and only harbor" capable of bringing the poor fishermen "to peaceful and life-giving shores": the Roman Church.[82] After singing the praises of "this highest and Universal Church" he diplomatically presents his golden rule for reform: bear proper witness.

> Now we, my brothers, if I may dare to include myself in your number, we, I say, who are like seven eyes in the stone, who bear the likeness of stars, who share the dignity of angels in our office of proclamation, let us observe, brilliantly reflect, and announce the words of life to the people, not only with our lips but also by our deeds. The tongue, indeed, proclaims the word of the preacher, but his life commends it. Moreover, since various people from all the world come together at the Lateran palace, it is imperative that there, above all other places, one should always find the proper kind of life.[83]

The rest of the letter is filled with variations on this thesis. "The office of bishop does not consist in peaked caps of sable" nor "blazing red garments" and fur collars, "but in uprightness of life."[84] He reminds them of the additional responsibility they have to "present yourselves as a model for upright living to others, not only to the faithful but also to bishops. In your life let them observe how one should act and what one should avoid." That includes everyday behavior as well: "No more childish games, enough of this biting eloquence and refined style. Beware of sounding like a fool and of engaging in nonsense."[85] In his concluding section he reminds his fellow cardinals one more time how heavy is their responsibility to bear witness to the faithful: "It is imperative that your life should

81. See B, 2:53 n.1; L, 2:263, prècis; and Friedrich Kempf, "Pier Damiani und das Papstwahldekret von 1059," *Archivum historiae pontificiae* 2 (1964), 73–89.

82. Letter 48.4, in L, 2:265; B, 2:55.

83. Letter 48.7, in L, 2:267; B, 2:57.

84. Letter 48.8, in L, 2:267–68; B, 2:57–58.

85. Letter 48.11, in L, 2:270; B, 2:60.

be a design, as it were a seal made of the hardest steel that produces a rule of life for others. A seal made of steel impresses its image on other metals without taking its form from them." It has the power to *re-form* other metals. Only by "presenting ourselves as a true model of living and a seal to the rest of the faithful" will the cardinals fulfill their function as reformers.[86]

While these remarks are addressed especially to the cardinal-bishops, Damian discusses reform principles with his secretary Ariprandus in Letter 54, written around the same time. Damian follows Paul's example when he criticized Peter (Gal 2:11–14): "What is the meaning of this, Blessed Paul, that you abuse your superior with such rebukes?"[87] Damian queries and then answers. "While appearing to rebuke Peter, he was in agreement with him, rather than his adversary," for the rebuke was given "in the service of obedience, and was not a disciplinary correction; it was not bold invective, but a harmonious meeting of wills."[88] Damian models his own criticism of the hierarchy on Paul's example and advises Ariprandus to do the same. "Be for [Fonte Avellana] a model they can imitate," Damian urges. "Your action will, therefore, be a shining example."[89] Public correction of the hierarchy follows the example of the vita apostolica.

Damian informs Ariprandus of three more reform principles. First, reform does not necessarily consist of "novelties of foreign invention." After all, Christ "observed the custom of his homeland ... [and] did not refuse to observe the traditions of men even in those things that seemed to have hardly any significance."[90] Secondly, correction is an essential tool of reform. "Be careful of one thing in particular, namely, that you never take offense at correction," for without "the polish of sharp correction the mildew" contracted would never be removed.[91] Thirdly, reform entails work. "This is certainly the correct order of things," Damian explains, that a person "is broken up like a level field by the plowshare of correction, and then is

86. Letter 48.12, in L, 2:271; B, 2:61.
87. Letter 54.13, in L, 2:352; B, 2:146.
88. Letter 54.16, in L, 2:353–54; B, 2:147.
89. Letter 54.17, in L, 2:354; B, 2:148.
90. Letter 54.2–3, in L, 2:345; B, 2:140.
91. Letter 54.4, in L, 2:345–46; B, 2:141.

planted with the gentle seed of holy preaching, [and] finally filled with an abundant harvest of good works." Without the reforming hand of authority, people would "never learn to write, and never become proficient in any suitable trade or manual skill, even though the Apostle says, 'The man who does not work, shall not eat.'"[92]

Despite Stephen IX's dying command to postpone the papal election until Hildebrand was present, once Stephen was dead Tusculan nobles succeeded in having one of their own elected as Benedict X.[93] The reform party fled to Florence, including Damian, who as cardinal-bishop of Ostia was the papal consecrator. Hildebrand returned May 5, but the reformers' election of Nicholas II did not occur until December. Consecrated on January 24, 1059, Nicholas drove Benedict out of Rome and a mere three months later (April 13) he convened the synod that promulgated the Election Decree. Sometimes overlooked is the fact that the same synod legislated against clerical marriages, encouraged lay criticism of clergy, and imposed the common life (vita communis) on canons—all of which were planks in Damian's reform platform.[94]

The principles of Damian's early years dictated this platform, and all are found in Damian's celebrated fictitious debate between an imperial attorney and a Roman lawyer, *Disceptatio synodalis.* The debaters will find the truth, because "God is not only truthful but is Truth Itself [*veritas eadem*]."[95] Oratorical or "evasive tricks" will make "Truth Itself desert one who is engaged in debate," so both attorneys will "rationally continue."[96] The Incarnation, the cornerstone of Damian's ecclesiology, is "the Word ... through whom finally the elements of all things were structured, who founded the

92. Letter 54.9–10, in L, 2:349–51; B, 2:144–46. In S, 72.10–11, he emphasizes the importance of the local priest in church reform and his role as instrument of reforming grace.

93. Cowdrey, *Pope Gregory,* 36, speculates that this request "may have arisen from negotiations in progress with the German court about the conduct of future elections" or because Hildebrand was trying to procure imperial approval of Stephen's candidate for pope, Gebhard of Flore.

94. See below, ch. 5. Berengar's Eucharistic teachings were also discussed.

95. Letter 89.48, in L, 3:346; B, 2:551.

96. Letter 89.70, in L, 3:355; B, 2:559.

Roman Church. Clearly it enjoys his privilege and is supported by his authority."[97] Anyone who denies "the Roman Church the privilege granted it" does violence to it.[98] To avoid injury the Church must "promote love and compassion throughout the world."[99] Its bishops "must demonstrate love and compassion."[100] They bear witness through "their special obligation" to preach.[101] In this instance they must preach that simony is "the sin of sin," because the simonist sells the Church "just as Judas Iscariot sold the Lord."[102] Instead, priests must take "as a model for your action" Peter or Paul, who "avoid[ed] giving scandal to the Jews as an example for our imitation."[103] Bishops and laity alike "are not to judge the external act, but you must rather carefully note the spirit and the intention with which it was done [*quo animo et qua intentione sit factum*]."[104] All must realize reform is change, and no one should "be ashamed to change his opinion for something better."[105] All must also acknowledge that successful reform comes only when society realizes that "the empire and the priesthood, by divine dispensation, are united in one mediator between God and men." This is Damian's goal for society: "Let us conspire to work together that the highest seat of the priesthood [*summum sacerdotium*] and the Roman Empire [*Romanum... imperium*] may be joined in harmony, so that the human race [*humanum genus*] which under both aspects of its nature is ruled by these two powers, should never again, God forbid, be torn apart."[106] In the end the Roman lawyer wins the debate "not by rhetorical arguments, nor flowers of oratory, nor finally by dialectical syllogisms, but rather purged of falsehood by recourse to reason."[107]

One could argue that the Lateran council of 1059 marked the

97. Letter 89.25, in L, 3:337; B, 2:542.
98. Letter 89.26, in L, 3:337; B, 2.542.
99. Letter 89.68, in L, 3:354; B, 2:558. See also 89.63 and 65, in L, 3:352; B, 2:556.
100. Letter 89.26, in L, 3:338; B, 542–43.
101. Letter 89.17, in L, 3:332; B, 2:538.
102. Letter 89.11, in L, 3:330; B, 2:536.
103. Letter 89.62, in L, 3:351; B, 2:556.
104. Letter 89.80, in L, 3:359; B, 2:563. See also 89.81, in L, 3359; B, 2:563 (*ad purae mentis*): 89.86, in L, 3:360; B, 2:564 (*quo animo et voluntate faciat*); and 89.87, in L, 3:361; B, 2:565 (*quo animo, qua mentis intentione*).
105. Letter 89.95, in L, 3:364; B, 2:568.
106. Letter 89.102, in L, 3:368; B, 2:572.
107. Letter 89.89, in L, 3:361–62; B, 2:565–66.

zenith of Damian's influence on official church legislation. It is certainly not, however, the peak of his influence on theological, cultural, and social matters, or even in the political arena. Probably right after Nicholas II's enthronement Damian is sent to Milan with Anselm of Lucca (later Pope Alexander II) as Nicholas's envoy to address the city's unrest.[108] In 1057 a group of laity, spurred on by the preaching of a deacon named Ariald, had risen in protest against the clergy. Ariald's message was simple. Christ told his disciples to let the light of their good works shine before all men (Mt 5:16). To do this they must bear witness through word and example: *imitatio Christi.*[109]

Damian's was the second papal legation to the city. Anselm had gone in 1057 with Hildebrand and only exacerbated matters. In December 1059 Damian wrote a full report of his mission, often called *On the Privilege of the Roman Church.* In the account he tells us the mission came as Damian was considering Hildebrand's request to "excerpt whatever specifically was seen to belong to the authority of the Apostolic See, and put it all together in some small volume as a new collection." Damian procrastinated, because he judged it "of little importance ... superfluous rather than necessary."[110] His mission to Milan changed his mind, for after preaching "on the privilege and primacy of the Apostolic See, the people became thoroughly well disposed.... Then, indeed, I clearly understood how helpful it is in ecclesiastical affairs to be aware of the prerogatives of the Roman Church."[111] Those prerogatives are twofold: "The privilege of the Roman Church should possess such power to preserve the law

108. Dressler, *Petrus Damiani,* 130; Leclercq, *S. Pierre,* 81; and Woody, *Damiani,* 189–90, place the legation sometime in 1059–60. See B, 2:230 n. 10. If later than 1059, this would affect the dating of Letter 65.

109. Andreas Strumensi, *Vita sancti Arialdi,* ed. Friedrich Baethgen (Leipzig: Hiersemann, 1934), MGH SS, 30,2,3, 1051–52 [1047–75]. See also Landulph, *Historia Mediolanensis,* ed. Ludwig Bethmann and Wilhelm Wattenbach, MGH SS, 8:32–100 (Hanover: Hahn, 1848); and Bonizo, *Liber ad amicum.* Andreas, *Vita,* 1051, tells us Ariald's father saw Ariald's light casting out the darkness of his mother's womb.

110. Letter 65.2, in L, 3:25, B, 2:229.

111. Letter 65.8, in L, 3:29; B, 2:236. Gyug, "The Milanese Church," challenges the idea that the conflict was "a critical moment in the transition from local to central."

of canonical equity and justice, and have at its disposal such vigor to exercise discipline in the ecclesiastical domain."[112] While the immediate issues were simony and clerical incontinence, dealing with these was complicated by Milan's resistance to Roman interference. It reasserted its traditional claim "that the Church of St. Ambrose should not be subjected to Roman laws and that the Roman pontiff had no right to judge or act in matters pertaining to that see." Consequently, "three days after I had announced the purpose that had brought me there, a rebellious cry sponsored by the clerical faction arose.... The shouting of the rioters grew ... and the whole city was aroused." Damian thought his death was imminent as he watched the crowd "thirsting for my blood."[113] Even in such dire straits his compassion surfaces, accepting the shouts "by the furious crowd, which, of course, one could well understand, given the circumstances."[114] After the mob finally quieted he preached a message of moderation and logic. He reminds them that Christ, the Word Incarnate, not the Roman or Ambrosian churches, is the source of authority through whom "all things were structured, who founded the Roman church. Clearly, it enjoys his privilege and is supported by his authority."[115] The first leaders of the Roman church, Peter and Paul, "won the Church of Milan through their disciples."[116] Then Damian demands that the crowd think logically: "Therefore, since the agents of your salvation came from the disciples of the Roman Church, it follows in the order of equity that the Roman Church is the mother and the Ambrosian Church is the daughter." He cites historical evidence of this ancient relationship and then concludes, as he had so many times before, with a mandate to utilize intellectual abilities to verify beliefs: "Therefore, search your written records, use whom you will to investigate the matter, and if you are unable to find what I say in your own sources, you may charge me with lying; but if you are successful, do not oppose the truth."[117]

112. Letter 65.2, in L, 3:24; B, 2:228.
113. Letter 65.3, in L, 3:26; B, 2:231.
114. Letter 65.4, in L, 3:26; B, 2:232.
115. Letter 65.5, in L, 3:27; B, 2:233.
116. Letter 65.6, in L, 3:28; B, 2:234.
117. Letter 65.7, in L, 3:28–29; B, 2:235–38.

At this point Damian's moderate approach is truly tested. After his sermon Damian discovered that "hardly anyone in the whole assembly was found to have been promoted to orders without payment." He was stricken with anxiety; how was he to react? "To exempt a few would have caused a dispute, ... to impose varying sentences" was contrary to justice.[118] Fortunately, Damian remembered Innocent I's comment that "where many have sinned, the crime cannot be punished." He thought about "the discretion used by holy pontiffs and the original authors of canons" when dealing with the ordinations of heretics and of the opinions of Fulbert of Chartres, Gregory I, and the apostles.[119] He recalled Leo IX's decree on reconciling heretics, in which he urges heretics to remember the role the Incarnation plays in reconciliation: "If the true high priest does not atone for us, using the nature proper to us, and the true blood of the spotless lamb does not cleanse us, then the true priesthood and true sacrifices do not exist in any other way in the Church of God, which is the Body of Christ."[120] Damian, thus "finding myself in a difficult position because I was unable to correct the malpractice of the Church on the mere authority of the canons," decided to reconcile the offenders on lenient terms. Determined to "make promotion to orders free in the future," Damian required of the guilty "a solemn irrevocable promise of free ordination for now and hereafter, first in written documents, then by giving their hand, and lastly by swearing an oath."[121] After the clergy so obliged, the laity, who were reportedly "more than a thousand," followed suit.[122] The last step was imposition of penance, and here Damian's compassion, thirst for equity, and moderation shines forth. For "those who simply paid fees ... in such a manner that many of them were hardly aware that it was sin," penance was light. "For those who paid more," the penance was greater, and so on.[123] "After all had been reconciled in this fashion," Damian declared in a striking reminder of his high esteem

118. Letter 65.9, in L, 3:29; B, 2:236.
119. Letter 65.10, in L, 3:30, B, 2:237.
120. Letter 65.11, in L, 3:31, B, 2:237.
121. Letter 65.12, in L, 3:33, B, 2:339–40.
122. Letter 65.22, in L, 3:37; B, 2:244.
123. Letter 65.24, in L, 3:38; B, 2:245.

for intellectual activity, "only those who were well educated [*litteris eruditi*]," chaste, and "serious in their behavior [*morum gravitate*]" could return to office.[124] As confident as Damian was in his dealing with the Milanese community, he is well aware that Rome may not accept his solution. "Whether I have erred in reconciling these men, I do not know," he admits. "But one thing I hope for," he concludes, is that "these two heresies have in this diocese been so impaired by prudent coercion, that with the help of God they will not in our time recover to fight again."[125]

Damian writes directly to Nicholas in the early months of his reign about another aspect of church life needing reform, the way scandals are handled. It is hard to ignore the perennial relevance of his message. "The genuine custom of the Roman Church seems to be observed in this way, that regarding other practices of ecclesiastical discipline, a proper investigation is held," Damian observes, "but a prudent silence is maintained concerning clerical sexuality for fear of insults from laymen [*de clericorum vero libidine propter insultationem saecularium dispensatione conticescat*]."[126] The situation "badly needs correction, so that precisely what all the people are complaining about should not be hushed up in council by leaders of the Church. . . . I do not see how something that is everywhere publicly discussed can be suppressed at the synod."[127] What Damian is focused on is the Church's accountability before the people. When leaders' behavior bears false witness in such a public way it is scandalous, and the Church must discipline the offenders.

As usual, Damian insists that discipline be applied with equity, not as it was currently done. "We indeed punish acts of impurity performed by priests in the lower ranks, but with bishops, we pay reverence with silent tolerance, which is totally absurd."[128] The situ-

124. Letter 65.25, in L, 3:38, B, 2:246.

125. Letter 65.26, in L, 3:39; B, 2:247. Unfortunately, Damian is wrong. Riots recurred in the city in 1066. Damian writes to the leaders of the Patarines around this time (Letter 129) to encourage the group to persevere in their reform work. See Andreas, *Vita,* 1051.

126. Letter 61.3, in L, 3:4; B, 2:207–8.

127. Letter 61.3, in L, 3:4; B, 2:208.

128. Letter 61.4, in L, 3:4; B, 2:208.

ation is upside down, for the more public the figure, the greater potential for good or bad his witness has. Leaders are highly visible in the community, so their witness is more visible. When a leader bears witness to wickedness "you cut yourself off from the members of Christ," and "invite others to do [wickedness] by your example."[129] Yahweh's reaction to the sexual conduct of Phinehas and the Israelites (Nm 25) is told "to teach us that the carnal sins of highly placed persons should be prosecuted with greater vigor" and verifies Damian's claims. It is why Yahweh was "silent regarding commoners, but vented his fury in condign punishment only on their leaders," why "eminent people must be more harshly punished."[130] When Damian asks Nicholas, "Is there anything worse that one can do than to exonerate lustful bishops when one is in a position to reform them?" we know how seriously Damian takes the work of reform.[131] He begs Nicholas not to be deceived by "improper compassion" but instead "discipline his subjects" vigorously.[132] By so doing he will win "grace, not only for himself, but also for the people," because everything a leader does affects those being led.[133] This is how Damian views the nature of leadership. It is another example of Damian's grasp of the relationship between the individual and the community, of the power actions have to communicate, and of the responsibilities leaders have to bear proper witness.

Damian's letter to cardinal-bishop Boniface of Albano (ca. 1059–60) also focuses again on episcopal leadership and reform. He complains that bishops "seize tyrannical power over the citizens of a town [but] they scorn the idea, I might say, of being fellow citizens."[134] Most times the bishops are not even members of the community they serve. A military commander "is chosen from the ranks" and stewards from serfs, "so then, why is it that only the Church of God is handed over to some outsider, some unknown man … while

129. Letter 61.11, in L, 3:9; B, 2:214; Letter 61.13, in L, 3:12; B, 2:216.

130. Letter 61.4–5, in L, 3:5–6; B, 2:209.

131. Letter 61.10, in L, 3:9; B, 2:214.

132. Letter 61.15, in L, 3:13; B, 2:218.

133. Letter 61.5, in L, 3:6; B, 2:209–10.

134. Letter 69.2, in L, 3:88; B, 2:299.

its own members are turned down?"[135] This practice opens the door to abuse, "as they do not enter by the door of the church, but rather through the secular postern gate" and become "thieves and robbers," not true bishops.[136] Damian's concern is, consistently, for the community and leaders' responsibility to serve the community. When a man "accepts investiture from the hands of a donor," "attracts such people with gifts," or "sells the election itself," he harms the community as well as himself.[137] In his closing Damian tells Boniface that if he wants to know more about Damian's reform ideas for the hierarchy, "you should take the trouble to look at the letter on the same theme I previously sent to your fellow cardinals."[138]

Damian was drawn back to papal reform in October 1061 when his fellow legate in Milan, Anselm of Lucca, was elected Pope Alexander II at Nicholas II's death. Discord erupted almost immediately. An embassy sent by Count Gerard of Galera and the abbot of S. Gregorio Magno traveled to Emperor Henry IV's court, and on October 28 their candidate Cadalus was elected as Honorius II. Undoubtedly their intention was to void the Election Decree. The battle lines were drawn. A court convened in October 1062 at Augsburg (for which Damian prepared his *Disceptatio synodalis*) left the matter unresolved. Battles with swords and words continued until Damian persuaded Anno of Cologne "to make every effort that a general council be held" in 1064 to end the schism with the recognition of Alexander II as true pope.[139]

Damian brought the full force of his literary skills to bear on Cadalus during the schism, consistently promoting the same moderate principles with a skilled caustic pen.[140] The situation is serious,

135. Letter 69.3, in L, 3:89; B, 2:299. Damian adds: "From where he might come, if a person is chosen by those over whom he is to preside, he is not considered an outsider."

136. Letter 69.2, ibid.

137. Letter 69.14 and 15; in L, 3:94; B, 2:303.

138. Letter 69.28, in L, 3:101; B, 2:309. He is referring to Letter 48.

139. Letter 99.6, in L, 5:105; B, 3:100. See Letters 87, 88, 89, 96, and 107; and Jasper Detler, "Das Papstwahldekret von 1059," *Beiträge zur Geschichte und Quellenkunde des MA* 12 (1986), 98–119; Cowdrey, *Pope Gregory*, 49–53; and Bonizo of Sutri, *Liber ad amicus*, 6 (594–96).

140. He reserves some of his most virulent epitaphs for him. See, for example, Letter 120.13, in L, 5:393–94; B, 3:390.

and he sees "danger everywhere threatening the state of the Church, the *sacerdotium* and the *imperium* recoil from one another."[141] His solution is predictable: proper witness. "How indecently confusing [*inhonesta confusio*] it would be for the Church brazenly to do the very thing against which it inveighs," Damian argues.[142] He repeats this maxim throughout. It is absurd (*absurdum*) that priests "should attempt to carry out the very thing they forbid their people to do, and to assert in deed what they attack in word."[143] Only a fool maintains "that the heads of churches must preach such things, but not observe them."[144] We learn this from Christ's "earthly life, no less than his preaching," for his witness in "his proposal for the direction in which our life should progress." Damian pleads in particular for religious leaders on both sides of the schism to imitate Christ's witness "which taught us in this way to bear quietly this rabid world, rather than take up arms." Damian then emphasizes that the kind of witness one is obligated to bear varies according to one's role in the Body of Christ. Thus, "within the *imperium* and the *sacerdotium* we must distinguish functions that are proper to each, so that the king may employ secular arms, while the bishop should buckle on the sword of the spirit, which is the Word of God."[145] When he writes to anti-pope Cadalus (Letter 89) after the massacre of papal forces, Damian's righteous anger is unleashed. "I recently wrote to you [Letter 88], enjoining you and earnestly admonishing you to refrain from such a bloody undertaking," Damian accuses. "But belching hellish flames like Vesuvius," Cadalus attacked, and "you and your army subjected this helpless and inexperienced people to such a slaughter that no one knows the number."[146] It is important to note the distinction Damian is making. While at one level he bemoans the loss

141. Letter 87.6, in L, 3:302; B, 2:508–9. 142. Letter 87.10, in L, 3:305; B, 2:511.

143. Letter 87.7, in L, 3:303; B, 2:509. 144. Letter 87.8, in L, 3:303, B, 2:510.

145. Letter 87.9, in L, 3:304–5; B, 2: 510–11. He criticizes Leo IX who "often became involved in acts of war," condemns ecclesiastical cases adjudicated by trial by battle, and asks whether any saints "had recourse to war?" Letter 87.13, in L, 3:308; B, 2:514–15.

146. Letter 89.3, in L, 3:327; B, 2:533; Letter 89.18, in L, 3:333; B, 2:538. In Letter 100.3, in L, 5:108; B, 3:102, Damian tells us that he "had to be on guard against the massed ambushes inspired by the fury of Cadalus" while crossing the Alps.

of life per se, at another level, he is disturbed because bishops were grasping "not sacerdotal, but royal and even tyrannical authority over the human race [*humanum genus*]."[147] This is a sin against the community. "After cutting off the members of the Church which is indeed [Christ's] body," Cadalus "with the aid of wild armed men" dared "to profane this sacrament of unity."[148] Writing to Henry IV (ca. 1065) Damian reminds him that he "function[s] as the defender of the Church [*qui aecclesiasticae defensionis officio fungeris*]." As such, Henry must end the chaos Cadalus is still causing and "help the Church in which the body of Christ is offered for the salvation of the world."[149] He accuses Henry of "supporting and flattering both sides" of the papal conflict so the empire will benefit. Damian finds this shortsighted and "shocking to believe," for "whoever attempts to divide the holy Church should fear, as the Gospel has it, lest he too be divided."[150] Even if Henry is "not openly promoting schism in the Roman Church, by approval or negligence," he is courting diaster.[151] When "the garment of Christ is torn ... the rending of this garment threatens division for the power of the king." Damian summarizes his thoughts.[152]

> And as both dignities, namely, the royal and the sacerdotal, are primarily joined to one another in Christ by the reality of a unique mystery, so are they united in the Christian people by a kind of mutual agreement. Each, in truth, needs the other for what he there finds useful [*utilitatis est indiga*], since the *sacerdotium* is protected by the defensive capability of the empire, and royal power is supported by the holiness of the priestly office. The king wears a sword, that so armed he may confront the enemies of the Church; the priest engages in watchful prayer, that he may appease God for the benefit of the king and his people. The former, using the scales of justice, is required to compose earthly affairs; the latter must provide for the thirsty a stream of heavenly eloquence.

147. Letter 89.17, in L, 3:332; B, 2:532.

148. Letter 89.9, in L, 3:329; B, 2:535.

149. Letter 120.3, in L, 5:388; B, 3:385–86.

150. Letter 120.5, in L, 5:389; B, 3:386.

151. Letter 120.7, in L, 5:390; B, 3:387. In Sermon 72.80–82, S, 423, Damian draws attention to the damage secular leaders can do to reform efforts (*elati quilibet atque sublimes a suae celesitudinis superbia corruunt, et omnia contradictionis atque infidelitatis obstacula destruuntur*).

152. Letter 120.8, in L, 5:390–91; B, 3:387–88.

> The former is established that he might compel evildoers and criminals by using the severity of legal sanctions; the latter is ordained to apply the keys of the Church that he has received, in binding some with the zeal of canonical vigor, while loosing others with the tenderness of ecclesiastical devotion.[153]

In early 1066 Damian writes to Alexander II and to two of Duke Godfrey's chaplains concerning remarks the clerics made in Damian's presence, that "one is not guilty of simoniacal heresy if he acquires a bishopric by purchase from a king or other earthly prince, so long as he was consecrated without payment."[154] Using arguments drawn from biology, the vita apostolica, Scripture, and logic, Damian reminds Henry that both *sacerdotium* and *imperium* are at fault when proper consecration procedures are ignored. Damian is, however, lenient in his judgment of the sinners, "because I must show compassion for my offending brother."[155] Simony and lay investiture are "to be avoided not only by bishops, but also by secular princes," Damian argues, but not all who obtain a church through payment or "in the same way hand over the churches" are guilty of heresy.[156] It is when individuals justify their actions "by certain subtle sophistries and argument" and with "stubbornness and inflexibility ... preach what is false" that they are rightly called heretics. Those "who express this idea ingenuously [*simpliciter*] and support it as their own opinion, should rightly be called foolish or stupid [*stulti vel ebetes*]."[157] The simonist must delude himself into believing that he "received

153. Letter 120.11, in L, 5:392–93; B, 3:389. Damian also has some definite ideas about how and when the *sacerdotium* should imitate the *saeculum*. See letter 97.22, in L, 5:82–83; B, 3:80: "Just as formerly that earthly senate [Rome] conducted all its discussions and directed and carefully exercised its common effort to subdue the whole non-Roman world to its authority, so now the custodians of the Apostolic See who are the spiritual senators of the universal church must earnestly engage in the exclusive effort to win the human race for the dominion of Christ." Attention should also be given to Damian's emphasis on utility. This emphasis is continued into the thirteenth century by new religious orders: Cistercians, canons regular, beguines, and Dominicans. See my *Theology of Work*, 109–13, 158, and 180–87.

154. Letter 140.3, in L, 6:104; B, 3:479. Letter 141 is written at the same time and addressed to the chaplains, and repeats the same argument.

155. Letter 141.6, in L, 6:115; B, 3:491.

156. Letter 140.15, in L, 6:110; B, 3:486.

157. Letter 140.16, in L, 6:110; B, 3:486.

from the prince only the earthly benefits of the Church, claim that you are some sort of steward," but stewardship of church property is a "function in the episcopal office."[158] Only "he who is consecrated" as bishop is the rightful steward, for as the infant Church bore witness, "property of the Church should be used for the needy and for dispensing other works of charity."[159] Proponents of lay investiture may argue that this property is "owned by some quasi-hereditary right," but this too is false. Churches must "be administered with spiritual moderation," not "by paying a subsidy for it," Damian insists.[160] "What a great scandal is caused" when simony and lay investiture flourish.[161] Here Damian's ecclesiology and social theology intersect, for the word scandal is a synonym for bad witness.

Damian believes that heresy is often the result of poor education. He argues that erroneous positions regarding the role of *sacerdotium* and *imperium* in investiture are similar to misunderstandings about the Incarnation. Some "people of sincere faith and faulty instruction in Catholic belief ... maintained that the mediator between God and men possessed two persons. But those who were endowed with such mental acumen that they could penetrate the mystery of the incarnate Word, have truly affirmed that both natures were united." This unity is the essence of the paradox of the Incarnation. "Not even in death could the divinity of Christ be dissociated from his body."[162] Yet, Damian accuses the chaplains, "you have no fear of dividing the Church, which is his body." The soldiers at the crucifixion "were afraid to rend the garment of the Lord, but you have no fear of tearing the Church to pieces."[163]

Concern for education, the role of the intellect in faith matters, compassion, individual culpability, stewardship, witness, the Body

158. Letter 140.7, in L, 6:106; B, 3:482.

159. Letter 140.9, in L, 6:107; B, 3:483. This repeats his argument from Letter 74.2, in L, 3:152; B, 2:370: "From [the first Christians' property] the Church was able to support not only clerics ... but could also give relief to various needy folk."

160. Letter 141.25, 18, in L, 6:126, 121; B, 3:502, 497.

161. Letter 141.18, in L, 6:121; B, 3:498.

162. Letter 141.19, in L, 6:122; B, 3:498.

163. Letter 141.20, in L, 6:123; B, 3:498.

of Christ, community interests: these concerns still inform Damian's reform ideology throughout the 1060s. In Letter 164 to Alexander II (1069) Peter is tired, frustrated at the lack of success in reform, and yearning for retirement from ecclesiastical politics. "I left the synod over which your holiness presided, then so worn out and drained, with my spirit so burdened with agenda [*ut mens mea tot oppessa negociis*]," Damian confesses and makes a hasty pledge: "Wherefore, I have made up my mind that as long as I live I shall absent myself entirely from Roman synods, unless unavoidable necessity compels me to go."[164] The pledge rings false, nevertheless, for Damian knows himself well enough to realize that he will not walk away from responsibilities as a reformer.

In Letter 167, written to Alexander around the same time we see more of the same. Damian feels vulnerable, sensitive, and underappreciated. He has been an unrelenting reformer and defender of Alexander "for whom I stood up bravely and fought against the whole world," pleading the pope's cause in councils, legatine missions, and clerical and lay assemblies.[165] Yet Alexander has not given Damian the real assistance he needs in the reform of his Gubbio diocese. He wonders if he was used by Alexander for his rhetorical skills: "Is this, in fact, why honors came my way, because I violently inveighed against your enemies, overwhelmed them with my biting words, both in my speeches and in my writings, praised you in the many tracts I wrote?"[166] If Alexander does not aid him in the real work of reform, then Damian will "be compelled to make public what I have until now suppressed in silence." If, however, Alexander does promote reform, Damian gladly "will put a curb on my freedom, place a finger on my lips."[167] It is ironic that Damian attempts to coerce Alexander into promoting his reform through fear of exposure when one of Damian's reform platforms attacks such behavior:

164. Letter 164.2, in L, 7:162–63; B, 4:166–67.

165. Letter 167.2, in L, 7:233; B, 4:235–36. In 1072 he was still active in papal business; he died on the way home from a legatine mission.

166. Letter 167.2, in L, 7:233–34; B, 4:236.

167. Letter 167.3, in L, 7:234; B, 4:236.

"[There are] two practices frequently employed by the apostolic See that need thorough correction ... first, that an anathema is attached to almost all decretal letters, and secondly, that no member of any diocese, whether cleric or layman, is permitted to expose the failings of his bishop."[168]

The passion for equity in disciplinary matters that we saw in *Gomorrhianus* finds its echo here in his attack on unwarranted anathemas: "Although according to the norms of justice, a greater delict is punished in one way, and a lesser in another, here the same indistinguishable penalty, namely, excommunication, is assigned to all." There is no proportionality between sin and punishment. "Whether they have sinned gravely or venially," they are all "deprived of God."[169] It goes against the canons, Gregory I, the stoics, and common decency when "from another man a human being receives the kind of punishment that almighty God himself does not expect."[170] Damian asks that "this customary formula [of anathema] be removed in the future from decretal letters." Damian then suggests that "in its place either an amount of pecuniary fine or some other penalty should be assigned." Damian's concern is for individuals, because these unjust anathemas could "result in disaster for their souls."[171]

His dedication to free speech and public participation in church government centuries before democratic society come to champion them is most noteworthy. He calls the prohibition against "any member of any diocese" openly criticizing a bishop "totally awry [*nimis absonum*]." His outrage is evident, and we hear underneath the condemnations Damian's anger at the distortions done to what a good bishop should be, humble and respectful of the laity's rights: "What kind of arrogance is this, what haughty disdain, and finally, what an excess of pride to allow a bishop, right or wrong, to live as he will, and what is the extreme insolence to deny his subjects the right to be heard?"[172] When the faithful questioned Peter's visit to

168. Letter 164.3, in L, 7:163; B, 4:167.
169. Letter 164.5, in L, 7:163; B, 4:168.
170. Letter 164.6, in L, 7:163–64; B, 4:168.
171. Letter 164.7, in L, 7:164; B, 4:168.
172. Letter 164.8, in L, 7:164–65; B, 4:168–69.

Cornelius (Acts 10:17–23), Peter "did not use his authority to rebuff the questions of his subjects, but humbly replied by citing his reasons." When his disciples criticized Peter, "he might have replied that the sheep committed to his care should not dare to accuse their shepherd." He might have "curb[ed] them by using the preeminence of his privileged position." He did neither. Instead, Peter "appeased them by his humble reply."[173] Peter is the bishop's model. "When a bishop is challenged about his actions, he should learn to give an account in all humility, not haughtily playing on the eminence of his high office, nor thinking he has been wronged when he is corrected by one of his subjects, but should consider him rather as a counselor or as a doctor who will attend to his wound."[174] The respect given to the laity must not be overlooked, nor Damian's continued championing of their right to criticize.[175] His attempt to ground church leaders within the community and the community's right to hold their leaders accountable is highly significant in the development of Western political thought and has not been given adequate attention.

Damian has more to say. Scripture (Mt 18:15–17) tells us what to do when sinned against. First, approach the offender alone, then with witnesses, and finally, "if he refuses to listen to you, report the matter to the Church." Damian is perplexed: "If a case involving any of the brethren is to be brought to the attention of the Church, why not one that involves bishops?"[176] Such an exception deeply offends Damian's sense of community and justice. It allows a bishop to "hide behind the dignity of his office and not appear in court, as justice required, to reply to the sons of his diocese who insisted that they have been aggrieved."[177] This "pernicious custom" must be eliminated.

> A free approach must be provided for just complaints, and appeals to a primatial see must be allowed for those known to be oppressed by their

173. Letter 164.10, in L, 7:166; B, 4:170.

174. Letter 164.11, ibid.

175. Damian's stance here verifies Becker's opinion about the connection between awareness of the laity's rights and simony complaints. See Becker, *Medieval Italy,* 5, n. 1.

176. Letter 164.15–16, in L, 7:168, B, 4:171.

177. Letter 164.17, in L, 7:169; B, 4:172.

> bishop, lest he who in his pride refuses to consider his brothers as his equals, should boast of the uniqueness of his high prerogative.... And he who does not speak humanely, but like rolling thunder terrifies others with his booming voice, should at length recognize that he is a man, and in humility learn to speak in human words.[178]

That these views are the last ones Damian was known to express on church reform makes them all the more memorable.

178. Letter 164.18, in L, 7:169; B, 4:172.

Five

RENEWAL OF RELIGIOUS LIFE

Regular Canons

Ariald is best known for his negative assaults on clerical simony and marriage in Milan during the Patarine crisis, but history also records some positive contributions he made to Western clerical life. Two of these are significant here: his emphasis on the power of clerical witness through *imitatio Christi,* and the promotion of *vita communis.*[1] His central message was succinct: Christ is the light of the world and the priest is to shine that light to the corners of the earth by preaching to the literate and by example for the illiterate.[2] If clerics would offer proper verbal and visual witness then the laity would join a Milanese financier in saying, "Lord Ariald, not only the learned but the unlettered realize that the things you say are useful and true."[3] Ariald's perception of *vita communis* as part of the solution for clerical problems is similarly significant. Realizing that clergy often had wives or concubines to maintain a household for them, Ariald believed that communal houses for priests would diminish their

1. See Phyllis Jestice, "A New Fashion in Imitating Christ: Changing Spiritual Perspectives around the Year 1000," in *The Year 1000,* ed. Michael Frassetto, 165–85 (New York: Palgrave Macmillan, 2002), 180.

2. Andreas, *Vita,* 4, 1051–52. See also Bonizo, *Liber ad amicum,* vi.

3. Andreas, *Vita,* 4, 1051–52. Note the use of utility as a criterion. See Letter 40.37, in L, 2:147–48; B, 1:430–31.

need for women partners.[4] In March 1051 Pope Leo IX indicated his belief in the ability of *vita communis* to eliminate clerical marriage when he proposed rules concerning "the food and clothing of canons" at St. Martin of Lucca, who had "delivered your church from priests with wives."[5] Neither of these mid-century promoters of the canonical life were pioneers, though; that distinction belongs to Romuald. Sometime after he founded Val di Castro, around fall 1005, Romuald realized the connection between an absence of communal living and the presence of clerical problems. If reformers wanted to solve the latter, then they should mitigate poverty and loneliness by promoting the former. To that end "Romuald had [some priests] live in community as canons; no more were they to dwell alone or with wives and children, but they were to submit to a superior and live together as brothers."[6]

Once again we find Peter walking in the footsteps of Romuald. Damian admiringly records this episode in Romuald's vita around 1042, and within a decade Damian's support of canonical life is known enough for the canons of Fano to seek his guidance during an internal crisis. Letter 39, *De communi vita canonicorum,* written about 1051, is the earliest medieval treatment of the revival of canonical life; it predates Hildebrand's reform proposals.[7] At the synod of 1059 Hildebrand proposed that the assembly review the recognized rule for Roman clergy, Louis the Pious's *Institutio canonicorum* (816/817).[8] Hildebrand succeeded in bringing the issue of canonical life to the forefront and is often given full credit for the spread of the canonical life. Much of the credit, however, belongs to Damian, because Hildebrand was merely "taking up the theme of some of Peter Damian's most powerful treatises."[9] Four years after the synod's

4. Andreas, *Vita,* 11–12, 1056–57; and Bonizo, vi, 595.

5. PL 143, 671.

6. VR 35 (230). Damian adds: "In the same zone Saint Romuald also built a monastery for young women." Becker, *Medieval Italy,* 106, implies that Romuald's preaching led to the establishment of canonical life in Lucca in 1025, but he offers no documentation.

7. See canon 120–22, in Mansi, 14, 231–32.

8. See my *Theology of Work,* 99–119, for the early history of canons.

9. Cowdrey, *Pope Gregory,* 46.

debate Damian wrote another treatise, Letter 98, *Contra clericos regulares proprietarios,* addressed to Pope Alexander II, to request legislation promoting canonical life. The two treatises together summarize the gist of Damian's envisioned reform for the canons. Like so much else that emanates from Damian's pen, his reform platform has value well beyond the intended target.

Damian's theology, particularly his ideas on witness, was highly influential in the development of canonical spirituality. Most historians consider him the "veritable founder" of the canons.[10] What he bequeaths to them is a profound awareness of their obligation to bear witness to society. Although historians have not explicitly acknowledged this essential element in canonical spirituality, they do endorse Caroline Walker Bynum's argument that canons' behavior is driven by "a new understanding of their obligation toward their neighbor ... their sense of responsibility for the edification of their fellow men."[11] This is witness. When Bynum states that the canon assumes that he is responsible "in whatever he says or does not only for the state of his own soul but also for the progress of his neighbor," she is summarizing Damian's message both in general and in these two letters.[12]

During the Carolingian era, canons—clergy serving collegiate churches—had been legislatively encouraged to live a modified common life, intended more perhaps to separate them from the larger secular community than to forge a spiritual community. By the tenth century even that modest goal had been abandoned. By the mid-eleventh century a movement to find a solution to the lax standards of many canons gained momentum. When Damian wrote to the canons at Fano, the reform of canonical houses was proceeding slowly and sporadically, "impelled by individual initiative."[13]

10. Fliche, *La réforme grégorienne,* 1:337. J. C. Dickinson, *The Origins of the Austin Canons and Their Introduction into England* (London: SPCK, 1950), 27, says the two were the canons' chief sponsors.

11. Bynum, "Spirituality of Regular Canons," 16 and 19–20.

12. Ibid., 9

13. Pierre Mandonnet, *St. Dominic and His Work,* tr. Marie Larkin (St. Louis: Herder, 1944), 242.

Damian was known as such a reformer. He agreed to address their problem, "namely, that some of you undertook to live by the rule in a house of canons, but that most of you did not agree to this, wishing only to reside individually in their own lodgings." Apparently, by mid-century the issue was raised frequently among canons, for Damian adds, "I am not surprised, because this is hardly rare."[14]

He begins his lecture. Some clerics mistakenly believe that they can engage in "carnal living . . . so long as they do not also retire from the Church's prayers and the administration of sacraments," but this is false.[15] The canon must live—bear witness to—what he is, just as a monk must, "in keeping with his name," live as a solitary. Thus a canon living on cathedral property cannot "share in the Church's common property, but reject the idea of living in community near their church." Damian turns to Acts 4:32–35, a passage he repeatedly refers to in his discourses on canonical life, to prove that canons' rejection of *vita communis* is wrong: "Certainly, this is not the pattern of the early church, and it deviates greatly from the disciples of apostolic origin by which all were united in heart and soul, sold their land and laid the money at the feet of the apostles, and distributed it to each according to his need. Not a man of them claimed any of his possessions as his own, but everything was held in common."[16] This brings him to the heart of the treatise, his argument concerning the value of the community to the individual. Community provides a "school of Christ" for each individual, where Christ "might be with you now and until the end of time."[17] Damian uses the metaphor again in an argument that includes a statement on the purpose of canonical life: to bear witness.

> If you stand before the people of God as possessing the words of life, a people for whom you were appointed to give good example and among whom you should shine as lights in this world; if you should wish, I repeat, to gather a harvest of souls among them and call back the errant to the right path of religious practice, you should first straighten what

14. Letter 39.2, in L, 2:98; B, 1:374.
15. Letter 39.4, in L, 2:100; B, 1:375.
16. Letter 39.6, in L, 2:102; B, 1:377.
17. Letter 39.14, in L, 2:110; B, 1:384.

is awry in your own lives, if that be necessary, and gathering in the school of Christ, you should remain together in a common way of life and in unanimity of spirit.[18]

A canon fulfills his function as example best within the protection of a community. This is not an attack on individualism but merely a reminder of the strength in numbers when pursuing a goal: "He who deserts the sheepfold of fraternal community willingly subjects himself to the teeth of the cruel beast."[19] Ultimately, the community's value is the sum of each individual's value, so Damian continues to remind the canons of their individual responsibility to bear proper witness: "Therefore, he who is to instruct others in the way of holiness must be careful lest, which God forbid, he appear to take the false path in anything."[20] Admittedly, it is always difficult to balance the two. The genius of Peter rests in his ability to see this juggling act as the crux of the canons' problem and to offer practical advice. Damian's bottom line is predictable: one attains personal salvation by saving others.

This is the reason why avarice is one of Damian's main targets. It puts the needs of self above the needs of others. Avarice deprives others of common goods, Damian argues. "Ananias and Sapphira were struck down bodily by the sentence of death not because they divided up common property, but because by retaining something that was theirs they did not share it with others." Damian spends a lot of time discouraging property ownership for the same reason he abhors avarice, because both threaten the well-being of the community. "Charity produces community, while avarice leads to disunity [*charitas quippe communionem facit, avaricia divisionem*]." Similarly, "when property is divided" into private ownership "there is certainly no unity in spirit."[21] The apostles manifested this rule when they took no purse, pack, bread, or money on their mission. They followed the instructions of Christ, who warned them "that they who were to teach others should themselves live blameless-

18. Letter 39.13, in L, 2:109; B, 1:383.

19. Letter 39.8, in L, 2:104; B, 1:378.

20. Letter 39.11, in L, 2:108; B, 1:382.

21. Letter 39.6, in L, 2:102; B, 1:377.

ly."[22] He also taught them to live by "a most necessary principle, that they should despise and avoid the filth of avarice, and not possess personal property." The apostles bore witness to the dangers of avarice for the benefit of others. Their witness is particularly relevant in times of change.

> Why was this done? Was it only for their benefit? But, come now, if it was done just for them, why was it recorded in writing unless it was also for us? "For whatever was written, was written for our own instruction." So why do we read these words in our churches, if it is not that the things we read we should also carry out in deeds? It was necessary especially for those who, throughout the changing times of succeeding centuries, should take their place in office to live in accord with their example.[23]

In Letter 98 Damian focuses more heavily on the vita apostolica. First, he establishes its authority as model: "Since we have the holy apostles and other apostolic men as our teachers, we must not follow our own opinion ... but place irrevocable faith only in those teachings that have been settled by approved doctors of the Church."[24] He allows "Augustine [to] come forward as a witness" and quotes lengthy passages from his *On the Clerical Life:* "I say 'he falls,' if he abandons his membership in the common life he has assumed, a state which is praised in the Acts of the Apostles."[25] Augustine is adamant on the issue. The primitive community donated all possessions to the poor or made it common property, so "whoever is discovered owning personal property ... where I am bishop, he cannot be a cleric."[26] Augustine's dictum, "that a cleric who possesses money cannot belong to Christ," is qualified by Damian: "I say this not of all clerics, but particularly of those who are enrolled under the title of canon and live together in common."[27] He turns next to Jerome, then to Prosper and to the *Instituto canonicorum* of 816/817. "Now, since the Holy Fathers do not disagree," Damian proceeds, "let us go to the source from which they drew their opinions.... It is, therefore, an

22. Letter 39.9, in L, 2:106; B, 1:377.
23. Ibid.
24. Letter 98. 3, in L, 5:88; B, 3:85.
25. Letter 98.5, in L, 5:89–90; B, 3:86.
26. Letter 98.6, in L, 5:90; B, 3:87.
27. Letter 98.7, ibid.

obvious fact that the Rule of the canons originated from the norms of apostolic life [*quod canonicorum regula ab apostolicae vitae norma prodierit*]."[28]

Next, he offers the first of two line-by-line exegeses of the classic description of the vita apostolica, Acts 4:32–35. His concern in the first commentary is for communal harmony: "If everything is held collectively, various personalities come together in one accord, because there is nothing over which they are found to quarrel. Therefore, if a cleric attempts to have his own income, he is not following in the footsteps of the apostles."[29] He cites Mark's description of the seventy disciples and talks about the problems that arise when clerics are possessed "by overriding avarice."[30] Disdain for episcopal authority, lack of self-discipline, worldliness, and disgust for liturgy follow, resulting in the ruin of "the assembly of clerics."[31] More importantly, witness is marred.

> If he is prudent in his speech, but does not bring his actions into accord with what he says, he can rightly be called a cripple on the road of the spirit.... But if his studied words are not accompanied by good works, he seems to be moving the well-shaped legs of his words without making progress.... Acceptable preaching does not acquit those whose words are proper, but whose lives do not conform; rather their guilty conscience violently reproaches them. Hence fittingly is the point made again.... In the mouth of a stupid man [Prv 26:9] a proverb is like a thorn, because as they say one thing and do another, their mind seems to harbor a contradiction.[32]

Damian's second commentary on Acts 4:32–35 reinforces his interpretation here. This time his focus is on verse 33, which he now sees as the key to the vita apostolica and, consequently, central to his social theology.

> In addition to what I said above, there is also the example given us by the apostles. For after Scripture first stated, "The whole body of believ-

28. Letter 98.17, in L, 5:95; B, 3:91.
29. Letter 98.18, in L, 5:95; B, 3:91–92.
30. Letter 98.21, in L, 5:98; B, 3:93.
31. Letter 98.22–25, in L, 5:98–100; B, 3:93–95.
32. Letter 98.26, in L, 5:100–101; B, 3:95–96.

ers was united in heart and soul," and at once continued, "not one of them claimed any of his possessions as his own, but everything was held in common," it immediately said, "The apostles bore witness with great power [*et virtute magna reddebant apostoli testimonium*] to the resurrection of our Lord Jesus Christ, and great was the grace in all of them"; and then added, "for they had never a needy person among them."

But what does the author of this sacred history mean to say when, in speaking of the attitude of the apostles and of the common life, he suddenly interrupted his discourse, and altering his style, as it were, proceeded to tell how constant they were in their preaching, "And the apostles bore witness with great power to the resurrection"? Why did he insert something else into the narrative which, once begun, he should have continued and brought to conclusion, except that he obviously wished to show that only those are fit to undertake the office of preaching who gain no profit from earthly goods, and while personally having nothing, own everything in common?[33]

Thus we have Damian's conception of canonical life. His advice is simple: "If any spiritual community is to maintain discipline and good order, it must somehow imitate the early days of the infant Church."[34] In the decades that follow Damian's treatises, canonical life spread and developed a distinct spirituality marked by an emphasis on witness.[35] Canons also included another favorite concept of Damian's in their spirituality: utility. When Damian advocates the vita apostolica he cites sources that emphasize how "it is necessary and indeed useful" and "of great use."[36] For Damian utility is a basic criterion for evaluating all matters. The concept is found throughout his writings from beginning to end. Creation is "for man's use"; light is given to man "that he might be at the service of others"; the Creator even "uses evil man for good purposes."[37] Damian decides

33. Letter 98.27–28, in L, 5:101; B, 3:96.

34. Letter 98.17, in L, 5:95; B, 3:91.

35. Damian lived long enough to see the success of his canonical reforms. See Letter 168.2, in L, 7:236; B, 4:238: "I call to your attention our canons . . . who seemed to be incorrigible despite my frequent attempts and great effort, but who now by God's grace have come to their senses and follow the practices of the canonical life."

36. Letter 98.13 and 14, in L, 5:93; B, 3:89 and 90.

37. Letter 5.2, in L, 1:94; B, 1:112; Letter 40.24, in L, 2:135; B, 1:417; and Letter 40.32, in L, 2:143; B, 1:425.

his vocation on the basis of what "is more useful for me"; he criticizes monks who "fail to practice useful trades"; he believes "everything harmoniously serves the utility of men: heaven, earth, and even hell," and that examining love and friendship is "both useful and upright"; and he says that the mind sorts thoughts as "either useful or unprofitable."[38] The prudent man decides whether to speak according to what "usefulness demands"; deeds made evident the "utility of fasting"; corporeal images are good because of "their usefulness for instruction"; the *regalis* and *sacerdotalis* need "the other for what he finds useful"; and fear of judgment day "is most useful" in fighting temptation.[39] This is but a minute sampling of instances where Damian employs the concept. His concern for utility must not be confused with modern utilitarianism; his is more limited, but still significant. It is consistent with his awareness of the social nature of actions. He employs the concept to remind others of the potential and ability of each word, action, and thought. This appreciation for the utility of an act is compatible with his promotion of witness. An act becomes useful to the community when it bears good witness.

These same messages are preached by regular canons. Near the turn of the twelfth century, for instance, Hildebert of Lavadin wrote to William of Champeaux after he decided to become a canon at St. Victor and abandon his intellectual activity. First he congratulates William for the witness of his life, but then he chastises him: "A man does not do all the good of which he is capable so long as he refuses to be useful." Refusal to utilize intellectual gifts renders the gifts useless. "What use, after all, is hidden wisdom?" Hildebert asks.[40] Philip of Harvengt emphasizes how witness mandates "that not only their life but their reputation is useful to [their] neighbor."[41] Adam of Dryburgh talks at length about the canon's obligation to offer "useful

38. Letter 8.4, in L, 1:102; B, 1:120; Letter 54.10, in L, 2:350; B, 2:145; Letter 108.18; in L, 5:204; B, 3:198; Letter 112.2, in L, 5:258; B, 3:259; and Letter 97.21, in L, 5:82; B, 3:80.

39. Letter 56.2, in L, 2:362; B, 2:154; Letter 137.8; in L, 6:93; B, 3:470; Letter 153.35, in L, 7:35; B, 4:32; Letter 120.11, in L, 5:392; B, 3:389; and Letter 50.81, in L, 2:331; B, 2:129.

40. PL 171, 141–43. See my *Theology of Work,* 111–13.

41. PL 203, 670.

sermons" and do "efficacious and useful" work.[42] Hugh of St. Victor sees this as the goal of witness, reformation "through the example of the good," and thus he defines the value of sanctity in utilitarian terms: "Indeed, the works of the saints which are very much in the estimation of men pertain not to dignity but to utility."[43]

Earlier canonical treatises also testify to a concern for witness. "[The canonical] order requires that they exhibit to others a pattern of holiness.... For a good life is necessary to us for our own sake," one anonymous canon writes. "Therefore we ought to live so that life agrees with name, and profession is carried out in deeds, so that if our order is holy our behavior should be holy, and just as men speak well concerning us, it is borne out by the witness of good action."[44] This is but a summary of Damian's theology. "Let them maintain gravity not only in speaking or acting, but also in walking or standing" while in their houses, so they may "draw [other canons] to better things by their examples," another canon writes, echoing both the Augustinian Rule and Damian.[45] Likewise, "let those going outside neither say or do anything at all contrary to the order or their goal ... and draw them to better things by examples of holy conduct."[46] That canons were drawn to the Augustinian Rule is natural once one considers that Damian's theology was at its foundation; they both have a theology of witness at their core. In his treatises for canons Damian included lengthy expositions of Acts 4:32–35; the Rule of St. Augustine is constructed around Acts 4:32–35. Damian is keenly aware of change; two of the Rule's most obvious characteristics are its adaptability to changing situations and its stress on the

42. PL 198, 557.

43. PL 176, 640.

44. PL 176, 897–98. See Caroline Walker Bynum, *Docere Verbo et Exemplo: An Aspect of Twelfth-Century Spirituality* (Missoula, Mont.: Scholars Press, 1979), 42, and my *Theology of Work,* 104–5.

45. [Peter of Porto?], *Regula clericorum,* PL 163, 709; Bynum, *Docere,* 38; and Ranft, *Theology of Work,* 104–5.

46. Ibid., PL 163, 717; and Bynum, *Docere,* 38. See *Regla tertia,* tr. de Bruyne, *Revue Bénédictine* 42 (1930), 320: "In walking, standing, in general deportment, in all your actions, do nothing that might be offensive in the eyes of anyone, let everything be in keeping with your holy vocation"; "to all brethren [the superior] should offer an example of good works."

impact one's life has on others.[47] While we have no evidence that Damian read the Augustinian Rule, we do know that canons read both Damian and the Rule. We know that Augustine, Damian, and canons viewed the vita apostolica as a model, realized the social implications of private lives, and acknowledged the individual's obligation to edify and educate, that is, "to be my witnesses," in Jesus' last words, "to the ends of the earth" (Acts 1:8). We know that canons played an essential role in the development of Western service sensibilities. I believe Damian helped point them in that direction.

Hermits

Historians have long observed that "it is much more than a coincidence" that the birth of regular canons and the general monastic revival occurred after and in the same region in which the eremitic movement established itself.[48] Neither is it a coincidence that the birth of organizations to implement new attitudes toward service and social responsibility arose after and in the same region as Damian's reform work. When Damian's message to hermits is examined, the connection between his social theology and these historical developments is manifested. We must also remember that Damian practiced what he preached. He did not merely cajole others into reforming religious life but did so himself. Before he even began writing about reform he had traveled extensively throughout Italy, lecturing about reform in cities, hermitages, and monasteries; after his writing mission commenced he continued to visit old monasteries and establish new ones well into his last years.[49] His life was a witness for reform. In his letters to hermits, however, he did not limit

47. Letter 119 deals with change on a philosophical level, but throughout his works Damian observes change as essential, pervasive, and good. For example, see Letter 21.9, in L, 1:201; B, 1:206: "These things happen ... so that they might be restored or transformed into something better." See my "Rule of St. Augustine," 145; Pope Gelasius II's letter, PL 163, 496; and *Regula,* in Luc Verheijen, *La régle de San Augustin,* 2 vols. (Paris: Etudes Augustinennes, 1967), 7.3 and 4.1, 5.

48. Dickinson, *Origins,* 38–39; and David Knowles, *The Monastic Order in England* (Cambridge: Cambridge University Press, 1940), 192.

49. See Letter 8; and intro., Letters, 1:67.

his remarks to the subject of witness but included two topics of special interest to them, asceticism and the virtue of moderation.

The first detailed writing on eremiticism (Letter 18) is addressed to his own community.[50] The date is uncertain (ca. 1045–50), as is his other treatise (Letter 50) to Fonte Avellana (1057–ca. 1063). Once again we see how Damian's early ideas are retained and developed in his later years. His introductory remarks in Letter 18 set the tone. The grandeur and beauty of the world form a stark contrast to the decaying state of monasticism, and Damian wants to reform this situation by bearing witness in writing "so that what one can now read in your living deeds [*ut quod in vestris nunc vivis operibus legitur*] may also be handed down in writing for the information of those who will come after us." Written witness is necessary in case "the regular observances of their home should at some time be lost through their failure to imitate it," but the living witness of hermits is, of course, superior to the written.[51] He describes at length "the way of life that now prevails at this hermitage" and then returns to his purpose in writing. "I was led to write these things with every good intention," he confesses, "that I might also provide beforehand for those who will come after you. It was done that when you read these remarks you might strive to persevere in the good work you once began, that the latter might learn from my writing what they must retain in imitating your example."[52] He charges them with the task of preserving that witness: "Inspect these few things that I have written here as a seal with which to stamp your manner of life and that of those that follow you. In your hands may its image never be defaced."[53] If they do so, they will not "sink from the strict eremitic life into the laxity of the monasteries."[54] This is how reform is achieved.

The longer and later Letter 50 expands upon these themes. Again he writes because "many monasteries have become so lax," and he wants to make sure Fonte Avellana does not follow suit.[55] He writes

50. The second part of *Dominus vobiscum* has a lengthy discussion on eremiticism.
51. Letter 18.4, in Letters, 1:161, B, 1:170.
52. Letter 18.17, in L, 1:167; B, 1:176.
53. Letter 18.19, in L, 1:168; B, 1:177.
54. Letter 18.18, ibid.
55. Letter 50.77, in L, 2:329, B, 2:127.

for the future. The request that he give instruction "in the rule of the eremitic life ... will be of great service to those who shall come after us."[56] If one follows in "Jesus' footsteps" then that witness will lead "many others [to] imitate the example of your noble fervor."[57] In his description of the hermits' routine he repeats the community's rule concerning food, clothing, worship, penance, and the like. His explanations of customs and exhortations are, however, more detailed and thus helpful in the analysis of his social theology. As always, he follows the rules of rational inquiry: "I think it is proper first to examine the source," so "before taking up the branches of my discourse, I should carefully investigate the origin of its roots and clearly explain who might have originated this institution."[58] The reader is likewise obligated by these rules, so if what Damian writes here is not enough, "if one does not refuse to investigate, he will be able to find this subject more fully explained in my other slight works."[59] Damian insists that "the disciples of truth," as he calls hermits, subject all aspects of life to introspection and rational endeavor.[60] "Amid the flood of thoughts that try to overwhelm you, consider your mind to be some sort of net that will hold proper ideas ... allowing idle notions to flow through," he advises. "Try to understand your thoughts and give close attention, not only to whatever might come to mind, but also to their source."[61]

While Damian is writing specifically about "what I see taking place in our congregation," he realizes there are many ways to serve God.[62] Indeed, Mary sat at Jesus' feet, but "Martha served the same Lord."[63] Nevertheless, Damian believes eremiticism is a "golden road" to God, because it is "so direct, so certain, so unencumbered."[64] In this he is endorsing the medieval hierarchy of vocations.[65] Da-

56. Letter 50.2, in L, 2:289; B, 2:79–80.

57. Letter 50.4, in L, 2:291; B, 2:81.

58. Letter 50.7, in L, 2:292; B, 2:82.

59. Letter 50.6, in L, 2:292; B, 2:82.

60. Letter 18.5, in L, 1:162; B, 1:171.

61. Letter 50.57, in L, 2:317; B, 2:115.

62. Letter 50.3, in L, 2:290; B, 2:80.

63. Letter 50.5, in L, 2:291; B, 2:82.

64. Letter 50.4 and 6, in L, 2:290 and 291; B, 2:81 and 82. See also Letter 18.18, in L, 1:168; B, 1:177.

65. He does not have as hierarchical a view of individuals, though, for throughout he insists "that the whole household of God be maintained with regular discipline and care,

mian sees eremiticism as superior partly because of the intense relationship binding individual and community together. In the Fonte Avellana community there is "such unanimity of will forged by the fire of mutual charity, that everyone considers himself born to serve all and not himself."[66] This unity extends even into death. If even a novice who had not completed a penance were to die, the brethren would "accept the whole penance and equally divide it among themselves." Damian's idea of community, that "when our own efforts are insufficient ... we are assisted here through the bountiful generosity of others," does not impinge on individualism.[67] The community must be aware of each individual's uniqueness. Thus the prior "must use moderation in applying strict rules."[68] He does not "appear to force the stronger ones to lessen their resolve to overachieve, or to present the weaker from applying their strength in attempting greater things." He must "carefully examine the strength of each of the brothers and should supply what is needed according to each one's ability."[69] Likewise, hermits should "gauge your strength in the balance of strict self-examination" to learn what they can and cannot observe.[70] Respect for individual needs does not damage the unity of the community, for "we read of many of our ancient Fathers who even while living together in common did not observe a common rule of life."[71]

Moderation is Damian's goal in asceticism as well as rules, and he explains why.

> I do not require any of the brothers to engage in prostrations, the use of discipline, or slapping his hand on the ground, or in praying with arms extended, or in other practices of holy fervor, but rather think that these things are not adapted to all the brothers, and so it seems more

---

and that every member work corporately at the duties proper to him, even the lay brothers." All members, lay brothers and monks, must accept "everything harsh and difficult" about the life. Letter 50.20, in L, 2:299; B, 2:92–93. Letter 152 is written in defense of the superiority of eremiticism.

66. Letter 18.15, in L, 1:166; B, 1:175.

67. Letter 18.16, in L, 1:166–67; B, 1:175–76.

68. Letter 50.76, in L, 2:329; B, 2:126.

69. Letter 50.41, in L, 2:309; B, 2:105.

70. Letter 50.31, in L, 2:305; B, 2:99.

71. Letter 50.32, in L, 2:305; B, 2:100.

> proper and more liberal that in these matters, one be given an option rather than prescribe them by definitive legislation.... I have ordained these things with such a measure of mild discretion after removing all rigor and austerity, so that a brother who is solicitous for his salvation will not dread this life-giving order, and still if he performs these tasks he may be fully confident in the mercy of Almighty God.[72]

Damian is true to his word: "In the matter of sleep ... we moderate discretion rather than harsh severity"; "it is left to [each brother's] discretion whether he chants the entire psalter, a half, or even a third, or omits it altogether"; when fasting, "whatever is allowed in summertime may also be permitted with discretion on Saturday during the winter"; he permits "wine to be drunk here if used with moderation."[73] During certain times of the year "one is permitted to live somewhat more relaxed."[74] Damian admits, "I do not take part" in extreme asceticism but aims "with some amount of discretion to moderate those milder commands" of the stronger brothers. When a former monk enters the hermitage "one should with modest disapproval criticize certain useless practices of monastic discipline" and "depreciate the monastic order by moderately taking it to task" without destroying it.[75] Compassion and common sense reinforce the need for moderation. "If it is noticed that someone of the brothers is sick we tenderly [*misericorditer*] care for him" and exempt him from fasting.[76] "Because those who were here enrolled began to grow ill, and because some wishing to enter the eremitic life seemed to be appalled at this severe practice," Damian takes "our weak stomach" into consideration and grants dispensations for wine, with the caveat that "we should at least try to be temperate in its use."[77]

The treatise includes one of Damian's clearest lectures on witness. He begins with a discussion on "how a hermit should live."[78]

72. Letter 50.48, in L, 2:312–13; B, 2:109. Also see Letters 118 and 139.

73. Letter 50.42, in L, 2:310; B, 2:106; Letter 50.45, in L, 2:311; B, 2:108; Letter 50.39, in L, 2:308; B, 2:104. See Letter 50.18, in L, 2:298; B, 2:91; and Letter 50.19, in L, 2:298; B, 2:91.

74. Letter 50.14, in L, 2:296; B, 2:87.

75. Letter 50.79, in L, 2:330; B, 2:128.

76. Letter 50.14, in L, 2:296; B, 2:88.

77. Letter 50.19, in L, 2:298–99; B, 2:91–92.

78. Letter 50.73, in L, 2:327; B, 2:124.

He warns about the dangers of false appearances, of "appear[ing] as someone always new."[79] One must look, dress, and act like a hermit if one is a hermit; if "you imitate Anthony you should not play Democritus." Hermits are obligated to "edify those who observe you." They must bear witness to the Truth at all times: "Therefore, be dignified when you walk, proper in your speech, slow to anger, and quick to forgive those who repent. In all things be an example of highest virtue, and, as one might say, always demonstrate that you are well-turned and well-rounded [*teretem atque rotundum*]."[80] His remaining task "at the end of this work [is] to add a few words" about the prior.[81] The addition is a brief but powerful discourse on the nature, utility, and necessity of life as witness.

> Since by your office you [the prior] are above others, you should also, if possible, surpass them by the way you live. It is truly a vivid and powerful sermon for your disciples, if in providing food for others the provider remains steadfast in rigorous fasting. He preaches best about nighttime prayer who, after a long period spent in chanting, gives signal to awaken the brothers. It is most eloquent to recommend silence if we ourselves curb our tongue. He who demeans himself by wearing torn clothes can profitably speak of poor garments. He who in fine attire stands out like a rich man, preaches in vain with John about camel's hair. One who avenges an injury is not very persuasive when speaking of patience. One who is eager to hoard money will hardly put out the fires of avarice in the hearts of others. He who seizes every opportunity for travel holds a sorry discussion on the rule of staying at home. But one who spends long years in his cell makes of his whole body a tongue that will praise stability, and when his mouth is silent, his mute members are eloquent because they call out in more varied ways.
>
> *Moreover, let your life always serve as a witness* [*vitae porro tuae semper habeto testem*] for it must speak of your hidden good deeds for the edification of the brothers and be able to cleanse your reputation of any devious suspicion.[82]

79. Letter 50.71, in L, 2:326; B, 2:123. Democritus is probably a magician.

80. Letter 50.72, in L, 2:326–27; B, 2:124.

81. Letter 50.73, in L, 2:327; B, 2:124.

82. Letter 50.74–75, in L, 2:327–28; B, 2:125. Translation and emphasis of the opening phrase of this passage, which is also the subtitle of this book, are mine.

This is the only time Damian uses *testor* in precisely the same way I do to designate the concept of witness. As explained in the introduction and illustrated in numerous citations throughout, Damian used other words—for instance, *exemplum, forma, exemplar, imitatio*—besides derivations of *testor* to indicate bearing witness. While his language's modernity here is significant, I do not want to overemphasize it at the cost of undermining the same sentiments expressed by other phrases and situations. In a letter written around this time to the hermits of Suavicinum, Damian uses *exemplum* to communicate the same message. As "all the saints bore with patience whatever could be done to them," so too must they. "As Scripture relates [*testatur*]," they must remember "that we are aided ... by the example of those who went before us" and imitate them: "So that God's commands do not terrify us, the example of the ancient Fathers strengthens us, so that by comparing ourselves to them, we may dare to think it possible to do what, because of our weakness, we would fear to undertake."[83] By "calling to mind the lives of our ancestors" we will "be encouraged" and "scale the heights of heaven."[84] In his vita of Dominic Loricatus (a Fonte Avellana monk whose living witness was a constant source of inspiration), Damian states these beliefs in yet another way, far-reaching in its implications: "I may also say that the remarkable life of holy men is more rewarding for those who hear it than a display of miracles. The former, in fact, prompts imitation, while the latter promote only admiration. Miracles teach how holy these men were, but their life shows how men today can be holy."[85] The passage is consistent with Damian's reason for writing Romuald's vita. Both vitae document Damian's criterion for sainthood, a criterion still adhered to today.

Damian's insistence on the centrality of witness in a hermit's life is present in his letter to the hermit Teuzo. Around 1055–57 the abbot of St. Mary in Florence "brought me in to arbitrate" and resolve the "enmity and long-standing dissension" that existed be-

83. Letter 76.6 in L, 3:161–62; B, 2:380.
84. Letter 76.7, in L, 3:162; B, 2:380–81.
85. Letter 109.28, in L, 5:221; B, 3:217–18.

tween Teuzo and his former abbot.[86] The original issue causing the rift was Teuzo's Donatist stand against simony. Teuzo judged sacraments administered by a simonist to be invalid, even going so far as to question whether "the pope himself [came] gratis to the apostolic throne." Furthermore, Damian reports, "you are said to render such a severe and haughty verdict on your brothers, that only once during a whole year did you receive the sacraments."[87] Damian is particularly upset by Teuzo's Donatist views.[88] By insisting that one know "'who ordained this priest' ... and 'who promoted [this bishop] to the episcopal office,'" Teuzo never rests and "will not let others live in peace."[89] Damian fears for the community, for "from this and similar silly indecision heresies and schisms often emerge, cutting off people who are uncertain from Catholic unity." He scolds Teuzo, urging him to remember the diversity of roles in the Church. "All do not share the highest power in handing down decisions" in the Church, that "the order of social life is then properly arranged when each one is satisfied within the bounds of his own rights. But where one oversteps the boundaries of another, then indeed every norm for right living is necessarily confused." Better that Teuzo "be occupied with [his] own problems, lest by excessive concern for the affairs of others we lose the fruit of our own work."[90]

And, according to Damian, Teuzo does have problems. When Damian arrived to mediate, their personalities clashed immediately. Damian says that Teuzo was irrational, quarrelsome, and eventually "seized me by the belt and violently put me out and slammed the door."[91] Undeterred, Damian asked forgiveness for "what I have said" and attempted mediation through letters, hoping "that this

86. Letter 44.5, in L, 2:224; B, 2:11–12.
87. Letter 44.27, in L, 2:237; B, 2:27.

88. So Jestice claims, "Peter Damian against Reformers." She also makes the puzzling comment that the controversy shows he is an opponent of ecclesiastical reform. I disagree with her description of Damian as raging; if Teuzo threw Damian out as reported, I believe the letter's tone is rather temperate, particularly when one is familiar with Damian's rhetoric. See also K. Cushing, "Of Locustae and Dangerous Men: Peter Damian, Vallombrosans, and Eleventh-Century Reform," *Church History* 74.4 (2005), 74–58.

89. Letter 44.27–28, in L, 2:237; B, 2:27.
90. Letter 44.28, in L, 2:237–38; B, 2:27.

91. Letter 44.5, in L, 2.224; B, 2:11–12.

correction of mine will not fail to bear fruit for you."[92] Teuzo's dilemma had started when he left his monastery before his training was complete. He sought no further guidance. "Even while you were still being formed in this new way of life, you went your own way, teaching before you learned," Damian reminds him. When Teuzo decided to live as a hermit in town, he revealed a flawed understanding of self and community. "The plaudits of the crowd" led Teuzo not to "judge yourself by the testimony of your own conscience, but rather according to the opinion of the flattering mob." Teuzo now lives a life of self-deception and has no community to offer correction. Secular society cannot be relied on, for it can easily misinterpret an eremitic witness in its midst; living witness has different meanings in different places. Eremitic witness does not belong in the city where its message cannot accurately be deciphered. "To be unacquainted with wine in the city would be a miracle, but to drink it in the hermitage is quite unbecoming," Damian explains. "In a hermitage a hairshirt is a garment, in town it is something to be wondered at."[93] Teuzo fails to grasp the realities of communication, and his failure to understand and render proper witness is the true focus of Damian's letter.[94]

Damian's solution is to teach Teuzo about witness: "Life is a better tool for edification when he preaches in living deeds [*visis operibus*], than some sterile language."[95] The preponderance of the letter is devoted to providing examples of how others taught through living witness.[96] He invites Teuzo to visit Fonte Avellana and "judge by your own observation what is being done in these woods."[97] He writes several biographical sketches of hermits so Teuzo has mod-

92. Letter 44.36, in L, 2:242; B, 2:33.

93. Letter 44.7, in L, 2:225–26; B, 2:13–14.

94. Discussion of Teuzo's opinion of simony is extremely brief. See Letter 44.27–28, in L, 2:237–38; B, 2:26–27.

95. Letter 44.17, in L, 2:231; B, 2:21. He repeats this principle verbatim in Letter 109.13, in L, 5:214–15; B, 3:210, indicating how significant he believed it and Dominic's life were.

96. Letter 109 contains a lengthier vita of Dominic, and it is Dominic's witness that Damian focuses on.

97. Letter 44.8, in L, 2:226; B, 2:14.

els to imitate: "I held up these models to you so that perhaps while thinking over the greater achievements of others, you might come to a decision about your own."[98] He also reminds Teuzo how intertwined the individual and community are. To concentrate on one to the neglect of the other ends in failure for both, for as Martin Storacus (one of Damian's spiritual guides) says, "What benefit comes to a candle ... if it gives light to others when at the same time the hungry flame devours it?"[99] Similarly, "a medicine is hardly acceptable if, while it retards the infected part, at the same time causes damage to the tissue that is healthy."[100]

When writing to Ariprandus, his secretary and fellow hermit at Fonte Avellana, Damian continues his argument on the superiority of living witness. The martyrs' execution bore greater witness than any words, for "they bequeathed to their followers an example that they might imitate." Damian urges Ariprandus to apply this lesson to his own life: "You too will find it easier to influence those who see you following in the footsteps of Christ, than to persuade those who hear you by any amount of words you speak."[101] Of course, the reverse is also true. Living witness can influence people negatively, a reality too often forgotten. Damian offers a warning of this to his hermits at St. Barnabas of Gamugno, who are guilty of laxity. Damian tells them that "we shall be guilty, not only of our own negligence, but also of the kind of life that others live; and while we ourselves fail by becoming lax, we also produce the cause of defection in those who come after us. For when their indolent life is pointed out to them, they ... use us as a shield in their defense." Bad witness is indeed "the source of their guilt."[102] It is often a source of scandal. When hermits render witness to a "life grown lukewarm," then they are "teachers not of erudition but of forgetfulness; not leaders in winning the battle, but the first who take to flight."[103] In another letter to the Gamugno community he repeats the lesson of a friend,

98. Letter 44.24, in L, 2:235; B, 2:25.
99. Letter 44:11, in L, 2:228; B, 2:16.
100. Letter 44.26, in L, 2:236; B, 2:26.
101. Letter 117.7, in L, 5:321; B, 3:319.
102. Letter 137.10, in L, 6:94; B, 3:471.
103. Letter 137.10–11, ibid.

Erlembald Cotta, who reported to him that after lodging at their hermitage and watching them "consorting with laymen, telling unseemly jokes and engaging in elegant wantonness ... he completely abandoned the very purpose of becoming a monk."[104] Their improper witness was responsible: "It is, indeed, proper that our life bear fruit, not only by avoiding detours and trackless deviations from the path of justice, but also by not depriving others by bad example of access to the service of God."[105]

Damian's correspondence with the Gamugno hermits (Letters 137 [after 1065] and Letter 142 [1066]) includes two other prominent planks of his reform platform, the condemnation of avarice and the promotion of good stewardship. In early letters he rails against avarice for the role it plays in simony.[106] He juxtaposes it to trust, and proposes shabby clothing and visits to graves as deterrents for the vice.[107] He repeats these sentiments, emphasizing the fatal effect avarice has on the unity of the community. Likewise, Damian reiterates to the hermits the theology of stewardship he had developed in previous letters. As early as 1042 Damian had lectured a layman and laywoman on obligations regarding their "extensive and long-lasting stewardship."[108] In Letter 110 Damian advises a wealthy prelate "to choose one virtue in preference to others, to which he is especially devoted."[109] He reviews possible options and argues that almsgiving would be the bishop's best choice. It aids in his personal salvation—"God accepts an alms for the poor from your hands, and securely holds it as an investment for you in his heavenly treasury"—but Damian sees the act more as one of justice and mercy than as one of charity.[110] His conclusion is based on his theology of stewardship:

104. Letter 142:2, in L, 6:128; B, 3:504.

105. Letter 142.3, ibid.

106. Letter 16.2, in L, 1:143; B, 1:153. See also Letter 3.2 and 3, in L, 1:87–88; B, 1:107–8; Letter 5.2, in L, 1:95; B, 1:112; and Letter 13.2, in L, 1:131; B, 1:144. Curiously he barely mentions it in *Liber gratissimus.*

107. Letter 21.14, in L, 1:205; B, 1:209; repeated in Letter 22.13, in L, 1:214; B, 1:215. Letter 50.56 and 61, in L, 2:317 and 319; B, 2:114–17.

108. Letter 2.2, in L, 1:85; B, 1:103. See Letter 64 to Anne of France and Letter 51 to Beatrice of Tuscany.

109. Letter 110.4, in L, 5:229; B, 3:225.

110. Letter 110.7, in L, 5:230; B, 3:226.

God made the world for everybody's use, not just certain individuals.[111] "Therefore, those who are rich should be regarded as dispensers rather than possessors, and should not consider what they have to be their own," Damian lectures. No one should "use their wealth for their own purposes, but they should function as administrators in the role as steward." Charity gives of itself; justice gives what is due, "hence, those who give alms to the poor, return what belongs to others, and do not disburse what is theirs."[112] Although the disbursement is in reality common property, it still is admirable, and "in the eyes of the loving Judge we are perceived as being merciful." Those who "turn their back on the poor ... will be accused of avarice but also of plundering." Then Damian uses the full force of his rhetorical skills to condemn those who fail as stewards: "Because you refused to provide for your fellow servants from the goods you received for their welfare, may the ravenous pits of hell devour you as you stand condemned of despoiling others of their property because of your passionate cupidity."[113]

Although the ideas are not new, Damian addresses some of his strongest statements on avarice and stewardship to the Gamugno community. This may be due to the high standard of behavior he demands of hermits. It may be that the new economic realities sweeping through Italy drove Damian to contemplate proper reactions to these realities. The embrace of poverty was central to the vita apostolica; Damian may have written to clarify principles at the core of that life. At a time when the relationship between secular and ecclesiastical authority and property was being reconfigured, Damian identified the vice responsible and the solution: "We must destroy avarice if we would live at peace and be independent of laymen."[114] Since it was the particular task of hermits to "bear fruit ... by not depriving others by bad example of access to the service of God," it is not surprising to see Damian use the opportunity of the hermits'

111. See Letter 5.2, in L, 1:94; B, 1:112; Letter 108.7, in L, 5:198 and 204; B, 3:192 and 198.
112. Letter 110.8, in L, 5:230–31; B, 3:227.
113. Letter 110.9, in L, 5:231; B, 3:227.
114. Letter 142.26, in L, 6:138; B, 3:516.

misuse of riches to preach on the subject in the strongest terms.[115] "You indiscriminately accept alms from laymen," he accuses them, "eagerly enlarge your holdings, and, in a word, both publicly and in private scurry to become rich."[116] Those who "amass riches" and "spend them for our own use" will never be happy, for "wealth induces anxiety in its owners and does not allow them to relax in security."[117] Only when one realizes why some are wealthy and some poor will happiness come: "One man is richer than others, not for the reason that he alone should possess the things he holds in trust, but that he disburse them to the poor." Damian does not stop there but repeats his earlier statement that stewards are not true owners. Again, it is a matter of justice, not charity: "He should distribute the goods of others, not as their owner but as their agent, and not merely through motives of charity, but of justice." He goes yet a step further and condones taking the wealth of others for the sake of justice. "Wherefore, he who takes from the rich to give to the poor is not to be thought a thief, but a dispenser of common property." He expands the application. Such a Robin Hood "who takes from the wealthy rather than from the unfortunate to provide for his brothers who are in need, or who supports some pious work, or, more importantly, who relieves the poor in their necessity, should not be counted as an avaricious man, but as one who justly moves common goods from one group of brethren to another." Justice is always the key: "Since giving of one's own bespeaks mercy, it is in the province of justice to distribute what belongs to others."[118]

No discussion of Damian's ideas on the eremitic life would be complete without mention of the discipline. The discipline did not puzzle or repulse then as it does now. Two elementary facts should be acknowledged at the outset. First, self-flagellation is not—cannot—be anywhere near as physically painful as scourging at the hand of another. One's arm reaching backwards simply does not

115. Letter 142.3, in L, 6:128; B, 3:504.

116. Letter 142.9, in L, 6:130; B, 3:507.

117. Letter 142.11, in L, 6:131; B, 3:508.

118. Letter 142.14, in L, 6:132–33; B, 3:509–10. See Letter 110.8, in L, 5:230–31; B, 3:227.

have the flexibility, strength, or range of motion that it does when extending itself forward. As the twenty-first century monk Thomas Matus confides from personal experience, the pain inflicted is minimal.[119] Secondly, self-flagellation must be set beside normal everyday existence. Sensation dulled by a harsh daily life requires unusual stimulus to gain one's attention. Self-flagellation does this by inflicting a new type of pain on an already pain-filled existence. Analysis of eleventh-century self-flagellation must keep these realities in mind. Damian could almost have modern readers in mind when he declares that "the discipline is thought to be more appalling than it actually is, and the fear of it is greater than the pain it inflicts."[120]

All discussion of Damian and the discipline should begin and end with the principle of moderation. Damian mentions the practice frequently. He tells us that although it was a forgotten practice, it "was by no means recently invented by modern ingenuity, but stems rather from the authority of Sacred Scripture."[121] Because of the example of Dominic Loricatus, renowned for his extreme use of the discipline, "the custom spread in our area, so that not only men but even noble women eagerly took up this form of purgatory."[122] Nevertheless, he willingly admits there are critics of the practice. Many believe it "to be harsh, even, perhaps, superfluous."[123] He disagrees, saying that when people scourge themselves, "they believe that they are partaking in the passion," and, therefore, he recommends it.[124] It is a qualified recommendation: "I meant for monks, and did not

119. See his comments, V5F, 4, n. 5 (97).

120. Letter 133.4, in L, 6:74; B, 3:453.

121. Letter 56.4, in L, 2:362; B, 2:155. He discusses it in Letters 18, 44, 45, 50, 56, 66, 76, 109, 133, 161, and 168.

122. Letter 66.26, in L, 3:66; B, 2:276; repeated in Letter 109.24, L, 5:219; B, 3:215. He also refers to Dominic's superb living witness. He "would more readily teach and direct you by the example of his outstanding life than anything I might achieve by my unskilled words." Letter 66.25, in L, 3:64–65; B, 2:275; repeated in Letter 109.21, in L, 5:217; B, 3:213.

123. Letter 44.20, in L, 2:233; B, 2:22. Letter 56 is written to answer the attacks of Peter Cerebrosus on the practice "after your frantic temper flared up against me." Damian is at his rhetorical (best? worst?), saying that the criticism arose "from an unsound brain and fury from a mind deprived of reason." Letter 56.14, in L, 2:366; B, 2:159; and 56.3, in L, 2:362; B, 2:154, respectively.

124. Letter 44.20, in L, 2:233; B, 2:22.

commission it to be brought to the attention of laymen or even clerics."[125] By the late 1060s Damian fears the practice among hermits is getting extreme, so he writes all his hermitages with a message of restraint. "When practiced in moderation [scourging] could be beneficial to you, but admittedly, when applied indiscreetly can be harmful." Moreover, potential members are "restrained from entering the hermitage" out of fear of the discipline. He wants to moderate its use.[126]

> Wherefore, using a mitigating norm of discretion, I ordain that no one in the hermitage shall be forced to practice autoflagellation.... Let no one, God forbid, rashly presume to go beyond this rule of moderation that I have prescribed. In this way I am not removing something that is good, but placing limits on what is superfluous. Nor am I denying the brothers something that contributes to their welfare, but setting discretionary bounds. If he wishes, each may take advantage of going as far as the law allows, but it will not be permitted to go beyond.[127]

He justifies his interference in personal piety by arguing that he is not "exceeding my authority, but [is] imitating the example found in God's law" which testifies to the use of "discretion in moderating the rigor of the punishment."[128] In his concluding sentence Damian's reservations are plainly evident; the discipline is inferior to other exertions: "Observe this norm in taking the discipline, chastise your spirit instead, and dutifully perform other virtuous deeds."[129]

He does, however, write the monks of Monte Cassino in spring 1069 to defend the practice. Apparently the monks had of late abandoned the practice altogether, because a cardinal "jeered at this practice ... despising it as something shameful, [and] utterly forbade you to ever again to engage in it."[130] The supposed shame was the naked-

125. Letter 45.2, in L, 2:244–45; B, 2:34–35.

126. Letter 133.4, in L, 6:74; B, 3:453.

127. Letter 133.5, in L, 6:74–75; B, 3:454. Unfortunately, Kenneth Russell, "Peter Damian's Whip," *American Benedictine Review* 41:1 (1990), 20–35, omits these passages from his study and thus reaches imbalanced conclusions.

128. Letter 133.6, in L, 6:75; B, 3:454. He cites Dt 25:2–3 as his example.

129. Letter 133.7, in L, 6:75; B, 3:454.

130. Letter 161.8, in L, 7:134; B, 4:138.

ness involved, for one "took the discipline while naked."[131] Damian gets especially upset at this reason. If Isaiah was not ashamed of his public nudity, "should a monk, who, so to speak, is not worth a farthing, blush to take off his clothes before a few of his brothers?"[132] It is a rejection of *imitatio Christi.* "While disdaining to be stripped and scourged with him, [you] deride his nakedness and all his sufferings" and refuse to bear witness to Christ's suffering and the apostles "whose example we are commanded to follow."[133] This in turn limits the monks' witness, for in the past their use of the discipline "attracted large numbers of people to follow your wholesome example, and has caused them to bring forth vigorous offspring." As Christ's scourging was a most powerful witness to his love for us, monks' bodily penance follows his example. Scourging's utility "is witnessed [*testes sunt*] not only by the monasteries that rejoice to walk in your footsteps, that is, those of their teachers, but also by a multitude of towns and villages that in common throw themselves joyfully into this same praiseworthy practice."[134] In addition, the discipline is a supremely autonomous statement of personal responsibility, for no one but the individual is in control. "It is not necessary, Lord, for you as judge to pass sentence on me," the penitent is saying. "I am laying hands on myself, I am taking vengeance on myself, and make myself responsible for my crimes."[135]

Monks

While visiting the Gamugno hermitage in winter 1067 Damian wrote the citizens of Florence about problems with their bishop, Peter, accused of simony. Earlier he had visited the city to mediate the conflict in person. His attempt "fared badly at the hands of

131. Letter 161.7, in L, 7:133; B, 4:137.

132. Letter 161.15, in L, 7:138; B, 4:142. See Letter 168.2, in L, 7:237; B, 4:239. Although the body is naked while scourging, "it appears to be garbed in sparkling attire before the eyes of God."

133. Letter 161.12, in L, 7:136; B, 4:140; and Letter 161.16, in L, 7:139; B, 4:143.

134. Letter 161.2, in L, 7:131; B, 4:135–36.

135. Letter 161.18, in L, 7:140–41; B, 4:144.

unruly crowds," and he decided to "put in writing" his opinion so no one could "falsify my words or alter their meaning."[136] He unequivocally states his premise: "Wherefore, ruling out the slightest possibility of rehabilitation, I anathematize and condemn the heresy of simony."[137] Next, he reiterates his anti-Donatist stance: "I believe without the slightest doubt that sacraments can be conferred by detestable ministers," and those ordained by simonists "should remain ministers."[138] These are not new pronouncements; "you often heard these things from my own lips." Moreover, Pope Nicholas II asked "everyone who thinks he has a just complaint against the bishop [to] knock at the door" of the Roman synod soon to be convened. Let them decide "the charge brought against him," because Damian is "hesitant to judge in a case involving such shaky controversy."[139] The controversy originated with Vallombrosan monks for whom he had little respect.[140] On the advice of Teuzo, their founder John Gualbert (ca. 995/1000–1073) left a Florentine monastery to denounce his abbot and his bishop, Mezzabarba, as simoniacs. A small group gathered around him, and after a short stay at Romuald's Camaldoli, they wandered about, settling finally at Vallombrosa. At first they lived as hermits, but their condemnation of Mezzabarba when he bought the Florentine episcopal seat in 1062 found them at the center of city life. The monks' protests soon led to armed conflict among citizens, monks, and clergy.[141]

Damian, of course, has strong opinions about them. His first major complaint is their Donatist stance. Damian is frustrated that they are still advocating that those "ordained freely by simonists ... are just as heretical as the ministers of their ordination." They are creating havoc in the city. They "reject and hoot at their Masses and all the

136. Letter 146.2, in L, 6:155–56; B, 3:533.

137. Letter 146.3, in L, 6:156; B, 3:533.

138. Letter 146.4, in L, 6:156–57; B, 3:533–34.

139. Letter 146.5–6, in L, 6:157–58; B, 3:534–35.

140. Letter 146.7, in L, 6:158; B, 3:535.

141. See Andreas Strumensi, *Vita sancti Iohannis Gualberti,* MGH SS, 30, 1 and 2; and *Iohannis Gualberti auctore discipulo eius anonyme,* MGH SS, 30/2, 1104–11. Cushing, "Of Locustae," wonders how involved Vallombrosans were in provoking the physical attacks.

sacraments dispensed by them," all because they fail to accept that the Spirit's gifts come "not because of any merit of [the priest's] but because of his ministry."[142] There is another issue bothering Damian.[143] He is disturbed because, as he sees it, the Vallombrosans are damaging the Body of Christ. The list of grievances is long. "According to a report, nearly a thousand people were deceived by this trumpery and nonsense and left this world without receiving the sacrament of the Body and Blood of the Lord," Damian laments. "In fact, they are convinced that no true sacraments can be administered by contemporary priests" and that they should not even enter some churches. Responsibility for this situation rests at the feet of "these monks [who] reach their decision on street corners, and defame the jurisdiction of synods ... disparage everything that smacks of clerics, and are careful not to offend laymen who, indeed, deserve to be more sharply and bitterly censured."[144] Damian himself has been personally "subjected to abuse" by them. "This is hardly conduct befitting a monk," Damian protests.[145] He calls them "sanctimonious men" who fall into heresy "by disdaining to follow the beaten path" and instead "wander over winding roads and dangerous pitfalls."[146]

In part, Damian is reacting to their hypocrisy and "irrational practices of the Pharisees."[147] Other primary sources agree with Damian that the Vallombrosans were Donatists who played a major role in Florentine unrest, but they also report positive innovations and renewal efforts. Damian fails to see, or at least to mention, these

142. Letter 146.10, 9, in L, 6:159; B, 3:536.

143. Damian has a troubled history with Florentine hermits. Damian wrote to Florentine clergy around 1055 to defend himself against "urban hermits ... [who] have schemed to excerpt from my current writings only that which could beget scandal for those unacquainted with the secrets of monastic fervor," that is, scourging. He claims they "have gained control over the people by nominally professing to be monks, who ... preside over tribunals ... [and] claim only for themselves the right to administer justice." They preach that if the discipline is allowed "all the sacred canons will surely be destroyed." Letter 45:3–4, in L, 2:245; B, 2:35–36.

144. Letter 146.17, in L, 6:163; B, 3:539–40.

145. Letter 146.18, in L, 6:164; B, 3:540–41.

146. Letter 146.19, in L, 6:164–65; B, 3:541.

147. Letter 146.18, in L, 6:164; B, 3:541.

positive aspects of the order. While he sees Romuald and his own innovations as restorative, he views John Gualbert's innovations, immersion in city life in particular, as damaging. Still, the complaints Damian records are valid. Their immoderation bothers him—excessively! Their "excessive purity [*nimia mundicia*]" and "excessive holiness [*nimia sanctitas*]" brought them to break "like infected branches, from unity with the body of the Church."[148] As a result "we can rightly compare this type of men to frogs or locusts, for as formerly these animals were a plague to the Egyptians, so now they devastate the Church."[149] Since Damian always defends the right and the obligation to criticize the hierarchy, one is led to assume that Damian sees their criticism as unjustified. He thinks it is interfamily bickering. "Shall we bare our teeth and snarl at one another, and like rabid dogs, tear one another to pieces with our jaws?" he worries.[150] This is not the way of monks. "Whoever wishes to be holy, should be so privately in the sight of God, and not pride himself on being better than his weaker brother" or attack him without reason. A monk must never forget his responsibility for the community's salvation as part of his own: "A young dog whose duty it is to ward off strangers, should never neglect his charge and begin attacking members of the family."[151]

Damian's opinion of other monks is, in contrast, quite high. He has such a close relationship with "the holy monks living in the heavenly school of Monte Cassino" that "the warmth of my affection for you glows in my heart."[152] He considers them a "holy and angelic community of brothers" whom he is "so preoccupied in thinking about."[153] His admiration for Cluniac monks is equally high. His three-month stay at their monastery in 1063 won his respect for their "strict and totally occupied order of the day" and their "continu-

148. Letter 146.19, in L, 6:165; B, 3:541.
149. Letter 146.20, ibid.
150. Letter 146.21, in L, 6:166; B, 3:541.
151. Letter 146.21, in L, 6:166; B, 3:542.
152. Letter 161.1, in L, 7:131; B, 4:135.
153. Letter 102.2, in L, 5:123; B, 3:118. Many of his letters to Monte Cassino are filled with tales and odd subjects, indicating he was quite comfortable sharing all sorts of thoughts with them.

ous effort to observe the Rule, especially your constant participation at Mass and in choir."[154] He sees Cluny as "a spiritual field where heaven and earth are engaged" and which "hold[s] me firmly bound by the glue of your love."[155] It is where "I happened to learn … outstanding examples of holy humility."[156] While reflections on monastic life are scattered throughout his letters and sermons, he writes three major treatises on the subject late in life (Letters 132 [ca. 1065–1071], 153 [after 1067], and 165 [1069]). While the dates document how long his early theology served him, the letters have the disadvantage of being written through the pessimistic lens of an aging man. The contrast in outlook is sharp when set beside early optimistic treatises, such as *Dominus vobiscum.* Of course, one should consider whether Damian's pessimism was warranted. Perhaps it was true that in his world "decency and right living have all but disappeared, and as vigorous church discipline gradually collapses, a pestilential flood of vice and depravity of every kind grows."[157] Eleventh-century Italy surely had its problems, and many of Damian's reforms "prove[d] to have been useless," akin to "planting seeds on a sandy beach."[158] In addition, his position of authority necessarily immersed Damian in problems. As legate, he went where the conflicts were. A few years after his appointment as cardinal-bishop he expressed his frustration with this situation. "I cannot avoid being a bishop, and grow weary of the episcopal burden" that leaves his soul "darkened by worldly affairs." It is "because of secular concerns" that he cannot "reach the heights of contemplation," and this fuels his resentment, perhaps leading him to exaggerate the decay.[159] The longer worldly affairs distracted him from contemplation, the more he resented and denounced them. The pessimism of his later works is probably the result of a combination of all these factors.

154. Letter 100.11, in L, 5:110; B, 3:105.
155. Letter 113.8 and 3, in L, 5:289 and 286; B, 3:292 and 289.
156. Letter 106.26, in L, 5:188; B, 3:182.
157. Letter 86.2, in L, 3:255; B, 2:460.
158. Letter 165.84 and 81, in L, 7:222 and 221; B, 4:225 and 223.
159. Letter 96.4, in L, 5:52; B, 3:47–48.

In many of his discussions on monastic life he marshals his pessimism to motivate reform. Because of worldly decadence monks must be "immensely grateful to God, that, in this age, you were chosen to live apart from the world in which it is obviously difficult for anyone to be saved."[160] A monk should feel privileged, for he has been "granted an abundant gift of grace" and thus "has Christ rescued you from the mouth of the cruel plunderer who sought to have you serve him as the world was falling apart."[161] The world is also undependable and transitory. "What in the world is so securely our own that we can safely trust it?" he asks Monte Cassino monks. "So never put your trust in any risky possessions." Instead, "go to Christ, the sailor's surest harbor, the safest and most quiet refuge."[162]

In a letter to Empress Agnes after she entered a monastery, he counsels her to remember that "the false happiness of this world is subject to so many calamities; since temporal power is affected by such changing conditions, and the state of affairs is thrown into confusion, ... what sensible person would not hold back from things so frivolous and fleeting?"[163] Monastic life, in Damian's view, is the easier, not the harder, choice. It offers guarantees and stability that secular life cannot. "Who is there that fortune does not influence, with dramatic variety now changing bad times into good and then good times into bad?"[164] One senses the exasperation Damian feels as he watches a world he cannot control. He takes refuge in what he *can* control. "All men, whether they be powerful or in want, all have the same origin and all will have the same end.... [This] we cannot alter," Damian states. "Between these two limits, however, there is a certain difference of lifestyle"—and this a person can control.[165] By choosing monasticism one chooses to control at least one aspect of life. Still, he is realistic and does not see monasticism as an escape or a grand panacea. "You have come," he says to Agnes, "not that [Christ] might solve for you your doubts and mysterious riddles, but

160. Letter 86.4, in L, 3:256; B, 2:461.

161. Letter 86.5, 4, in L, 3:257, 256; B, 2:461.

162. Letter 86.86, in L, 3:298; B, 2:504.

163. Letter 104.29, in L, 5:150; B, 3:155.

164. Letter 104.26, in L, 5:158; B, 3:154.

165. Letter 104.31, in L, 5:161; B, 3:157.

to open the door to the heavenly kingdom."[166] Much work must be done before entrance into heaven is attained, but religious life is a more dependable way than unpredictable secular life. One has only to look at the Roman emperors and note how uncertain their lives were, "how few of the emperors died a natural death." Hannibal, Cleopatra, Anthony, Pompey: all were subjected to "an ill-fated change in fortune."[167] Empress Agnes "once the wife of the earthly emperor" left behind the fickleness of secular life and now as "bride of our Redeemer" had the steadfastness of religious life.[168] Never one to miss an opportunity to emphasize the witness component in monastic life, Damian tells her what "an edifying example of imitating the Savior" her entrance into the monastery was; "to have seen you and those of your company at that moment was a marvelous spectacle to behold."[169] Her witness is greater than that of most people, because her choice was more extreme: "Who, moreover, will fear the loss of possessions that will pass away, when he beholds the voluntary poverty of a woman whom just a few years ago he saw ruling so many kingdoms?" He writes of this not so she will be offended "but rather that wherever your outstanding virtue is proclaimed, it may provide great edification for those who read of it."[170]

Damian has much to say about monastic virtues in a letter to his nephew Marinus, a "raw recruit" at St. Apollinare in Classe who needs "to be more fully trained."[171] Given their relationship and his youth, Damian thinks "that care of your welfare more urgently depends on me," so he starts "giving you advice."[172] He discusses chastity, sobriety, moderation, restraint of speech, courtesy, and obedience in turn, emphasizing how exercise of each defeats its corresponding vice. His approach is lenient, even indulgent. "Let the practice of virtue grow apace with your bodily development that custom may lighten what the weakness of human frailty finds abhorrent," he

166. Letter 104.10, in L, 5:150–51; B, 3:147.
167. Letter 104.25–27, in L, 5:158–59; B, 3:153–54.
168. Letter 104.33, in L, 5:162; B, 3:158.
169. Letter 104.11, in L, 5:151; B, 3:147.
170. Letter 104.16, in L, 5:153; B, 3:149.
171. Letter 132.2, in L, 6:57; B, 3:139.
172. Letter 132.3, in L, 6:58; B, 3:439.

advises the youth.[173] He gives practical advice: "Do not resent correction." Avoid "complaining ... against a negligent superior." "The first raft available after shipwreck is the straight forward confession of sin." "When you are in good health" do not take unnecessary medication. And so on.[174] He illustrates each with historical and scriptural examples. "But why do I protract this long narrative?" Damian asks. His answer is as we have grown to expect: "I do so only that you should choose just a few from the many who are available, and use them as a model as you strive to fashion the beauty of the spiritual man."[175]

He continues his advice, and just as he "decided to call a halt to my writing," he adds a bit more. His first addition is a warning about mixing secular interests with monastic life. They are not compatible. "Beware, my dear son, lest as you go on living in the monastic cloister, you take part in discussing secular affairs," Damian cautions.[176] This is a particular sore point for him, because he knows the power they have to distract the monk. "What is this foolish preoccupation with these and other inane things, but to divert our mouths from the clear waters of divine praise and to soil our lips with filth and mud?" he argues. Such behavior also impedes the required diversity of roles in the Body of Christ; a monk's role differs from a lay person's. "In truth, what business has a monk involving himself with the trifling affairs of laymen? To what purpose should I carry within the confines of the monastery the noisy courts of justice, the tribunals of judges, or the courts of kings?"[177] He explains his vehement insistence on this division of labor. A monk must concentrate on being what a monk is supposed to be, perfect: "I am not content that you be mediocre, my son, for I wish to see in you the very best, the most perfect [*Nichil mediocri inte contentus sum, fili, totum summum, totum perfectum est quod in te sentire desidero*]."[178]

173. Letter 132.10, in L, 6:61; B, 3:443.

174. Letter 132.12, in L, 6:63; B, 3:444; Letter 132.13, ibid; Letter 132.14, in L, 6:63; B, 3:444–45; and Letter 132.16, in L, 6:65; B, 3:446.

175. Letter 132.19, in L, 6:66; B, 3:447.

176. Letter 132.24, in L, 6:69; B, 3:449.

177. Letter 132.25, in L, 6:69; B, 3:450.

178. Letter 132.30, in L, 6:71; B, 3:451.

Letter 153 to the Pomposa community offers a more formal analysis of monastic life. As Damian sees it, "our order has fallen away from holy fervor" and continues "to fall further downward every day." He believes that "a spark of fire seems to remain," so he writes this "letter of exhortation" not "as an insult to yourselves" but to encourage reform.[179] He begins by reminding them that the spiritual health of a community is dependent upon each individual's effort: "God ... examines the deeds of every person and office, of every rank and order, on a balance of careful examination, and ... has different scales for each order."[180] Each must live up to his responsibilities according to his position in the community. Entering a monastery is only a first step. "What use is it, I ask you, for someone to have completed a part of a journey if he does not reach the destination?"[181] In the first seven sections Damian discusses his understanding of the Benedictine Rule. Its strengths are vast. It is wise, "drawn up with so much discretion and specially tempered with a scale of such moderation."[182] It is flexible, "made like a full, spacious mansion, capable of taking in all types of people, boys as well as old men, the strong and the weak, the delicate and those who differ in various ways by a difference in their practices."[183] However, Benedict wanted monks "to observe not merely what he wrote down" but more. The Rule is limited, a path which leads to better things. Consequently, "he who has decided to be content with the Rule of the blessed Benedict alone has limited himself to the narrow possession of the mountain of Ephraim" (see Jo 17:15).[184]

The relationship between rest and labor is discussed next. That "the labor of a good work comes before the rest of contemplation" is his thesis.[185] He explains. "Rest in the joy of the most perfect contemplation" is the goal of every monk.[186] His "entire way of life and

179. Letter 153.3, in L, 7:15–16; B, 4:14–15.

180. Letter 153.5, in L, 7:17; B, 4:16. See also Letter 153.26, in L, 7:29–30; B, 4:27: "The spring that flows in the center is the sum of individual springs."

181. Letter 153.6, ibid.

182. Letter 153.22, in L, 7:27–28; B, 4:25.

183. Letter 153.26, in L, 7:29; B, 4:27.

184. Letter 153.11, in L, 7:20; B, 4:19.

185. Letter 153.34, in L, 7:34; B, 4:32.

186. Letter 153.32, in L, 7:33; B, 4:31.

renunciation of the world strives for nothing other than rest." He poetically describes rest as "catching sight of the truth." Here is the paradox: "This rest is only acquired if first a person is engaged in the various labors of its battles."[187] Jacob had "to toil in service" for two seven-year periods before he attained rest, and monks must follow his example.[188] Unfortunately, too many monks "adopt inactive lives of indolent idleness" and never "bear the fruit of the active or contemplative life."[189] Indeed, if they do perchance bear fruit, "it is not that they seek the fruits of spiritual profit in them."[190]

This brings him to a discussion about secular studies. His complaint is the same. Some monks pursue secular knowledge without seeking spiritual profit from it, and in the Body of Christ "spiritual studies," not "the rules of Donatus," are the domain of religious.[191] Read outside the context of his lifelong advocacy of rational investigation and the division of labor, the passage seems anti-intellectual. Properly contextualized, Damian's point is consistent with the principles established early in life. It is not the utilization of rational powers that Damian objects to—Damian has already instructed these monks to "now go, read, run through and turn over the pages, investigate them carefully [*age nunc, lege, percurre, revolve folia, sollenter investiga*]"—but to a monk's misdirection of those powers.[192] His attack focuses on "the trifles of the external arts," "superfluous teachings," and "superfluous notions" which monks must "strip off" if they wish to attain their designated goal, "the solid truth of right reason."[193] A monk "should not know how to debate the merits of cooks, he should not ... be so skillful as to bring forth witty or captious words," or the like. Instead, "let him withdraw from external affairs, let him guard his mouth from idle conversation, let him seek the secret place of his mind [*mentis sue latibulum petat*], where he may burn with all his efforts to see the face of his Creator."[194] Other

187. Letter 153.31, in L, 7:32; B, 4:29.
188. Letter 153.34, in L, 7:34; B, 4:31.
189. Letter 153.38, in L, 7:36; B, 4:34.
190. Letter 153.39, in L, 7:37; B, 4:34.
191. Letter 153.40, in L, 7:37; B, 4:35.
192. Letter 153.22, in L, 7:27; B, 4:25.
193. Letter 153.40–41, in L, 7:37–38; B, 4:33.
194. Letter 153.44, in L, 7:39; B, 4:37.

kinds of knowledge were fine "when they were in worldly service, but it is different for those of us" in monastic service. Damian makes sure readers know who and what he is criticizing: "We have said these things against those monks who are entangled in the absurdities of the superficial arts."[195] It is the conditional clause that established the meaning of Damian's concluding advice on this matter: "Beyond this, it is useful that every brother who has abandoned the world with his whole heart unlearn the things he already knows *if they prove to be harmful* [*si noxia probantur esse*]" (italics mine).[196]

A much lengthier section follows on the gift of tears, a gift Damian holds in great esteem.[197] It is a behavior rather foreign to modern sensibilities, but Damian's succinct definition clarifies why he valued it so highly: "Tears serve as mediators of peace in forging an alliance between God and humans."[198] This is the essence of the gift. He mentions numerous functions and benefits of tears, "but if I wanted to run through all the gifts of tears, the day would likely conclude before the abundance of examples should be exhausted."[199] The remaining two discussions are practical, one on what "is appropriate for those who administer" monastic offices and an interesting one on what should be done "to distinguish the different age-groups, and to tailor garments, so to speak," appropriately.[200] The latter reveals psychological insight into adolescence. He acknowledges that youths "have a great need for the weightiest aids of exhortation because you endure the harsher struggles of the flesh's fire," which can sometimes rage "like restless Vesuvius."[201] He is similarly discerning in his discussion on the trials of "old holy men" who know that "if you lose now, you cannot recover" in another battle.[202] A short

195. Letter 153.43, ibid.

196. Letter 153.44, ibid.

197. Apparently Romuald was not as big a proponent of tears as Damian, for Romuald "would often remind [his disciples]: 'Be careful not to weep too much, because excessive tears harm the eyes and damage the brain.'" VR, 31 (223).

198. Letter 153.45, in Letters 7:40; B, 4:38.

199. Letter 153.46, in L, 7:41; B, 4:39.

200. Letter 153.57, 70, in L, 7:47, 55; B, 4:44, 55.

201. Letter 153.74, in L, 7:57–58; B, 4:54.

202. Letter 153.81, in L, 7:63; B, 4:60.

warning against false witness and exhortation to proper witness concludes the treatise.

> To wit, holy Church ... is also lined within and without with pitch, so that outside she is caressed in fraternal sweetness and within she will be united in the truth of mutual love. For whoever loves inwardly, but outwardly is at variance with the brothers owing to the unsuitable harshness of his practices, has pitch, to be sure, on the inside but does not have it on the outside.... One who presents himself outwardly as worthy of love and conserves inwardly a loving nature, who displays the fruit of kindness outwardly with the branches of the Word ... he is lined with pitch both within and without.[203]

Damian's last treatise on monastic life, Letter 165, is often cited as a premier example of *contemptu mundi* literature, yet in a way that categorization misses the point. Damian's concern is not with the state of the world but with monks' involvement in it. It is the monk's failure to keep a freely made vow to renounce the world that Damian deplores. His long introduction makes this clear; it is the individual monk who is responsible for the sorry state of monasticism, not the world. "We who are known to have renounced the world," Damian prods, "why do we again fall back into it?" No external power forced monks to this renouncement. It was "of our own accord" that "we have determined, moreover, that what once was rightly ours should now be ours no longer."[204] Damian does not claim that all things earthly are damned, only that they "have vowed, not to men but rather to God himself to consider them an everlasting abomination [*sed et perpetuam eorum abbominationem non homini, sed, Deo potius professi sumus*]."[205] It was "in the contract we made with our God ... [that] we promised to renounce the world and everything for which it stands."[206] When a monk, therefore, "returns to those [things] he has left behind ... he is like the stupid traveler who cannot return to the place on which he irrevocably turned his back, and has not reached the destination toward which he planned to go."[207] As his

203. Letter 153.91, in L, 7:69; B, 4:65.
204. Letter 165.2, in L, 7:171; B, 4:175.
205. Letter 165.3, in L, 7:172; B, 4:176.
206. Letter 165.5, in L, 7:173; B, 4:176.
207. Letter 165.6, in L, 7:174; B, 4:177.

verbs indicate, Damian sees the contract as a free, personal decision.

After this reminder of personal responsibility, Damian presents a series of lectures on monastic problems and solutions. Avarice is his first target. He sees no problem with money per se—"by worldly standards it is just possession"—but "when one is acquiring it . . . dangerous ambition often takes over," and one starts "to reclaim what we have given up."[208] Noteworthy is Damian's statement that it is "their attitude toward what they [own] [*sed non diversas circa haec, quibus fruuntur, exhibent voluntates*]" that determines whether monks, poor or rich, are avaricious.[209] This interferes with the monk's specific goal to be a worshipper of Christ, not money, for as "Truth itself says, . . . no one can worship God and money at the same time."[210] The avaricious monk is also shortsighted and forgets what eschatology teaches, that while earthly treasures come and go, true riches are "kept for you in heaven."[211]

The next section is quite long and focuses on the problems inherent with "those who were only recently so fervent in despising everything that belonged to the world, now eagerly returning to the whirlwind of secular affairs." Again, it is not the activity itself that Damian decries but a monk "forgetting all that he had promised."[212] Again Damian emphasizes the importance of inner dispositions. A person's decision to change his life is meaningless if all he has done is "put aside secular attire, but has not changed his attitude [*qua qui saecularem vestem non cum mente deposuit*]."[213] The problem is all the more worrisome because it renders erroneous witness: "We should not be surprised that those who observed all of this are scandalized."[214]

Wandering interferes with nearly all aspects of monastic life. "A monk who travels about cannot observe the fast," "not watch in nightly prayer vigils," not genuflect, observe silence, or read and

208. Letter 165.8, in L, 7:175; B, 4:178.
209. Letter 165.13, in L, 7:178; B, 4:181.
210. Letter 165.9, in L, 7:176; B, 4:180.
211. Letter 165.16, in L, 7:180; B, 4:183.
212. Letter 165.21, in L, 7:182–83; B, 4:185.
213. Letter 165.22, in L, 7:183; B, 4:186.
214. Letter 165.23, in L, 7:184; B, 4:187.

pray enough.[215] Charity, chastity, and tears of compunction diminish, while contact with all that is bad in the world increases: "A monk who goes out among the people ... will come in touch with murderers, perjurers, and the incestuous, with arsonists and adulterers." It is "totally out of place to associate with those who are separated from God, especially for monks who are united with God with such a special and, I might say, such a domestic familiarity [*domestica familiaritate*]."[216] His concern, once again, is with monks' failure to honor their commitment, not with society (although in this instance his pessimistic outlook leads him to say parenthetically that "for years now, all sorts of crime have sprung up throughout the world, every shameful act now flourishes, and daily this condition becomes more widespread the closer we come to the end of the world").[217]

A bigger problem for the wandering monk, however, is "the love of costly attire."[218] As we have seen, the connection between clothes and witness was well established in his early writings. Always he insists that clothes communicate a message. "In a hermitage, a hairshirt is a garment, in town it is something to be wondered at," we heard him say to Teuzo.[219] Here he reminds monks that it is their duty to make sure that clothes reflect beliefs, for "from a person's attire one can infer what his inner disposition is like, and from his external appearance can judge the quality of his purpose."[220] John the Baptist "came with a new message" and dressed accordingly.[221] He is the monk's model, as is Isaiah in his nakedness. Damian cautions moderation, though, lest one "use the uncouth appearance of their garb to win approbation of the crowd ... so that they may boast their self-esteem."[222] Sometimes "when occasion demands," good clothes are necessary to communicate a message effectively. If monks remain focused on their message they will "not [be] affected

215. Letter 165.24, in L, 7:184; B, 4:187–88.
216. Letter 165.31–32, in L, 7:189; B, 4:132.
217. Letter 165.31, in L, 7:189; B, 4:192.
218. Letter 165.36, in L, 7:192; B, 4:195–96.
219. Letter 44.7, in L, 2:226; B, 2:14. See Letter 24 for discussion in an even earlier work.
220. Letter 165.37, in L, 7:193; B, 4:196.
221. Letter 165.38, in L, 7:194; B, 4:197.
222. Letter 165.43, in L, 7:196; B, 4:199.

by the luxury or distressed by the coarseness" of their clothes, but only care, as Judith did, whether they are effective vehicles for their message.[223]

The monk "addicted to the vice of wanderlust" suffers the loss of solitude and "will not be able to reach the heights of perfection."[224] Furthermore, wanderers do not live up to their intellectual and spiritual potential. The soul loses "its ability for inner deliberation, in countless ways dissipated itself ... and because it pretends to be acting intelligently, is blinded to the point where it is unaware of what it is doing."[225] Now he tempers his tone as moderation takes over. His condemnation of contact with the secular world is not total. He understands the duties of Martha. Monks need to remember, though, that their role in the Body of Christ is that of Mary.

> Nor do I wish to imply by these words that a monk should obstinately purpose to remain at all times in retirement, nor that on occasion he should not agree to leave the monastery when extreme necessity demands. Yet I rather advise that he do so temporarily and only rarely, with the knowledge that by wandering through the world he cannot practice the spiritual life, not reach the heights of perfection even if he makes every effort to do so.[226]

Despite necessary exceptions, a monk best serves the community following Mary. The surest, safest way a monk can save others and self is not by worldly activity, but by the witness of one's life.

> And so, it frequently happens that he who is not content to look after himself, and leaves the monastery to promote the salvation of others, is forced to put himself in danger, and like a man reaching out to help someone who is grasping for air in a shipwreck in a stormy sea, he puts himself in jeopardy of drowning in the furious waves. In the

223. Letter 165.46–47, in L, 7:198; B, 4:201.

224. Letter 165.48, in L, 7:198–99; B, 4:202. In Letter 169.2; in L, 7:244; B, 4:248, written about 1070, Damian confesses that this was his personal plight: "Because I am surrounded by the darkness of so many secular interests I am unable to see the brightness of the interior light, and cannot lift my confused and insensible mind to the contemplation of spiritual truths."

225. Letter 165.58, in L, 7:205; B, 4:208.

226. Letter 165.60, in L, 7:207; B, 4:209.

> dark night of this life it is safer for us, as we stand on the shore, to produce a light for those who have suffered shipwreck, than out of compassion for them to swim out at the peril of our lives, so that when we have shown them the right direction, they may reach the safety of the harbor.[227]

This is Damian's ideal, monasticism bearing witness and the world responding. Unfortunately, as he grows older Damian sees both sides failing. "Formerly, indeed, the world felt a need for those who would announce the good news; but those days are over and times have changed," he laments. His frustration is personal as he reviews the failure of his witness "to implant spiritual ideas in the minds of worldly men."[228] No one can convince, "I will not say the people, but even one person" to repudiate sin.[229] "Was there ever a simonist who on the basis of my advice and warning willingly resigned his office? What violent usurper of another's rights ever restored the inheritance he had stolen?" he asks in frustration. "What public officer ever allowed a poor debtor to go free without paying interest on his loan? What debtor ever acted in good faith to guarantee the rights of the heirs of his creditor?" It is from this vantage point of disappointment and impotence that Damian describes the world. "Everything in the world is confused, and all the decrees of religion and faith are brought to naught," his diatribe begins. "Justice is sold," "laws are subject to corruption," "money to be sure has influence on the laws," "avarice, the root of all evil, becomes ever more pervasive": these are the realities Damian focuses on as he tries to understand his failures.[230]

His indulgence in self-pity is short-lived, though, and soon he is back on message. It is not his assigned task, or any monk's, to convert by preaching. "How can we be so bold as to rudely involve ourselves in the office of preaching, which was never delegated to us?" he queries.[231] Monks must fulfill the function proper to their own life, not

227. Letter 165.66, in L, 7:211–12; B, 4:214.
228. Letter 165.73, in L, 7:216; B, 4:218.
229. Letter 165.75, in L, 7:217; B, 4:219.
230. Letter 165.77, in L, 7:218–19; B, 4:221.
231. Letter 165.79, in L, 7:220; B, 4:222.

that of others. "You should judge it unnecessary to involve yourself in fruitless labor" and concentrate on being a good monk. "When people come, one should give them salutary advice, but at no one's urging should you lightly put aside the treasure of your own life of solitude." Let imperial assemblies and papal bulls come and go. The good monk will "show his respect ... but hold himself aloof," saying, "Let it suffice for me constantly to weep for my sins, let it be enough for me to demonstrate that I am dead to this world."[232] Damian's own failures make this advice urgent and personal. His pain is obvious.

> Monks, I beg you, do not rush into the courts of kings under the guise of ecclesiastical concern; do not disturb princes in audience with them, as if you were carefully using the occasion to advise them on their spiritual welfare. Believe one who has experience in these matters, believe one who has grown weary in zealous pursuit of these goals. I have often spoken with his majesty the emperor, telling him what I thought should be said, and at papal invitation I have participated in councils. But one who pursues these matters in our own day, seems to be planting seeds on a sandy beach.[233]

Damian is particularly exasperated by bishops who when challenged "would become furious, promptly they would attack and insult us" and declare that they, not Damian or his reform colleagues, "came to this council to decide on this matter."[234] Even years later Damian's anger at this "novel presumption" that the hierarchy is not subject to criticism is evident: "At one time I replied to them, Venerable fathers and lords, just as it is your special prerogative to judge, so also is it allowed lesser members of the Church to speak their mind in the council, nor does any canonical authority forbid younger men to propose what they think is for the well-being of the Church."[235] Still, his failures haunt him. He wants his example to save others from similar frustration: "I have briefly brought up these matters, so that one without this experience might learn from me how much

232. Letter 165.80, in L, 7:220–21; B, 4:223.
233. Letter 165.81, in L, 7:221; B, 4:223.
234. Letter 165.82, in L, 7:221; B, 4:224.
235. Letter 165.83, in L, 7:221–22; B, 4:224.

it behooves him carefully to avoid such affairs." His life bears witness to the power of one's life to guide others, be it to imitate or to avoid. "From one who has preceded him, one may learn whether he can trust the unknown waters of some subsequent enterprise," Damian teaches. "And so, it should suffice that I have tried to do these things, not for me alone but for all my brothers, that when one's effort proves to have been useless, it should serve as a warning, not just to one individual but to many."[236]

His last lecture concentrates on end times and for the need to be "preparing for the advent of the Antichrist."[237] He feels his age, projecting his individual plight onto all. Everyone "has become feeble with age" and "men now grow old in their youth."[238] I have referred a few times to Damian's lack of grace in growing old. As early as 1058 he was complaining that "my eyes grow dim … clouded by mucus. Wrinkles are appearing and my gums give signs of the ruin of my teeth. My head … sprinkled with grey hair now grows snowy white. My voice becomes hoarse and my strength is failing."[239] These types of remarks are plentiful. Taken together they paint an unflattering picture of a man preoccupied with the physical process of aging. "I was already experiencing the infirmities of old age, and," he reports at age fifty-seven, "I had begun to totter with uncertain steps." Still, in this condition he was able to journey over the Alps to Cluny, indicating exaggeration—or extreme determination.[240] In 1064 he declined to visit Monte Cassino "for my advanced years make it likely that my death is imminent."[241] He even reports the increasing loss of libido through the aging process. "I who am already an old man can licitly and securely look at the face of an old woman lined with wrinkles," he confesses. Still, all sexual appetite is not gone, so "like boys from the fire I guard my eyes at the sight of more beautiful and

236. Letter 165.84, in L, 7:222; B, 4:224–25.

237. Letter 165.85, in L, 7:222; B, 4:225.

238. Letter 165.89, in L, 7:225; B, 4:228.

239. Letter 57.18, in L, 2:379–80; B, 2:178.

240. Letter 103.3, in L, 5:143; B, 3:139. He brags about this feat in Letter 113.13, in L, 5:291; B, 3:295.

241. Letter 106.2, in L, 5:175; B, 3:169.

attractive faces."[242] He complains to his older brother Damianus that "my unhappy spirit" is "afflicted with sorrow as I carefully watch the day of my death coming ever closer, and appearing before my eyes as if it were present." He notices his hair "turning white" and is disconcerted when he sees "that in whatever group of people I find myself, almost all are younger than I am." Only after his physical death fills him with fear is he reminded of the fear of divine judgment for that life, a sequence I find surprising, given his verbose eschatological pronouncements. It reveals, I think, a rather human side of him: "Nor is my unhappy spirit satisfied with this dread sight alone, fixing the limits of its attention on the death of the body, but is soon hauled before the judge, there to muse, and not without great trepidation, over what can be held against it."[243] He continues, fretting about men who "are daily snatched away prematurely by death," but then he puts aside his fears by recalling that as God "has called us from afar ... he strengthens us" so we can "confidently approach the throne of glory."[244] He concludes with a reminder about the monk's goal: "Let us occupy all our senses in seeking after this life-giving banquet, so that in becoming insensible to all worldly affairs, as truly dead to the world we may live for God alone." The monk is then ready "to hear these words from the mouth of Truth itself ... 'You shall eat and drink at my table in my kingdom.'"[245]

242. Letter 143.2, in L, 6:143; B, 3:522.
243. Letter 138.2, in L, 6:97; B, 3:473. Damian is complaining to a brother older than he.
244. Letter 165.90–91, in L, 7:225–26; B, 4:228.
245. Letter 165.93, in L, 7:227; B, 4:230.

Six

REFLECTIONS ON SECULAR SOCIETY

The Exercise of Authority

When Damian first articulated his concern for stewardship in Letter 2, he did so while lecturing margrave Boniface of Tuscany on the nature of his authority. God, not humans, "committed so many thousands of people to your rule, placed the necks of your enemies under your feet, and so gloriously [has] distinguished you above all other powerful men in the kingdom," Damian tells him, so Boniface must remember that "if you are zealous in keeping his commandments he will advance you through earthly goods to those of heaven."[1] This is Damian's starting point. Secular authority, although temporary, is good, a gift from God, but one that comes with responsibilities. Throughout his long career, when secular leaders fail to live up to these obligations Damian does not hesitate to chastise them. When Duke Godfrey of Tuscany "neglect[s] this principality in which almost 100,000 people live," Damian is relentless and "repeat[s] in my letter what I have often said to you in person," that "you owe an accounting to the severe judge for all over whom you preside by reason of your authority." Here his advice is practical:

1. Letter 2.2, in L, 1:84–85; B, 1:103.

delegate. "What you are unable to carry on your own shoulders, you will be strong enough to bear by employing another to whom you have given the task."[2]

More advice follows: "When the sternness of justice is weakened, the rule of law is destroyed," so Godfrey must remember to "always take steps to safeguard justice in dealing with the people committed to your charge."[3] Godfrey has this power over people not because of his own actions, but because it is his specific function in the Body of Christ. "All the members of the Church are not assigned the same office, for one duty is proper to a priest, another to a judge," Damian explains, and "the prince's sword is quite different from priestly symbols of dignity." It is the prince's task as "God's agent [*Dei minister*]" to use the sword when needed or else "the sword will surely grow rusty." If Godfrey were to neglect his secular duties "and spend the greater part of the day attending masses and saying prayers," he would become "the agent of the adversary, the devil."[4] Furthermore, society will "be thrown into turmoil unless human affairs [are] remedied by a return to equity and justice." To strengthen his argument Damian tells Godfrey the story of Emperor Theodosius whose failure to enforce the law rendered society chaotic, until he finally began "to put fear into the hearts of evildoers by using the power of his imperial authority and to restore general peace. And thus the world, which through his inactivity had begun to fall apart, was revived through the rule of equity and justice."[5] When Godfrey does not change, Damian writes him again with the same message. Even though Godfrey is "outstanding among your peers by reason of decency of an upright life," he must fulfill his specific role in the community, "the strict application of justice" and not the functions of others.[6] "Let evil men see in you a prince, and not deride you as a priest," Damian scolds.[7] "It is required of you ... to enforce jus-

2. Letter 67.4, in L, 3:71; B, 2:281–82.

3. Letter 67.5, ibid.; and Letter 67.21, in L, 3:78; B, 2:289.

4. Letter 67.7, in L, 3:72–73; B, 2:283.

5. Letter 67.14, 18, in L, 3:76–77; B, 2:286, 288.

6. Letter 68.2, in L, 3:79; B, 2:290.

7. Letter 68.20, in L, 3:87; B, 2:297.

tice and to oppose with the force of legitimate authority those who are about to act unlawfully."[8] If Godfrey does not know how, "use as models the lives of others who checked the evil deeds of men by enforcing justice."[9]

Given secular authority's origin in God, its intimate relationship with ecclesiastical authority follows. As early as April 1047 Damian endorsed the exercise of secular authority in the ecclesiastical world; Emperor Henry III commissioned him "not once but frequently" to chasten the pope for not using his own "keen-edged sword" to "re-establish downtrodden and degraded justice."[10] This is how it should be. The reverse is also true. Damian is ever insistent that the task of each member of the Body of Christ be acknowledged and protected. "Since within the *imperium* and the *sacerdotium* we must distinguish functions that are proper to each," Damian points out in a letter to Bishop Oldericus of Fermo in 1062, "how indecently confusing it would be" for the *sacerdotium* to perform the tasks of the *imperium*.[11] Both authorities must respect their differences while still pursuing the same heavenly goal. Both should likewise remember that because of this intimate relationship, what affects one affects the other. "Be careful," Damian warns Henry IV, "lest while allowing the *sacerdotium* to be divided, your empire too, which God forbid, should be divided."[12] The goal of each branch of authority, he tells Duchess Adelaine of Turin, can only be achieved if with "mutual efforts" each will "join forces against the devil."[13] In 1063 he praises Archbishop Anno of Cologne for using his sacerdotal authority to safeguard the imperial power of the young Henry IV: "He was aware that each dignity is in need of the services of the other; that while the priesthood is protected by the defenses of the realm, the latter is supported by the sanctity of the priestly office [*Sciebat enim, quoniam utraque dignitas alternae invicem utilitatis est indiga, dum et sacerdotium regni tuitione*

8. Letter 68.4, in L, 3:80; B, 2:290–91.

9. Letter 68.20, in L, 3:87; B, 2:297.

10. Letter 26, in L, 1:244–46; B, 1:240–42.

11. Letter 87.9–10, in L, 3:305; B, 2:511.

12. Letter 120.8, in L, 5:390; B, 3:387.

13. Letter 114.2–3, in L, 5:295; B, 3:297.

protegitur, et regnum sacerdotalis officii sanctitate fulcitur]."[14] Because of Anno's efforts "the Empire and the Church enjoy through your good offices the peace we all desire," so Damian prays that "the Author of both authorities" may grant him "eternal peace."[15]

Perhaps Damian's clearest declaration on the relationship of the two types of authority and their corresponding duties is written to the Emperor Henry IV.

> And as both dignities, namely, the royal and the sacerdotal, are primarily joined to one another in Christ by the reality of a unique mystery, so are they united in the Christian people by a kind of mutual agreement. Each, in truth, needs the other for what he there finds useful [*utilitatis*] since the *sacerdotium* is protected by the defensive capability of the empire, and royal power is supported by the holiness of the priestly office. The king wears a sword, that so armed he may confront the enemies of the Church; the priest engages in watchful prayer, that he may appease God for the benefit of the king and his people. The former, using the scales of justice, is required to compose earthly affairs; the latter must provide for the thirsty a stream of heavenly eloquence. The former is established that he might compel evildoers and criminals by using the severity of legal sanctions; the latter is ordained to apply the keys of the Church that he has received, in binding some with the zeal of canonical vigor, while loosing others with the tenderness of ecclesiastical devotion.[16]

On one occasion Damian praises Cencius, the prefect of Rome, for combining the two types of authority in his own person; when Damian lost his voice in the middle of a sermon, Cencius finished it for him. "You, especially, obviously imitate the example of this priest and king [Christ] when on the bench you hand down legitimate decisions at law," Damian says, and "in the Church lift up the minds of people assembled there."[17] Damian does, nevertheless, advocate the superiority of papal authority over imperial. Surprisingly, he bases his conclusion on logistics, not theology. In a letter to Pope Alexander II, Damian diplomatically emphasizes "that while a pope

14. Letter 99.3, in L, 5:104; B, 3:99.
15. Letter 99.6, in L, 5:106; B, 3:100.
16. Letter 120.11, in L, 5:392–93; B, 3:389.
17. Letter 145.3, in L, 6:151; B, 3:528–29.

presides over the whole world, the earthly authority of most kings is limited.... Thus, when a king dies, only the kingdom which he heads is deprived of his leadership, but when the pontiff of the Apostolic See passes away, the whole world is orphaned by the loss of its common father."[18]

Damian's correspondence with secular leaders was considerable. Twenty-nine letters are addressed to nobles, three more to judges, and one to a lawyer.[19] In 1042 he asks margrave Boniface to use his secular authority to perform "your extensive and long-lasting stewardship" and to "protect the monasteries that lie in your area."[20] Letters written after mid-century reiterate these concerns. Four ask members of the nobility to protect ecclesiastical interests, two lecture on the need to secure secular goals, and six remind the nobles to do both.[21] Damian's overarching concern for both secular and ecclesiastical authority is the same: justice—with compassion. He realizes this is not an easy task. He thanks Anne, queen of France, for influencing her husband, Henry I, "to govern with equity and compassion," but he warns Godfrey, "do not be over-compassionate."[22] The line between the two is fine, and rulers must realize that the latter jeopardizes the entire community as much as the former. Both lead to "complete disorder for his people" and the leader himself.[23] This rule applies to all authority, secular and religious; Damian cites John the Deacon's dictum: "He who fails to correct when it is possible for him to do so, makes himself guilty of the other's fault."[24] This reality reinforces the importance of secular authority in Christian society, for the lay ruler's specific role is enforcement. "What is more holy,

18. Letter 108.4, in L, 5:197; B, 3:190.

19. Letters to noblewomen: 51, 64, 66, 71, 104, 114, 134, 130, 143, 144, 149. Letters to men: 1, 2, 15, 17, 20, 43, 67, 68, 83, 85, 120, 135, 145, 148, 151, 153, 179. Letters 21, 23, and 170 are to judges, and Letter 25 is to a lawyer. See appendix 2.

20. Letter 2.2 and 4, in L, 1:85; B, 1:103–4.

21. Letters 43, 83, 114, and 154 are concerned with protecting ecclesiastical interests; Letters 143, 155 with secular interests; and Letters 51, 64, 67, 68, 120, and 145 with both.

22. Letter 64.2, in L, 3:22; B, 2:226; and Letter 68.3, in L, 3:80; B, 2:290.

23. Letter 67.12, in L, 3:75; B, 2:285.

24. Letter 61.9, in L, 3:8; B, 2:212, See also Letter 120.7, in L, 5:390; B, 3:283.

more pleasing to God, or more preeminent in Christian living than to enforce justice and to oppose with the force of legitimate authority those who are about to act unlawfully?" Damian asks. "The people who are your subjects [are] kept for harm through the maintenance of a just regime," so rulers must prioritize their tasks accordingly.[25] A ruler, Damian informs Henry IV, "is required to compose earthly affairs ... by using the severity of legal sanctions," and then cites Romans 13:4: "It is not for nothing that he has the power of the sword."[26]

He cited the same verse to Godfrey, adding that "from these words you should understand that the prince's sword is quite different from priestly symbols of dignity. You do not buckle on your sword to stroke or caress the evil deeds of violent men, but to prepare to cut them down."[27] Laws must be enforced with regularity, for if the sword "is always left in the scabbard and is never bared to inflict vengeance," it is useless. Judges join rulers in this responsibility; "the former clearly carries a sword that he may unsheath it to punish those who live to flaunt justice."[28] By fulfilling these secular tasks, rulers and judges contribute to the building of a peaceful physical community which in turn strengthens the spiritual community. "There can be little doubt that he who takes pains to build the physical structure of a church," Damian tells a senator, "has a part in erecting this spiritual temple."[29] A ruler must remember that secular duties supersede personal piety; his own salvation and the welfare of the community are dependent on the proper prioritizing. "Take care, lest out of devotion to your own prayer," Damian warns Cencius, "you neglect the governance of such an innumerable population entrusted to you, and disregard the general well-being of the common people, which expects justice from you."[30] Only the ruler "who did justice while he lived deserve[s] the very name of Justice after death."[31]

25. Letter 68.4, in L, 3:80; B, 2:291.
26. Letter 120.11, in L, 5:392–93; B, 3:389.
27. Letter 67.6, in L, 3:72; B, 2:282.
28. Letter 67.7, in L, 3:72–73; B, 2:283.
29. Letter 83.5, in L, 3:243; B, 2:450.
30. Letter 155.3, in L, 7:76; B, 4:72.
31. Letter 155.5, in L, 7:78; B, 4:73. In Letter 38.43, in L, 2:97; B, 1:372, Damian admits his preoccupation with justice, asking the addressee, Bishop Gislerius of Osimo, "to forgive the zeal for justice I displayed" and not to think it "a kind of arrogance."

Interestingly, Damian's most significant discourses on social responsibilities are written to or about female members of the nobility. In 1057 he writes to congratulate Duchess Beatrice on the decision made by her and her husband, Godfrey, to live in continence. The focus of the letter, however, is on the social duties of rulers. He acknowledges that "rarely this occurs," that a person "at the summit of earthly dignity … bring[s] forth a harvest of good works," but Beatrice has accomplished this.[32] The value of chastity rests in its ability to grant women more autonomous power. "Now you are free of that ancient curse in which it was said to the first woman, 'You will be in the power of your husband and he shall be your master.'"[33] He refers to Sarah and Abraham: "Notice that as a result of her chastity, she to whom Abraham had previously given orders he was now commanded to obey, so that now he was to listen to her in everything."[34] She must provide the model, much as *Historia ecclesiastica tripartita* tells us Empress Galla did.

> "She showed special regard for the lame and infirm," it says, "not employing slaves or other servants, but doing so herself, going to their homes and serving each as he had need." And then it continues, "So, too, going through the hospitals belonging to the churches, she waited on the sick, with her own hands cleaning their pots, tasting the soup, handing them spoons, breaking their bread and serving them food, diluting their wine with water, and performing all the other duties regularly taken care of by slaves and servants." … But if perhaps some flatterer were present, and in the interest of royal dignity, would tell her to desist from her zealous service, she would say, "It is the duty of empire to distribute gold; but on my part, I perform this service in the name of the empire which has bestowed all good things on me." Nor was she satisfied to stand alone in performing these hospitable deeds, but also urged her husband the emperor to engage in the same acts of devotion. … This woman set an example which her husband might imitate and offered him words of holy advice.[35]

32. Letter 51.2, in L, 2:335; B, 2:132–33.
33. Letter 51.3, in L, 2:336; B, 2:133.
34. Letter 51.4, ibid.
35. Letter 51.6, in L, 2:337–38; B, 2:134–35. Damian is quoting Cassidorus, *Historia tripartita,* 9.31.546–47.

After more *exempla* about marchioness Guilla of Tuscany and Helena, mother of Constantine, Damian tells Beatrice to "walk in the footsteps of holy princesses, take as your model their way of life, that by keeping them in mind you may learn what you should accept and what you should avoid."[36]

Damian has deep respect for noble women, believing that God "uses women to achieve a more glorious triumph."[37] Duchess Adelaine of Turin, a ruler of extensive lands in northern Italy and Burgundy who governs them "without a man's help," sees her power as unexceptional, because all authority comes from God. "Why should one wonder, father," she asks Damian, "that God saw fit to grant me, his unworthy servant, some small degree of power over men?"[38] Thus Damian writes to "encourage you to join with the lord bishop, so that through your mutual efforts" they may reform the local clergy. He admits that it may "seem improper that I should write especially to you on the incontinence of clerics," but he does so because "I felt that you possessed adequate means to correct the situation." She has the means because her application of justice throughout her lands has earned her the respect of all: "Those who wish to settle their disputes flock to you for your legal decision."[39] Her reputation among church leaders is stellar; when "I was speaking with many bishops and heads of monasteries, there was not one of them who complained of having suffered any inconvenience from you." Nor could Damian himself see any injustices when he stayed "in the monastery of Fruttuaria, where I was a guest for almost ten days [and] I could see good evidence of your humane and agreeable treatment of the churches."[40] She needs only to continue in this way. "Never abandon the practice of generosity and justice," he ends, "and thus, let your every legal decision promote the glory of almighty God, that when you have finished your stewardship" heaven will await.[41]

36. Letter 51.9, in L, 2:340; B, 2:137.

37. Letter 114.8, in L, 5:297–98; B, 3:299.

38. Letter 114.4, in L, 5:296; B, 3:298.

39. Letter 114.2–3, in L, 5:295; B, 3:296–97. He adds, "as a woman you are as strong as a man."

40. Letter 114.11, in L, 5:300; B, 3:301–2.

41. Letter 114.18, in L, 5:304; B, 3:305–6.

When he writes Countess Guilla, wife of marquis Rainerius II of Monte S. Maria (before 1067), his concern is not clerical reform but secular. Guilla comes to her power not through inheritance as Adelaine had, but through marriage. Unfortunately, the house she married into "is morally deficient." Damian's mandate to her is challenging: "Break the pattern of customary evil that you have found, abolish the practice of confiscating the property of the poor, prevent unjust taxes and impositions on the serfs, and following the example of King Josiah establish a new order of affairs."[42] His concerns focus solely on social justice. "In imitation of this holy king, you too must destroy the practices of long-standing disorder, and introduce a new regime of wholesome and blameless deeds."[43] In particular she must overthrow avarice, the cause of so much injustice. "Do not live by plundering the poor, but recoil from food acquired through violence," Damian lectures. He offers a practical solution: labor. "And since the Apostle commands everyone to work with his own hands 'so that he may have something to share with the needy' you should intensify your farming, and thus your barns will be filled with abundant crops to be used in assisting the poor." Hilary of Arles should be her model, for even though he was an educated nobleman, "because of his great compassion" he "helped the needy ... by working as a farmer."[44] Not only is Adelaine responsible for her own actions, "but I must further add that you should make restitution upon discovering things that have been stolen before your coming here."[45] He anticipates objections. His answer is based on an unbending principle: morality is blind to gender.

> But perhaps you will reply to all this, that unless your husband take the lead in these matters, a weak instrument such as you can hardly hope to

42. Letter 143.4, in L, 6:143–44; B, 3:522.

43. Letter 143.5, in L, 6:144; B, 3:522. This is also evident in Damian's last dated letter (1070), to Judge Moricus. Here he says to someone whose life's focus was the safeguarding of justice that the only way you "rescue your soul [is] by almsgiving and be[ing] constant in performing the works of mercy." Letter 170.9, in L, 7:250; B, 4:253.

44. Letter 143.8, in L, 6:145–46; B, 3:524.

45. Letter 143.9, in L, 6:146; B, 3:524.

succeed. Nor will I disagree with what you say, for since by God's will a wife's dedication is to her husband, the weaker sex usually needs the authority of a man [*Verum plane nec diffitemur, quia cum ad virum mulieris sit divinitus decreta conversio, indiget plerumque sexus infirmior auctoritatis virili*]. But when a wife's opinion is more correct, it is proper that a husband not stand in her way by using his authority.... Besides, if a husband were never to follow the advice of his wife, the Lord would not have said to Abraham, "Pay heed to everything that Sarah has to say to you."[46]

Such advice is consistent with Damian's long-standing principles. In April 1051 he argued that in God's judgment "the same law applies both to men and to women."[47] He remained faithful to that belief; in his last dated letter (1070) he included an *exempla* concerning God's harsh judgment of men who swore falsely against two women in court.[48] Most importantly, throughout his entire life Damian maintained that women are spiritually equal to men, and therefore have the same spiritual obligations. Since the spiritual realm is superior to the secular, spiritual authority transcends secular authority. Damian accepts the inferior position of women in secular arrangements, but he is reminding Guilla that this inferiority does not apply to matters of the spirit. The superiority of spiritual claims require that she proceed to enforce them in the secular realm, no matter how difficult it be. "Therefore, as far as possible, you should not delay returning whatever was acquired through injustice," he concludes. "Reform the manners of your house, suppress violence and violations of the peace, and through discipline curb the administration of your estate that has gone unchecked." If Guilla rules with justice then "after your brief stewardship has run its course, you may be worthy to pass to the reward of your eternal inheritance."[49]

We also get a fair idea of Damian's thoughts on social justice in two of his three letters to prefect Cencius. Besides what has already

46. Letter 143.10, in L, 6:146–47; B, 3:524–25.
47. Letter 38.34, in L, 2:91; B, 1:366.
48. Letter 170.6–7, in L, 7:249–50; B, 4:251–52.
49. Letter 143.11, in L, 6:147; B, 3:525.

been discussed, Damian also justifies Cencius's preaching based on the scriptural concept of the priesthood of believers [1 Pt 2:9: "You are a chosen race, a royal priesthood"]. "Can there be any doubt that you were following the example of [Christ]?" Damian ask. Thus, with prescient wisdom Damian advocates a theological concept that was only fully developed centuries later by Luther. When doing so, he takes the opportunity once again to preach on the importance of witness, this time, the witness of the priesthood of believers.

> It follows, therefore, that by the grace of Christ every Christian is a priest, and hence has a perfect right to proclaim his wondrous deeds [*Constat ergo quemlibet Christianum esse per Christi gratiam sacerdotem, unde non inmerito debet eius annunciare virtutem*]. . . . Now there are two things most necessary for the proficient preacher, first, that he abound in spiritual thought, and second, that he be preeminent for his virtuous life. But if any priest is deficient in either quality, namely, outstanding for his way of living, and eloquent in his teaching, one's life is undoubtedly more important than one's teaching. The fruit of good works is sweeter than the bare leaves of one's words, and renown for virtue is a more powerful example than eloquence or urbane and elegant speech.[50]

Those who do not possess the gift of eloquence consequently need not worry; "every simple priest of upright life, who even though deficient in the richness of speech, by his outstanding deeds stills shines, as it were, with the brilliance of his exemplary life, and those whom he fails to teach by his words, he inspires by the example of his intense spirituality."[51] Damian wants Cencius to contemplate the implications of this truism. After reminding Cencius of the two different duties of a priest, as shown in the example of Moses and Aaron, Damian asks him: "For as you control the people by virtue of your jurisdiction as prefect of the city, and by reason of your judicial power, what else are you doing but fulfilling the office that Aaron held? And when by holy exhortation you call upon the same

50. Letter 145.3–4, in L, 6:152; B, 3:528–29. It is only at Vatican Council II that this concept is fully developed and promoted by the Roman Church.

51. Letter 145.5, in L, 6:152; B, 3:529.

people … what is that but loyally carrying out the spiritual design of Moses? So, well done, my energetic man; continue functioning like two men in the field of the Lord!" The Christian leader fulfills his role in the Body of Christ "at times by composing a case in court by justly weighing the evidence" and at other times by "using words of saving exhortation in the church." In short, Cencius should "follow in the footsteps of Moses in matters that pertain to God, and again over issues that are of secular concern, act in the role of Aaron."[52] People should "see in you the two-edged sword," a person who will "fight implacably to defend the holdings of the churches, punish the violent oppressors of the poor, hold the line of justice and equity, and constantly dedicate your whole being, not to family affairs, but to the welfare of the city." If Cencius seeks justice for both and his life bears witness to this search, then he will be honored as "the father of your country" and the Church's "worldly defender."[53]

The Laity

Appreciation for the laity's role in the Body of Christ is well documented in Damian's early letters. That appreciation guides his theology throughout his life. His first and last dated letters are to laymen. Not once do we hear a note of condescension in his correspondence with them. Always he treats them as his equals before God. As spiritual equals the laity have a right and an obligation to judge the clergy; I have cited many instances of Damian's defense of lay criticism.[54] This means that the laity could also draw conclusions from their judgments and act accordingly; when "members of a parish are given good reason to withhold obedience to their parish churches by not paying them their legal tithes," Damian condones such action.[55] His respect is not limited to lay leaders. He understands why, "given the circumstances," the laity in Milan turned into any "furious crowd" during the Patarine conflict.[56] He listens to the objections

52. Letter 145.7, in L, 6:153; B, 3:530–31.
53. Letter 145.8, in L, 6:154; B, 3:531.
54. See above, ch. 2, and Letter 17.
55. Letter 74.7, in L, 3:155; B, 2:374.
56. Letter 65.4, in L, 3:26; B, 2:232.

Florentine citizens have about their bishop.[57] His respect for the laity is shown in his concern for "various needy folk" in parishes and in the spiritual counseling he offers his siblings and relatives.[58] He gushes with admiration for Gerard di Faroaldo who, during a famine in Ravenna, "cut his crops and even sold some of his property to provide food for as many people as possible."[59] He congratulates the people of Faenza for peacefully agreeing "to follow unanimously what together you determined to do."[60] When Damian came to the conclusion in *Dominus vobiscum* that "the Church of Christ is so joined together by the bond of love, and in each it is mystically complete," he was not making an abstract statement.[61] He firmly believed that "whatever is fitting for the whole, is in some way fitting for each part."[62] He emphasized this repeatedly: "Whatever function is assigned by nature to a particular member can be said to be performed by the body which is its whole ... that the part functions for the whole and the whole for its parts."[63] He was stating what he believed and lived. He considered it his vocation to teach others of this reality. Whether people be lay or cleric mattered not, only if they be good or evil.

That he offers spiritual guidance to the laity is in itself something to note.[64] Before mid-century Damian had established this inclusive principle, that the laity were quite capable of living a deep spiritual life; four of the thirty-seven letters from this period are concerned with lay spirituality.[65] His letter to a Ravenna nobleman is the earliest example of his lay spiritual guidance. He reminds the judge that the Office "should be performed by all Christian faithful as a daily task," not just by religious.[66] He must "never allow yourself to forget these offices instituted by the Church." The command

57. Letter 146.

58. Letter 74.2, in L, 3:152; B, 2:374. See Letters 93, 94, 123, 132, 138, and 158.

59. Letter 110.24, in L, 5:240; B, 3:237.

60. Letter 147.3, in L, 6:168; B, 3:544.

61. Letter 28.11, in L, 1:262; B, 1:255.

62. Letter 28.15, in L, 1:263; B, 1:256–57.

63. Letter 28.22, in L, 1:268; B, 1:260.

64. See my *A Woman's Way*.

65. Letters 15, 17, 21, and 23.

66. Letter 17.2, in L, 1:145; B, 1:156. One has to wait until modern lay institutes are founded to see the Office promoted for the laity in any seriously concerted way in the Roman Church.

is the same for everyone: "If there are psalms to say, say them."[67] He advises Beatrice of Tuscany to do as he does, "always emulate such noble deeds" as those of St. Helena. Born an innkeeper's daughter, Helena overcame class and gender limitations and "was able to do ... what empresses descended from ancestors of the highest nobility could not achieve ... be inscribed in the register of saintly women."[68] For Damian, the essence of sanctity is universal and constant. It does not vary from one social or religious stratum to another, nor does his instruction to follow good example vary. "Hold up this predecessor of yours before you as a mirror, and use as models the lives of others who checked the evil deeds of men by enforcing justice," he advises Godrey.[69] "Be another Benjamin ... follow also in the footsteps of Judas Maccabaeus," he tells Cencius.[70]

Here is another reason why Damian places such emphasis on witness: imitation is the surest, most reliable way to achieve sanctity, and bearing witness shines a light on the model to be imitated. "For like a golden star you appeared to illuminate the darkness of those who pursued earthly goals," he tells Empress Agnes, "and by your shining example you restored light to those who followed you."[71] The variable in sanctity, then, is the model, that is, the way in which each person bears witness. As long as each model remains faithful to the message all models are equal. These principles nourish Damian's appreciation of lay sanctity and his recognition of the spiritual equality of all individuals in the community. In heaven, Damian counsels Countess Blanche, "none will differ from another in any way, but all will associate unanimously in a common exercise of will." In heaven all will see "how it is possible for [God] to observe the singular as if he were unconcerned about the universal, and how he beholds universals as if he took no notice of singular affairs."[72]

67. Letter 17.19, in L, 1:155; B, 1:164–65.
68. Letter 51.8–9, in L, 2:339–40; B, 2:136–37.
69. Letter 68.20, in L, 3:87; B, 2:297.
70. Letter 145.8, in L, 6:153–54; B, 3:531.
71. Letter 144.2, in L, 6:148; B, 3:278.
72. Letter 66.38–9, in L, 6:148; B, 3:526. Blanche may be fictitious. See B, 2:248–49.

While Damian writes at length throughout the years about the trials and tribulations of religious, he is quite cognizant of the challenges and hardships of the laity. One need only read once again his letter to the grieving parents Amelric and Ermilina to see how aware he was of the laity's difficulties.[73] We see his understanding of the complexities of lay situations also in a letter to another nobleman, Albert. "Perhaps you will say, 'My mother often exasperates me, disturbing me and my wife with her harsh words. We cannot bear such reproach and insult and will not tolerate her abuse and disgusting scolding.'" Such personality conflicts are the things of lay life, Damian counsels, and Albert must resolve them. "You will be more richly rewarded if, while suffering annoyance, you accept it with gratitude and, amid all her sarcastic censoring, you humbly reply with courtesy."[74] The reason why children must honor their parents is rooted in the nature of the relationship as much as in God's command. "Think for a moment how cruel it is to snub and despise those from whom you have your very being," Damian chides Albert. If one does reflect, then "with what great humility you should submit to those who gave you birth and to whom you are indebted for what you essentially are by nature. Since you cannot be in doubt of what you received from them as a boy, how much more should you repay them with gratitude now that they are older?"[75] There is another, less altruistic but very human reason why children must honor their parents; their witness is an example for the next generation: "It normally happens, moreover, according to the just plan of God, that he who is humbly subject to his parents will enjoy the obedience of his own children when he too becomes a parent."[76]

Given Damian's emphasis on the role social responsibilities play in the pursuit of sanctity, he naturally has much to say about marriage. The new type of marital bond that he advocates is already well developed in his early writings. We saw the emphasis Damian places on Romuald's rejection of society's time-honored tradition of set-

73. See Letter 15.

74. Letter 85.6, in L, 3:252; B, 2:457.

75. Letter 85.5, ibid.

76. Letter 85.3, in L, 3:250–51; B, 2:456.

tling disputes through bloodshed.[77] Damian continues Romuald's campaign against blood feuds by redefining the marital bonds that held early medieval kinship groups together. Letters 19 and 36 are devoted to defeating an attempt to intensify the power of the kinship group by narrowing permissible degrees of consanguinity in marriage. When visiting Ravenna in 1044 he learned of "a great dispute over the degrees of consanguinity" taking place at the law school there, because "at the request of courtiers from the people of Florence" they debated whether marriage "might now legally be contracted by counting four degrees on one descending line and three in the other," the combination thus meeting the canonical requirement of seven degrees.[78] Damian sees right through this blatant attempt to manipulate numbers in order to increase the power of the kinship group at a time when social forces were working against it.[79] Whereas Romuald's entrance into San Apollinare bore witness to his demand for social change, Damian's witness is written as well as lived. "I argued verbally with those who were pontificating in these matters," Damian confides, but two bishops pursued him to also "set down in writing what I had orally stated."[80] He tolerates no numerical manipulation. "You should not say that four generations on this side and four on that make eight generations, but rather that these persons are related to one another in the fourth degree."[81] In typical rhetorical style he defends his "undue extension of remarks," because he considers the issue to be highly significant: "I judge it imperative to write these things so that the cancer which daily grows larger as it creeps along may not spread its contagion through the vitals of the Church."[82]

Damian ends this letter by stating that his motive in the debate

77. VR, 1 (173).

78. Letter 19.2, in L, 1:171–72; B, 1:180–81.

79. See Giovanni Miccoli, "La storia religiosa," *Storia d'Italia* 2.1 (1974), 472–507.

80. Letter 19.2, in L, 1:172; B, 1:181.

81. Letter 19.22, in L, 1:186; B, 1:193. He argues in this first letter that the first person does not count as the first generation, but he questions this opinion in Letter 36.

82. Letter 19.31, in L, 1:192; B, 1:198.

was concern for the community's future.[83] As Becker observes, when Damian argues "in favor of more severe medieval consanguinity provisions, he was working in fact to enhance prospects of sociability among humankind."[84] Damian wants marriage to conform to his model of relationships promoted in *Dominus vobiscum* and to leave tribal models behind. His life's crusade against ecclesiastical concubinage is consistent with this goal. Emphasis on the physical aspects of a union reinforces the archaic model; Damian wants abstract, sacramental elements to define a new model. In one of his letters to Cencius he cites Sirach 26:1–2 ("a good wife makes a happy husband ... a staunch wife is her husband's joy") and then discusses the two lives, "the spiritual and the physical ... the former lifts up one's spirit and holds it aloft with a longing for heaven, the latter burdens it with worldly affairs." Yet Abishag, a Shunammite woman, was good for King David. "Inquire of Solomon and he will explain to you the mystery of this girl: 'Acquire wisdom,' he says, 'and gain understanding.'" This is the image of marriage Damian promotes. Marriage is a physical state, but he believes it is also capable of spiritual realities. His belief in the potential of marriage to include the abstract leads him to continue the metaphor: "Let us, therefore, embrace wisdom, that is, a life of holiness, as our wife, that we might beget noble offspring, worthy of our inheritance."[85]

His letters to Countess Blanche and Empress Agnes give us further insight into Damian's view of marriage. After the death of her husband, Blanche entered a monastery, and Damian writes a letter of direction filled with marital metaphors. The kind of marriage Damian builds his metaphor on is one "cleansed of all the filth of passion [*passionum squaloribus*]." Too often Damian's rhetoric gets in the way of balanced interpretation and leads us away from the context of his remarks. If we place the comment in the context of Damian's efforts to expand society's expectations of marriage beyond

83. Letter 19.32, in L, 1:193; B, 1:199.
84. Becker, *Medieval Italy,* 185, n. 23.
85. Letter 135.2–4, in L, 6:78–79; B, 3: 457–58.

the physical to the sacramental, however, then his attack on passion makes sense.[86]

> As the body becomes spiritual, it will be in harmony with the soul, and the whole man will in no way disagree with the will of its creator. Then will the words of the bridegroom be fulfilled: "Come, my spouse, the time of pruning is at hand." For when a shoot is pruned, whatever is superflous is cut away, leaving behind only what is useful [*utile est*]. Consequently, all that the creator has made remains, while whatever the devil has added is taken away. There each one's secret will be laid bare before the eyes of all. There, with all hearts united by the bond of mutual love, none will differ from another in any way, but all will associate unanimously in a common exercise of will.[87]

In Damian's metaphor of divine union as marriage is his theology of human marriage. "Surely the holy soul is rightly called the loved one and the bride of Christ because it is joined to him by faith and love," Damian insists. "O how sweet this relationship and how unspeakable the joy that wells up in the heart of man when creator and creature take their delight in mutual love."[88]

In the first of six letters to Agnes, Damian's presupposition is the superiority of "the Spouse of heaven" to any earthly spouse, but this is not an attack on marriage. To the contrary, his use of the marital metaphor is a strong affirmation of the dignity of marriage. Damian views Agnes's earthly marriage to Henry III respectfully and agrees with her decision to enter a monastery for the very practical reason that no other human suitor is acceptable: "What, therefore, were you to do? Your husband had been emperor, he was the very peak of royal power ... and since nowhere on earth could you find a suitable husband, one who appealed to you [*qui tuis placeret oculis*], you violently rushed to embrace the Spouse of heaven."[89] Furthermore, he tells her that "I make these things known" so others will be edified and follow her example.[90] He wants these ideas on marriage to

86. Letter 19 (1046) and 36 (ca. 1050) predate Letter 66 (end 1059–Oct. 1060).

87. Letter 66.28, in L, 3:67; B, 2:278, including phrase "filth of passion."

88. Letter 66.5, in L, 3:44–45; B, 2:252–54.

89. Letter 104.13, in L, 5:152; B, 3:148.

90. Letter 104.16, in L, 1:153; B, 3:149.

disperse throughout society. He continues to praise her for her decision to marry Christ, but never at the cost of demeaning earthly marriage. Even the sexual act is elevated to an emotional level in his metaphor. He writes about "the intimate delight of your bridegroom, to that sweet union where two hearts are like one," where he will "pour the essence of divine love into your innermost being, and ignite the secret recesses of your heart."[91]

In those instances where Damian praises a spouse for renouncing sex, he carefully emphasizes that there are other elements in a marriage that should remain intact. This is his message to Beatrice when she and Godfrey agreed on mutual continence. She is to follow the example of Abraham and Sarah after she "purposed to live in chastity." Instead of diminishing the marriage, other nonphysical aspects of their relationship rose to the forefront. "As a result of her chastity" she had a new voice in the marriage, because Abraham no longer "controlled her as master." When three visitors unexpectedly arrived, Abraham "did not give orders to the slave girl Hagar, did not charge the servants." Rather, "he and his wife served the guests and did not decide to delegate this duty of graciousness." Together they "carried out the task of hospitality."[92] Together Amelric and Ermilina mourned their dead child; together Godfrey and Beatrice performed good works.[93] This oneness of heart is true for harmful behavior, too. Damian chastises a nobleman named Albert for misdirecting his affections for his wife: "Out of love of your wife you are despising and slighting your holy mother." Albert must correct this error and use his own love to restrain "your lovely wife from every offense to her mother-in-law."[94] Appreciation of the power of love in marriage is again seen in his correspondence with Queen Anne of France. It is "blessed love" that "render[s] your prudent husband

91. Letter 104.23, in L, 5:156–57; B, 3:152. This is consistent in medieval exegesis of Song of Songs, which, however, Damian rarely mentions. The exception is Song 1:12 (five times) and 4:11 (five times), both of which focus on fragrance.

92. Letter 51.4–5, in L, 2:336–37; B, 2:133–34.

93. See Letters 15 and 148.

94. Letter 85.4, 9, in L, 3:251, 254; B, 2:456, 458–59.

pleasing in the eyes of God." Marital love is demonstrated by "tender advice" and dual concern for "the purse that is their body" and "the gold of their soul therein contained."[95]

Damian adds another note in his letter to Anne, one about her children. We clearly hear Damian's own love for children in his remarks. "Because you merited to receive from God the gift of children, rear your noble offspring so that, from the very day you nursed them as babies, they may be fostered to love their creator," he encourages. Damian's appreciative attitude toward children and the parent-child relationship is evident in early letters. After the death of both of his parents while Damian was still young, two older siblings, Damianius and Rodelinda, became Damian's substitute parents; in the late 1060s Damian fondly recalls his visit with "my eldest sister of blessed memory, who had been a second mother to me."[96] Besides the obvious example of his personal grief at the death of a child he probably never met—"I was overcome with instant sorrow, and bitter pangs of compassion pierced my heart"—in *Dominus vobiscum* he discusses the role children play in salvific history; they are the benefactors of witness.[97] After retelling a story from Joshua 22:10–28, he tells us "why I have introduced this bit of history." It is so all will remember that "they meant their work to be a witness for their children."[98]

We have seen how Damian willingly undertook supervision of his nephews. "By reason of your tender years, which need another's help," Damian provided the necessary help to his nephew Marinus, "although you are not my son."[99] Sometimes we see Damian almost project actual parental claims, as when a nephew goes to France to study and Damian asks a bishop for his "compassion for the youth, namely, my sister's child, to provide for him from your paternal piety," and "look upon my image in this boy, observe the appearance of my countenance in this one."[100] He feels a particular duty toward his

95. Letter 64.2–3, in L, 3:22; B, 2:226.

96. Letter 149.14, in L, 6:178; B, 3:552; and Letter 138. John of Lodi's vita should be read with these letters in mind.

97. Letter 15.2, in L, 1:140; B, 1:151.

98. Letter 28.27, in L, 1:271; B, 1:263.

99. Letter 132.3, in L, 6:58; B, 3:439.

100. Letter 125.2, in L, 6:26; B, 3:412.

nephew Damianus and follows his vocation carefully. "I suffered it badly," he confesses to Damianus when he heard the youth's choice of monastery, because as uncle Damian is still monitoring his upbringing as he goes "forth from your home."[101] Damian has specific goals in mind: "I want the power of your prior and the discipline to check this aberration of indiscretion, with you left unharmed."[102] In another letter to Damianus, Damian shares with him a story that Empress Agnes "reported to me yesterday," about Otto I and Queen Adelaine's attempt to make their daughters marry against their will.[103] Damian's sympathy is obvious in the retelling, and not solely because the alternative the daughters chose was religious life. His concern is about both the royal couple's improper child-rearing and the natural hardships of puberty; Damian writes that "indeed there is no virtue that endures harsher struggles in the flower of adolescence than the one that ardent desire assails."[104] He extends his understanding of adolescence to novices. "Now that you are almost grown-up," he counsels, "put aside the toys of a nursing baby in all things."[105] Damian's sympathy is also evident in a metaphor comparing unreformed monks to bastards: "We are like an illegitimate child who rejoices that he is known by his father's name, while the degenerate nature of his origin holds him back, by law, from inheritance."[106] Another metaphor comparing the duties of a priest to that of a mother likewise reveals Damian's view of the parent-child relationship. The priest "must be the soul of compassion, fondling the Church's children like a forgiving mother, always gathering them to her breast and nourishing them with the richness of her teaching."[107]

101. Letter 158.6, in L, 7:90; B, 4:85.

102. Letter 158.5, in L, 7:89–90; B, 4:85.

103. Letter 123.3–4, in L, 6:13; B, 3:401–2. One daughter defeated the proposed marriage by hiding "two young chickens" under her clothes "until they had completely putrefied" and the stench drove suitors away.

104. Letter 123.3, in L, 6:12; B, 3:400. See Letter 153.74, in L, 7:57; B, 4:57.

105. Letter 153.72–73; in L, 7:56–57; B, 4:53. Damian has quite a lengthy discussion on the training of youthful novices here. See Letter 153.70–77; in L, 7:55–60; B, 4:51–56.

106. Letter 153.3, in L, 7:16; B, 4:14–15.

107. Letter 67.6, in L, 3:72; B, 2:282.

Because he so earnestly believes in the value of monastic life, however, he seems harsh when children encroach on that domain. In his letter to Blanche he constructs an imaginary speech by a devil wherein he tempts Blanche to leave the monastery to tend her child. In the temptation we see how well Damian understands the duties of a good mother and yet how eager he was to have them abandoned for what he considered to be a higher calling.

> "Go home," [the devil] says, "and still fulfill the purpose of your holy profession. Guide your family, live a life of virtue, observe a grave and modest regimen toward your son and others his age, afford your insecure son the example of a mother who does not flaunt the law, and do not let him fall back into the company of flatterers." Therefore, in fabricating these ideas, the evil spirit hardly worries over the ruse to draw you back into the world, so long as he is sure that by a secular life he will dominate your thinking.[108]

Leaving one's children for monasticism, however, is an ancient custom. Sources record the heartbreaking scene at the harbor as Paula (347–404) left her children to sail for the desert; Melanie the Elder's (342–ca. 409) scene of departure was hardly less dramatic.[109] Modern sensibilities may make us cringe a bit when faced with Damian's endorsement of the practice, particularly given his avant-garde vision in so many other areas.[110] Nevertheless, his attitude is consistent with monastic history and his principles. The distractions of caring for children should be minimized or eliminated when pursuing monastic life. Hence, he congratulates the Monte Cassino community when "I discovered in that fertile field ... that I did not find there schools for boys, which often weaken and dissipate the rigor of the religious life."[111] After telling a story about a fellow monk and

108. Letter 66.16, in L, 3:57–58; B, 2:266–67.

109. "Little Lexotius piteously stretched forth his hands from the shore. Rufina, a grown-up girl, by her tears silently besought her mother to stay," while Paula's "frame was wrung with anguish." Jerome, *The Pilgrimage of the Holy Paula,* tr. Aubrey Stewart (London: Palestine Pilgrims Text Society, 1887), 2. For Melanie the Elder and full discussion, see my *Women and Spiritual Equality,* 63 and 51–71.

110. One senses this in Blum's comments, L, 1:29.

111. Letter 119.84, in L, 5:385; B, 3:382.

his five-year-old son getting lost one night, Damian concludes that "everyone of us monks" must realize that because "boys are subject to the wiles of the malicious adversary," much patience is needed to deal with their pranks.[112]

Secular Studies

While Damian was happy not to find a boys' school within Monte Cassino, he was a strong proponent of education and spoke admiringly of the educated. The cathedral in Besançon is a "heavenly Athens"; "old Guarempatus, a most upright man [is] superbly educated in the arts and in medicine"; the nun Offa gave Bella "a splendid education"; and a monk from St. Vincent's monastery was "skilled in many arts and crafts, in writing and secretarial work."[113] He arranged for an abbot to be "both teacher and sustenance" for a nephew, "receiving him yet rude and untutored ... to return him to us later with the twins of the trivium and quadrivium as a wife."[114] In Damian's mediated agreement for Milan's clerical crisis "permission to function was returned ... only [to] those who were well educated," chaste, and upright.[115] Although he decries the married clergy of Turin he admits that they "are otherwise decent people and properly educated in the study of the arts."[116] Conversely, he speaks disparagingly of the uneducated who indulge in activities reserved for the educated. When three archpriests question "an opinion we expressed in a sermon," Damian's defense includes an ad hominem attack on "those who are rustics and untutored (or actually illiterate) [*rusticos et inperitos* (sic) *ac litterarum prorsus ignaros*]" and know "almost nothing but how to plough up fields."[117] The pontiff-elect, Gerard of Florence, whom Damian supported in 1058, is "well educated, a man of brisk intelligence," while his opponent cannot "explain fully for me—I will not say just one psalm, but even one line

112. Letter 119.88, in L, 5:386; B, 3:384.

113. Letter 111.2, in L, 5:248; B, 3:247; Letter 70.16, in L, 3:108; B, 2:318; Letter 83.10, in L, 3:245; B, 2:452; and Letter 142.29, in L, 6:139; B, 3:517.

114. Letter 125.2, in L, 6:26; B, 3:412.

115. Letter 65.25, in L, 3:38; B, 2:246.

116. Letter 112.2, in L, 5:259; B, 3:260.

117. Letter 121.2–3, in L, 6:3–4; B, 3:393.

of a homily."[118] Damian is highly insulted when "those who have barely learned how to run through the alphabet syllable by syllable are made judges over me."[119]

His attitude toward knowledge in general is grounded in a deep appreciation for the workings of the mind. Interestingly, many of his most astute observations are addressed to women. "The human mind by nature is not able to remain unoccupied by thoughts," he instructs his sister (probably Rodelinda). "It either exerts itself in serious matters or delights in the frivolous; and while thinking about useful things [*utilibus rebus*], it is protected from the invasion of attacking thoughts. Nor does depravity find an opportunity of whispering into its ear where the mind, intent on what is useful, keeps close counsel with sober thoughts." He believes that it is "highly useful [*utile*] to meditate on time," temporal and eternal.[120] "No small advantage accrues to our mind" by so occupying it. "And so, as the rational mind thinks through these matters, it comes to the notion that it too will not pass away with time, but will survive without end," he teaches. "Therefore, no little benefit derives from diligently analyzing these things." He then suggest to his sister that if she wants to follow up on the topic of time "you should read St. Augustine's work *On the City of God,* St. Jerome's *Explanation of the Prophet Daniel,* and also the *Apocalypse* with its commentaries, in which you will surely find sufficient discussion on this subject."[121] This is not devotional reading; it demands an educated reader with a keen mind. That this is recommended to a laywoman should be viewed alongside Damian's championing of the spiritual equality of women and men; he sees equality in the intellectual realm as well.

He discusses other theories on the psychology of the mind with Agnes. "If eyesight is of such importance even in dumb animals," he begins, "how much more certain it is that when human minds, endowed with reason, wish to distinguish what they perceive, they afterwards visualize in their imagination the images they acquired

118. Letter 58.5, in L, 2:392; B, 2:194.

119. Letter 121.9, in L, 6:8; B, 3:392.

120. Letter 93.2, in L, 5:27–28; B, 3:27.

121. Letter 93.3, in L, 5:28–29; B, 3:27–28.

from their outer senses. And even though, through deliberation, these impressions never propose what one should do, still, as they frequently intermingle with our thoughts, they at times cause them to depart from their purity."[122] This theory prefaces his main message, not to let images of past life distract one from present goals. "At the sight of secular things and worldly lifestyle the old conflict again erupts," so Damian rarely revisited "the house where I was born," and Agnes should follow his example.[123] That he defended his thesis with a theoretical explanation indicates that he believed Agnes would comprehend. Reasoned explanations are necessary in good spiritual guidance, because the mind is where spirituality is formed. When he writes "something for [his sister's] edification, I approach the innermost recesses of your mind," because the Holy Spirit's "special seat, nevertheless, is attributed to the mind, which presides over the subject body with a certain authority of direction."[124] He often speaks of his own spiritual life as centered in the mind: "I stand for questioning before the tribunal of my own mind and straightforwardly investigate myself with severe self-inspection."[125] Control of the mind is extremely difficult. It is always engaged. Lack of activity and silence challenge one's ability to direct thought properly or to defeat temptations. "I have certainly learned and have sufficiently—and more than sufficiently—experienced that the farther you retreat from the occupations of the world or from secular contacts, the more trouble you have struggling with the bothersome din of attacking thoughts," he confesses to his sisters.[126] Yet if this challenge is met, the rewards are eternal, "because when the human mind does not focus itself on outer worlds," he reminds Agnes, and "because when the human mind is everywhere encompassed by the cloisters of silence it is led up to the highest places of the air."[127]

122. Letter 149.13, in L, 6:177; B, 3:551.

123. Letter 149.14, in L, 6:178; B, 3:552. He went back once at night and once to visit his dying sister.

124. Letter 94.11, in L, 5:38; B, 3:35–36.

125. Letter 101.3, in L, 5:121; B, 3:116.

126. Letter 94.8, in L, 5:36; B, 3:34.

127. Letter 124.4, in L, 6:22–23; B, 3:408–9.

He repeats some of his theories to men. He seems particularly impressed by the fact that the mind is in perpetual motion. "The human mind is not able to remain entirely empty or unoccupied with love of something," he instructs Abbot Mainard of Pomposa.[128] The discourse on the psychology of the mind found in Letter 93 to his sisters is found verbatim in a letter written to the hermit Adam, although he does add a reminder about the limitations of the mind. "The mind, no matter how brilliant, cannot comprehend as it is, nor any speech of the human tongue explain" the mysteries of Judgment Day.[129] This is the principle that informs reason's most basic characteristic, its limitation. This postulate is fundamental to Damian's worldview: "There is still something great that, in our corruptible flesh, the vision of the human mind cannot attain."[130] The mysteries of life "which cannot be conceived by any natural capacity of human reason and cannot be discerned by any insight or application of the mind, must be gathered only from statements," he explains to the patriarch of Constantine while discussing the Filioque clause, "which the supreme and incomprehensible Truth asserts" in Scripture.[131] Interpretation of Scripture is often difficult, but through the years "many apostolic and Catholic men ... explained the orthodox faith in simple terms and left to posterity a record": tradition. "Surely they were under obligation to investigate these matters carefully and diligently, and to define the rule of faith with certainty; we must simply follow the path along which our forefathers have preceded us."[132] The mind can grasp physical matters but it is limited and does not have the ability to comprehend the divine. Through certain people the Spirit has shed light on the mysteries of divinity, and we must "receive with the purity of faith that which came to us from [tradition] as through streams of truth, and we gladly accept this drink as if it were drawn from the primary source of the divine fountain."[133]

128. Letter 153.7, in L, 7:19; B, 4:17. Also see similar remarks to the hermit Adam, Letter 92.2, in L, 5:19; B, 3:15.

129. Letter 92.8, in L, 5:25; B, 3:25.

130. Letter 82.5, in L, 3:235; B, 2:442–44.

131. Letter 91.10, in L, 5:7–8; B, 3:6.

132. Letter 91.16, in L, 5:11–12; B, 3:9.

133. Letter 91.17, in L, 5:12; B, 3:9.

This leaves plenty of room for secular knowledge in people's lives. That Damian personally found satisfaction in such knowledge is gleaned from those letters in which he uses secular knowledge extensively, with little apparent theological benefit, for example, Letters 49 and 108. These incidences are not typical, though; he usually employs it as a means to an end. In *De Divina omnipotentia* Damian, "formerly a rhetorician, but now a philosopher of Christ," as he calls himself elsewhere, places the full weight of his secular education behind his investigation into the concept of omnipotence.[134] In Letter 86 he borrows freely from *Physiologus, Bestiarius, Etymologies,* and *Hexameron* to serve his purpose, that "in the animals man might discover what should be imitated and what avoided ... [so] as rational man is instructed by things that lack reason, he may move unencumbered toward his creation along the road of wisdom."[135] And while most of his metaphors and *exempla* are scriptural, a large portion are mined from secular knowledge.[136] The legion of sources that he borrows from is easily available and the list of classical authors he refers to directly in the text should persuade the skeptic of his appreciation for secular knowledge.[137] Cicero, Sallust, Juvenal, Horace, Demosthenes, Grillius (a fourth-century grammarian), Plato, Xenocrates, Pythagoras, Thales, Euclid, Xenocrates, and Vergil are either identified and cited, cited anonymously, paraphrased, or referenced.[138] For Damian, utility determines employment. If secular

134. Letter 165.1, in L, 7:170; B, 4:173. Resnick, *Divine Power,* 6, says the treatise makes "a positive contribution ... raising issues—and proposing solutions—that will occupy the attention of philosophers and theologians for centuries."

135. Letter 86.10, in L, 3:259; B, 2:464.

136. His knowledge of secular matters is seen in the following examples: Letter 57.33, in L, 2:388; B, 2:189 (mythology); Letter 66.4, in L, 3:43; B, 2:251 (the marketplace); Letter 67.5, in L, 3:71–72; B, 2:282 (medical and pharmaceutical treatments); Letter 69.13, in L, 3:93–94; B, 2:303 (legal matters); Letter 74.5, in L, 3:153–54; B, 2:372–73 (mortgages, rents, and leases); Letter 762, in L, 3:160; B, 2:378 (musicians and mathematicians' tasks); Letter 79.4, in L, 3:141; B, 2:399–400 (duties of knights, lords, and vassals); Letter 97.15–20, in L, 5:78–82; B, 3:74–79 (fashion); Letter 119.33, in L, 5:360; B, 3:358 (theater); Letter 121.2, in L, 6:3; B, 3:393 (astronomy); Letter 151.8, in L, 7:6; B, 4:4 (shipping); and Letter 153.2, in L, 7:15; B, 4:14 (money-lending practices).

137. B, 4:297–368.

138. Cicero in Letter 156.6, in L, 7:82; B, 4:78; Horace, Letter 137.10, in L, 6:94; B, 3:471;

knowledge is useful, Damian includes it. Curiously, direct citation and attribution is found only in works written during his last seven years. Prior to 1065 only one letter cites and attributes an author or a work, Justinian's *Institutes* in Letter 19.[139]

Damian is even more generous with his use of history, but, again, the chronological breakdown is curious.[140] Prior to 1059 little history is found in his writing other than that concerning the German empire and that most commonly when writing about current affairs. Letter 40 (1052) and Letter 51 (1057) cite Cassidorus's *Historia ecclesiastica tripartita* concerning Eastern history. Beginning with Letter 69 (1059/1060) and ending with Letter 89 (1062), Damian reinforces his arguments with historical examples from the early Middle Ages. The invasion of the Huns is told at relative length in Letters 69 and 89; some Frankish history is presented in Letters 71 and 72. From 1062 to 1065/1066 Damian's letters include numerous précis and references to Roman history and only one about the early medieval era. In these latter writings Damian is particularly taken with history from the Roman Republic, its wars with Carthage, and Roman emperors.[141] What I deduce from these groupings is that Da-

---

and Sallust, Letter 162.5, in L, 7:144; B, 4:147. See appendix 3 for classical references. Juvenal in Letter 142.24, in L, 6:139; B, 3:514; and Horace, Letter 44.34, in L, 2:241; B, 2:32, are cited anonymously. Vergil in Letter 117.17, in L, 5:327; B, 3:324 and Letter 132.6, in L, 6:59; B, 3:440–41; and Grillius, Letter 106.3, in L, 5:175; B, 2:169, are paraphrased. Examples of the references Damian makes: Xenocrates's academy in Letter 44.3, in L, 2:222; B, 2:9; Ciceronian eloquence in Letter 98.16, in L, 5:94; B, 2:90, and Letter 117.17, in L, 5:327, 330; B, 3:324,328; Cicero's law in Letter 96.9, in L, 5:56; B, 2:52; Euclid, Phythagoras, Nichomachus, Plato, Cicero, Demosthenes in Letter 28.4, in L, 1:257–58; B, 1:251–52; Pythagoras and Plato in Letter 117.3, in L, 5:324; B, 3:317; Pythagoras in Letter 10.10, in L, 1:118; B, 1:132; Thales in Letter 121.2, in L, 6:3–4; B, 3:393; Plato in Letter 119.68, in L, 5:376; B, 3:373–74; and Martianus Capella in Letter 10.10, in L, 1:117; B, 1:132.

139. Letter 19.2, 10, 12, 18, 30, in L, 1:172, 178, 179, 182, 183; B, 1:180, 185, 187, 191, 197.

140. See Letter 160.7–9, in L, 7:106–7; B, 4:103–4, in which he explains why those who think that reading about history "serves no useful purpose" are wrong: "This age long past is made to serve us at the present time." Letter 160.9, in L, 7:107, B, 4:104.

141. See Letter 89.14, in L, 3:331; B, 2:5; Letter 97.13, 18, in L, 5:77, 80; B, 2:72–74 and 77; Letter 104.26–28, in L, 5:158–59; B, 3:154–56; Letter 111.15, in L, 5:255; B, 3:257; and Letter 120.4, in L, 5:388; B, 3:386. The exception is Letter 72.13, in L, 3:120; B, 2:330–31, where he places an ordination in the reign of "wicked Anastasius"; and Letter 51.8, in L, 2:339; B, 2:136–37 in an example involving Helena for Duchess Beatrice. For Roman emperors, see Letter 89.4, 13, 14, 15–21, in L, 3:327–31, 332–35; B, 2:534, 536–40; Letter 104.24–25, in L,

mian had an active, thirsty mind which eagerly drank when it came across new material. Through discussion or study or intellectual restlessness Damian's attention probably shifted from time to time. He saw a new set of historical events as an effective means to illustrate his argument and used it accordingly.

What we have left to do is to reconcile Letter 117 with these realities. Written to his secretary Ariprandus after 1064, *De sancta simplicitate* addresses Ariprandus's regret that he "sought first the approach to the light of truth before learning the blind wisdom of the philosophers," that he entered the hermitage uneducated.[142] Damian's parting remark, that if "this learning of the world ... should have limited use by those who are trained in the classics, how much more carefully should it be withheld from those who would like to learn?" captures the difficulty scholars have had in reaching a consensus regarding Damian's attitude toward secular knowledge; he admits to limited use yet wants it withheld.[143] Much of the confusion, however, is resolved if his remarks are placed within the larger context of his social theology. In general his attitude toward secular knowledge grows from his beliefs concerning the Body of Christ and the division of labor therein. As usual, it possesses an internal logic. A brief review of his early writings will refresh the reader's memory concerning the relevant principles. In his first treatise he reveals his openness to reason in matters of faith, telling his readers the correct sequence in seeking truth: "We read, we believe, and therefore are convinced."[144] After presenting a scriptural argument he tells them that "I would still like to argue with you from reason."[145] In Romuald's vita Damian approvingly reports that Romuald was writ-

---

5:157–58; B, 3:153–54; Letter 108.4–5, in L, 5:196–97; B, 3:190–91; Letter 120.5, in L, 5:389; B, 3:386; and Letter 149.16, in L, 6:179; B, 3:553.

142. Letter 117.2, in L, 5:318; B, 3:317.

143. Letter 117.25, in L, 5:331; B, 3:328–29. Blum, *St. Peter Damian,* 134, says "it is difficult to judge conclusively." Older historians most often did judge him, though, negatively. See J. A. Endres, "Petrus Damiani und die weltliche Wissenschaft," *Beiträge zur Geschichte der Philosophie des Mittelalters* 8.3 (1910), 15–17. Newer works are frequently more nuanced.

144. Letter 1.11, in L, 1:43; B, 1:70.

145. Letter 1.67, in L, 1:79; B, 1:99.

ing a book.[146] To Judge Bonushomo he writes a lengthy exposition of the pros and cons of secular knowledge and admits its usefulness and necessity for those in the world. "Since you fill a position of some importance in the world, and cannot completely avoid using the language of the world in your contact with your associates, or at times devoting yourself in some degree to literary studies, you should follow this norm," to engage in secular studies, just not as vigorously [*omnino vivacem*]."[147] Bonushomo should "steer a middle course [*sit medie temperata*]," remembering that ultimately "all spiritual wisdom should have the upper hand."[148] For those, "especially for laymen, who find themselves totally unable to excel in the affairs of both worlds, they should ... subordinate those things which they cannot completely despise," that is, secular learning.[149] In short, Damian sees no problem with people in the world pursuing worldly knowledge as long as they prioritize and do not let the secular dominate the spiritual.

Ariprandus is not a judge but a hermit. A monk has a different function in the community, a function that is not dependent on secular knowledge. His primary function is to bear living witness to the spiritual. He does this through means which, logically, differ from those of a judge. Ariprandus "will find it easier to influence those who see you following in the footsteps of Christ, than to persuade those who hear you by any amount of words. Nor does almighty God have any need for our grammar to attract men to himself, since at the outset of man's redemption ... he did not commission philosophers and orators, but instead sent simple and unlettered fishermen."[150] Damian's point to Bonushomo and Ariprandus is the same. One's function in the community determines whether and how much one should pursue secular knowledge. A judge needs secular knowledge; a monk does not.

146. VR, 33 (225).

147. Letter 23.10, in L, 1:220; B, 1:221.

148. Letter 23.6, in L, 1:217; B, 1:218; and Letter 23.7, in L, 1:219; B, 1:219.

149. Letter 23.13, in L, 1:222; B, 1:222.

150. Letter 117.7–8, in L, 5:321; B, 3:319. See Letter 132.30, in L, 6:72; B, 3:452; Letter 141.6, in L, 6:165; B, 3:490–91; and S, 57.11, for the same sentiments.

This insistence on a division of labor surfaces in a letter to Desiderius. After establishing the superiority of mystical knowledge over earthly, he directs the abbot's attention to his specific role in a monastic community's attempt "to understand mystical and higher things." The goal is the same—"Christ to whom the assembly of all the saints bears witness"—but the abbot has greater responsibilities to attain this wisdom, for "insofar as you are the eye for those entrusted to your direction, you should engage in the pursuit of spiritual goals and take care to provide not only for yourself but also for them."[151] Likewise, because a priest fulfills a spiritual function in the community Damian speaks disparagingly only about his lack of knowledge in spiritual matters. That he "had so little and so poor an acquaintance with the teaching of the alphabet that it was clear that he was hardly able to read a bit of writing syllable by syllable," Damian accepts, but when a priest habitually leaves wine in the chalice after consecration, Damian criticizes him as "certainly negligent and indolent."[152]

The model for all this division of labor is found in the vita apostolica: "The apostles themselves, the leaders of the Christian teaching and those foremost in our discipline, had different tasks among themselves."[153] Later on in the same treatise when Damian is discussing the role of secular studies in the monk's life, we see this principle holding up his argument. He is upset, because he sees monks "labor on the trifles of the external arts for this reason, to profit more fully from divine studies."[154] In this they are deceived, for in the division of labor "we [are] forbidden to strive after vain teachings of this sort after having accepted this sacred order of living [*post acceptum sacrum ordinem*]."[155] In a long metaphor based on the Mosaic law concerning

151. Letter 82.5, in L, 3:235–36; B, 2:443–44.

152. Letter 123.7, in L, 6:14–15; B, 3:403.

153. Letter 153.19, in L, 7:25; B, 4:23. Further on Damian roots his theology in 1 Corinthians 7:7: "For I would that all people were even as myself, but each one has an undivided gift from God, one after this manner, another after that." Letter 153.27, in L, 7:30; B, 4:28.

154. Letter 153.40, in L, 7:37; B, 4:35.

155. Letter 153.41, in L, 7:38; B, 4:35.

marriage with captive women (Dt 21:12–13), Damian does, however, concede that once she shaves her hair, cuts her nails, and removes her clothes "so that she may strip off the outer covering of fables and of fictions ... to reveal the solid truth of right reason," she is an Israelite.[156] Accordingly, "we may choose as if in marriage the art of any discipline whatsoever, once it has been cleansed of every superstition, insofar as once she has become an Israelite she may enter into marriage with an Israelite as a result, and, being very fertile, she may deliver the offspring of spiritual works."[157]

Unfortunately, Damian does not address his own education or his utilization of it, thus opening the door to accusations of hypocrisy. He does, however, address the issues of talent and individual vocation, and these lead us away from judgments of hypocrisy. Twice Damian mentions Ariprandus's impressive intellectual gifts, but still insists that that does not mean he should engage in secular learning.[158] "How, then, do you know that almighty God, the treasurer of merits, has not endowed you with the discrimination and agility of a talent more subtle than usual, for the purpose of now somehow giving you a sign of future reward?" Damian asks him.[159] Ariprandus must remember that God gives the talent and God decides what that talent is for, because "men are not chosen for battle in the army of the spirit only because of their own decision, but he who inspires them to be converted to him, arranges in their regard each moment of their life and time, so that some he invites to his service who have already reached a ripe old age, and others are enjoying the full vigor of surging youth."[160]

Here, I think, is Damian's understanding of his own vocation. In his decision to become a monk he was cooperating with God's individualized plan for him. It is a plan, which for a reason that Dami-

156. Ibid.; B, 4:36.

157. Letter 153.42, in L, 7:38; B, 4:36.

158. Letter 117.2, in L, 5:318; B, 3:317 ("you ... having a docile mind and facility for study"); and Letter 117.11, in L, 5:323; B, 3:321 ("your talented mind").

159. Letter 117.11, in L, 5:323; B, 3:321.

160. Letter 117.6, in L, 5:320; B, 3:317.

an does not comprehend, includes the use of his intellectual talents. While Damian accepts his unique vocation I think it frustrates him, hence his occasional ambivalence and resentment. The logic seems elementary; a monk serves the community by seeking divine wisdom, so there is no need for secular wisdom. Why, then, is he called to pursue both? We see the difficulty he has in accepting what he considers to be an illogical situation, particularly after he is consecrated bishop, and "these burdens were thrust upon me."[161] A mere year afterwards he pleads for permission to retire to "the haven of quiet" of his hermitage.[162] Months later he writes again, adding old age to his list of excuses. The argument he lays out is a good example of Damian's ambivalent attitude toward earthly wisdom: he wants to retire and devote his life to the pursuit of divine wisdom, so he taps into his knowledge of human history to make his case.[163] His requests for retirement continue to his death. "Inasmuch as you are angry with me for wishing to relinquish my episcopal office," he explains to a fellow monk around 1070, "I will say that you are not viewing the matter with the eyes of the spirit. Because I am surrounded by the darkness of so many secular interests, I am unable to see the brightness of the interior light and cannot lift my confused and insensible mind to the contemplation of spiritual truths."[164] Damian is not a hypocrite, but a person carrying a burden he wishes on no one.

At some level Damian made peace with his predicament, sometimes with humor: "Truly I would rather weep than write," he complains to Pope Alexander II. "In fact, I should weep the more because I am unable to weep."[165] A firm believer in the proposition

161. Letter 57.3, in L, 2:370; B, 2:165.

162. Letter 57.33, in L, 2:388; B, 2:189.

163. Letter 72. He narrates the history of thirty-four cases where retirement was allowed. While the main characters are obviously religious, he situates them within secular history, for example, Leo, archbishop of Ravenna, retired "while Otto III was happily reigning, [and] Frederick became his successor." Letter 72.66, in L, 3:146; B, 2:365.

164. Letter 169.2, in L, 7:244; B, 4:247–48.

165. Letter 164.2, in L, 7:162; B, 4:166. Blum, L, 5:318, brings attention to Damian's "tragic humor" in his tale concerning the learned Walter, in Letter 117.14, in L, 5:325; B, 3:322–23.

that a monk's role in the Body of Christ is as a living witness pursuing divine wisdom in solitude, he also believed that his vocation differed from the norm. He is an exception. Frustration comes when we see Damian allowing himself what he denies to others, and we conclude it is rooted in an exaggerated sense of self-importance. The opposite is true. His motives are altruistic, for what he really wants is to spare others the trials he has suffered. His is the harder path. He truly believes that the fullest Truth and the greatest happiness are divine, not human, wisdom. "And oh, to how many this earthbound, sensual wisdom has not granted a happy life," he laments.[166] "For him, however, whose mind is opened by the gift of the Holy Spirit, there is little need of this graded learning because he easily grasps everything by the natural vigor of his nimble talents," Damian tells Ariprandus.[167] The wisdom given by the Spirit satisfies a person's search for meaning; secular wisdom does not. Therefore, "it frequently happens that some men who are wise in sensual things enjoy a long life and are never able to find what they are looking for."[168] Damian longs for the day when he can devote himself completely to spiritual studies, for then he will find the happiness that comes with Truth. His patience sometimes wears thin when monks cannot realize this. "If I may speak with some irritation," he complains in Letter 153, "among their number are those who follow the crowd of grammarians, who, having forsaken spiritual studies, desire to learn the absurdities of the earthly art, and, who, trivializing the Rule of Benedict, take pleasure in applying themselves to the rules of Donatus."[169] Here he is criticizing the improper prioritizing of secular studies over spiritual studies, not secular knowledge per se.

One must remember in all this that for Damian all knowledge, secular and spiritual, is reducible to one truth, Christ. "Do not sup-

166. Letter 117.13, in L, 5:325; B, 3:322.

167. Letter 117.12, in L, 5:324; B, 3:321. Graded learning refers to "grammar school where boys are ... called 'abecedarians,' others 'syllabarians,' still others 'nominarians,' while others 'calculatorians.'" Letter 117.11, in L, 5:323, B, 3:321.

168. Letter 117.16, in L, 5:326; B, 3:324.

169. Letter 153.40, in L, 7:37; B, 4:34–35.

press the truth, but with all your strength defend it in every undertaking and dispute," he advises Judge Moricus. "Whoever resists the truth to gain human favor is indeed guilty of denying Christ, who is Truth Itself."[170] This identification of Christ with Truth permeates all his writings and is constantly reinforced by his use of *Veritas* as a nomenclature.[171] Besides his argument that different people pursue Christ—Truth Itself—in different ways, everyone, secular master and religious alike, must recognize that divine wisdom is superior to earthly wisdom. Hence Damian articulates a postulate that is often considered as the summation of the medieval intellectual's approach to knowledge.

> Clearly, conclusions drawn from the arguments of dialecticians and rhetoricians should not be thoughtlessly addressed to the mysteries of divine power; dialecticians and rhetoricians should refrain from persistently applying to the sacred laws the rules devised for their progress in using the tools of the syllogism or fine style or oratory, and from setting their inevitable conclusions against the power of God. However, if the techniques of the humanities be used in the study of revelation, they must not arrogantly usurp the rights of the mistress, but should humbly assume a certain ancillary role, as a maidservant to her lady, so as not to be led astray in assuming the lead, not to lose the enlightenment of deepest virtue, nor to abandon the right road to truth by attending only to the superficial meaning of words.[172]

Damian sees no problem with investigations into "the method and order of speech ... by young lay students in the schools" in secular matters. He willingly grants "to the wise of the world the things that are theirs."[173] What must be acknowledged are the limits of secular

170. Letter 170.8, in L, 7:250; B, 4:252.

171. Approximately one-fifth of his letters contain the nomenclature, many with multiple uses. See my "The Role of the Eremitic Monk in the Development of the Medieval Intellectual Tradition," *From Cloister to Classroom,* ed. E. Rozanne Elder, 80–95 (Kalamazoo, Mich.: Cistercian Publications, 1987), for the relevance of Damian's use of *veritas* in intellectual history; it helped resolve monasticism's ambivalence toward intellectual pursuits which in turn paved the way for monasticism' leadership in the universities that followed.

172. Letter 119.26, in L, 5:356; B, 3:356. See Kurt Reindel, "Neue Literatur zu Petrus Damiani," *Deutsches Archiv für Erforschung des Mittelalters* 32 (1976), 405–43, for scholars' appraisals.

173. Letter 119.29, in L, 5:357; B, 3:355.

knowledge and the superiority of divine wisdom. The two are not mutually exclusive nor must laity and religious engage solely in their respective realms. In fact, Damian often encourages intermingling, as long as their respective limitations and ranking are respected. Hence, he tells Hildebrand and Albert of Monte Cassino (1069) that "one indeed takes treasure from the Egyptians with which to build a tabernacle to God, if he reads the poets and philosophers, using them astutely to penetrate the mysteries of heavenly wisdom"—something Damian has done his whole life.[174] This is, after all, simply an elucidation of what he wrote to Honestus, a nobleman "involved in secular affairs" in his very first work.[175] "Because the Truth and Wisdom of God," he wrote when explaining the change from the Old to the New, "came also to teach men on earth, what he had formerly commanded to be observed physically under the shadow of allegory, he later enjoined on his disciples to be understood spiritually." Created things are "empty, that is, a shadow or image of a thing, not the thing itself," he lectured, revealing his own training in secular philosophy, "not the very truth but imitations of truth."[176] Damian concludes by reminding Honestus that the individual must use all knowledge wisely. "I have indeed supplied all the weapons" Honestus needs to attain Truth. He is responsible for their wise use: "You have at your disposal all that is necessary for such an engagement. Use the means before you as you shall judge expedient."[177]

174. Letter 160.16, in L, 7:130; B, 4:134.

175. Letter 1.74, in L, 1:82; B, 1:101–2.

176. Letter 1:55, in L, 1:70; B, 1:91.

177. Letter 1.74, in L, 1:82–83; B, 1:102.

CONCLUDING REMARKS

Allowed to speak for himself, the real Peter Damian emerges. He is a man of his time in presentation, a man who transcends his time in content. With acute sensitivity to his surroundings, he experiences life first as a son and brother, then as orphan, student, master, hermit, theologian, author, preacher, prior, papal legate, and cardinal, and finally as hermit once again. His many roles afforded him a vantage point for viewing eleventh-century Italian society that few others had, and he took full advantage of that opportunity. That he recorded his observations and reflections is most fortunate, for they form a unique historical source for the period. That he was a premier theologian whose message still speaks to us today is more than fortunate; it is a treasure.

It is indeed refreshing to find a theologian who applies such sound principles to everyday situations. He is a social commentator and critic par excellence. He responds to the particular issues of his day with universal wisdom. His guiding axiom is simple: let your life bear witness to your beliefs. Or, as we might say today, practice what you preach. Accordingly, he chides popes and bishops when they fall short of Christian ethical standards. He insists that lay people are members of the priesthood of believers and that their function within the Body of Christ is essential. He listens to the complaints of the laity in Milan and encourages them to criticize clerics when needed. He lectures secular rulers on stewardship and the proper use of authority. In a society dominated by strict class divisions and almost exclusively concerned with the rights of rulers, Damian champions the rights of the ruled. He attacks avarice relentlessly and identifies the damage it does to a growing society. He tells the upper class to distribute the goods they control to the lower classes. When he sees injustice, he tries to remedy it. If he finds disparity in ecclesiastical discipline, he rails against it.

Damian also uses his theological principles to open doors. He offers a new kind of spiritual direction to women and men, clergy and laity. He rejects a rigorous approach in spiritual matters and elevates the importance of intention when determining guilt or innocence. He maintains that marriage and child-rearing are based on emotional attachments beyond kinship and legal arrangements. By applying his theology to the intellectual world Damian sets the stage for society's full engagement; since Christ is Truth Itself, the Christian not only may pursue knowledge but must do so. From his first letter to his last Damian endorses intellectual activity. He does not want his arguments accepted blindly but asks that they be rationally critiqued. He constantly tells people to think for themselves. He encourages both men and women to educate themselves, and he provides educational opportunities for some family members. He spends time and energy on acquiring a substantial library for his community. He embraces his own intellectual talents and considers it a duty to utilize them to the fullest. He promotes introspection, inserts autobiographical remarks in his writings, and has a deep love of tears, all of which foster the new concepts of individual and self then developing in Western society.

Damian's theology is a near-perfect blend of extreme ideas and moderate judgments. He has an inordinate intolerance for sin, yet advocates leniency for the sinner. He challenges the gift culture as a means of ecclesiastical advancement and rails against clerical misconduct, yet insists that offenders be treated fairly and enjoy equity before the law. He admires extreme asceticism but insists it be practiced judiciously. His ideas about the individual, the community, and the relationship between the two are radical in conception, but his application of them to real-life situations is measured. His key contribution to the Papal Election Decree is a radical idea moderated in practice. And so on.

Does this mean that Peter Damian himself was perfect? Of course not. He was an imperfect man who often reflected his imperfect world. The purpose here, however, is to judge not the man but his theology. While it too is not perfect, it possesses many attributes that make a theology timeless. Damian's principles are universal, his topics comprehensive, and his judgments sound. Any society—especially one experiencing many of the same problems as eleventh-century Italy—that ignores Damian's theology does so to its own detriment. Peter Damian deserves to be heard. We will be all the richer if we listen.

Appendix 1

SELECT INDEX TO THE WRITINGS OF PETER DAMIAN

The following lists of citations to key topics treated by Peter Damian are not complete. They should be considered merely a starting point for those interested in researching Damian's legacy further. All citations are to Blum, *Letters,* and only the letter and section numbers are given.

Writing/books: 17.2, 25; 18.20; 19.2, 30; 21.2; 23.2–3; 25.16; 27.12; 37.5; 38.5; 40.2, 115, 120, 122; 44.35; 45.9; 47.8; 54.2; 55.12; 57.16, 18, 20, 24, 35; 58.6; 59.16; 62.2, 3; 66.17, 31; 69.23; 70.21; 72.36; 74.4; 75.4; 80.29; 81.36; 84; 86.69; 87.14; 88.31; 94.27; 95.2; 96.2, 11, 25; 98.16; 99.2; 102.25, 32; 103.5; 105.23; 107.7; 108.2, 7, 12; 109.2, 9; 112.37; 116.4; 117.19; 118.25; 119.75; 121.2, 9; 123.2, 9, 17; 126.21; 132.23; 137.8–9; 140.13; 141.2, 13, 14, 25; 142.22; 146.2, 5–6; 152.12; 153.54, 56, 67–68, 95; 156.2, 15; 160.11; 164.2; 167.3, 5; 168.13; 177.7; 179.2.

Appendix 2

ADDRESSEES OF THE LETTERS OF PETER DAMIAN

The numbers in the table below do not add up to the total number of letters Peter Damian sent, since many of the people to whom they are addressed fit into multiple categories. For example, Duchess Beatrice of Tuscany is counted under "female nobility," "laity," and "women."

Addressee	1040–59 (Letters 1–65)	1059/60–65 (Letters 66–128)	1065–70 (Letters 129–70)	Undatable
bishops	23	14	2	2
canons	1	1	1	
communities	3	7	7	
family		3	3	
female nobility	3	5	5	
hermits	9	8	7	
hierarchy (other than bishops)	6	5	5	
Hildebrand	4	3	2	
judges, lawyers	3		1	
laity	12	6	9	2
male nobility	6	5	6	1
monks	13	19	10	4
popes	8	8	3	
priests	7	3	5	3
women	3	7	6	

Between 1062 and 1067, Damian wrote eleven letters to women. Damian's most prolific writing years were 1057 (8 to 10 letters), 1058 (7 to 9), 1059 (11), 1062 (7 or 8), 1063 (11), 1064 (11), 1065 (17), 1067 (8), and 1069 (11).

Appendix 3

SELECT REFERENCES AND TOPICS IN PETER DAMIAN'S SERMONS AND LETTERS

SERMONS

Saints, discussed or cited on their feast days

Alexius (Sermon 28)
Anastasius (3)
Andrew (57)
Anthimus (19)
Apollinaris (30, 31, 32)
Barbatianus (65)
Bartholomew (41, 42)
Benedict (8)
Boniface (20)
Cassian (39)
Christopher (33)
Columba (66)
Donatus (38)
Eleuchadius (6)
Fidelis (54)
Flora (34, 35)
George (13)
Hilarion (38)
Hilary (2)
John the Apostle (63)
John the Baptist (24, 25)
Lawrence (22)
Lucilla (34, 35)
Luke (53)
Mary (45, 46)
Mark (14, 15, 16)
Matthew (49, 50, 51)
Peregentinus (22)
Rufinus (36)
Severus (4, 5)
Stephen (37)
Valeria (17.1)
Vitalis (17.1, 17.2)

Miscellaneous topics

Exaltation of the Cross (Sermon 48)
Christmas (61)
Church dedication (72)
Hermits (21, 73, 74)
Invention of the Cross (18)
The Lord's Supper (10)
Mary's birth (67, 68)

Topics treated in Sermon fragments

Pancratus (Sermon 76)
Synods (75)

Authors cited in Sermons

From antiquity: Horatio, Livy, Ovid
Christian Fathers and theologians: Ambrose, Augustine, Eusebius, Flavius Josephus, Gregory I, Hippolytus, Jerome, Leo I, Rufinus, Sozomen, Sulpicius Severus, Tertullian
From the medieval period: Alcuin, Bede, Cassian, Scotus Erigena

Sermons focused on the following topics

LETTERS

Classical authors and mythological figures cited or referenced

Historical references

Ancient history

There are no references to Roman history prior to the 1050s.

Early medieval history

Otto II fighting Saracens: 72.52–53
Pepin: 72.39
Robert Guiscard: 87.13
Rulers of Asia and Bithynia: 89.103
Vandals: 72:59

Stories about early medieval history are found in Letters 69–89 (1059/60–62)

Miscellaneous references

Chess: Letter 57.31
Dice: 57.31, 32
Science: 10.8; 28.4; 86; 119.68; 121.2
Wines: 132.6, 22

The chief sources for Letter 86 are *Physiologus, Hexameron,* and *Etymologies*

Appendix 4

BIBLICAL CITATIONS IN PETER DAMIAN'S LETTERS

Number of New Testament citations

Letters	1–30	31–60	61–90	91–120	121–50	151–80
Matthew	39	56	65	57	17	48
Mark	7	12	10	7	4	4
Luke	39	32	29	48	20	36
John	24	41	39	43	17	19
Acts	19	32	20	28	5	22
Paul	103	111	89	107	118	258

New Testament verses cited four or more times

Matthew: 3:16 (5 times); 6:21 (5); 6:24 (6); 11:30 (4); 16:19 (6); 18:16 (7); 22:13 (5); 24:29 (4); 25:41 (7). 5:1–10 (6); 8:18 (5); 8:20 (10).

Luke: 2:14 (4); 9:58 (4); 9:62 (7); 10:1 (4); 10:39–40 (5); 21:34 (4).

John: 1:3 (9); 1:29 (6); 1:32 (4); 12:24 (4); 20:22 (4).

Acts: 2:3 (4); 4:32–35 (7);

Romans: 6:4 (6); 8:32 (4); 15:4 (9).

1 Corinthians: 5:8 (5); 7:13 (5); 7:7 (40); 9:27 (4); 10:4 (4); 11:29 (4).

2 Corinthians: 3:6 (6); 6:2 (4); 6:14–16 (7).

Galatians: 4:4 (4); 2:11 (4); 2:20 (5); 3:13 (5); 6:17 (4).

Ephesians: 4:8 (4); 5:5 (7); 6:14, 17 (10).

Colossians: 2:3 (4).

2 Thessalonians: 2:8 (5).

1 Timothy: 2:5 (5); 5:22 (4).

Hebrews: 10:27 (5); 10:38 (4); 13:13 (5).

1 Peter: 3:9 (5).

2 Peter: 2:22 (7).

Revelation: 1:5 (5); 1:7 (5); 3:15 (5).

Old Testament verses cited four or more times

Genesis: 3:5 (5); 3:6 (4); 3:18 (4); 27:27 (6).

Exodus: 3:14 (4); 16:3 (4); 17:11 (5).

Leviticus: 10:1 (4).

Joshua: 7:25 (5).

1 Kings: 20:42 (4).

2 Kings: 5:26 (5); 5:27 (6).

BIBLIOGRAPHY

Acta Sanctorum. Edited by Jean Carnandet. Reprint: Paris: V. Palme, 1963.

Adelman of Liége. *Epistola ad Berengarium*. In R. B. C. Huygens. "Textes latins du XIe au XIIIe siècle." *Studi mediévali*, 3rd series, 8 (1967), 476–89.

Anderson, C. Colt. *The Great Catholic Reformers*. New York: Paulist Press, 2007.

Andreas Strumensi. *Vita sancti Arialdi*. Edited by Friedrich Baethgen. Leipzig: Hiersemann, 1934. MGH SS, 30, 2, 3, 1047–75.

———. *Vita sancti Iohannis Gualberti*. MGH SS, 30, 1 and 2.

Anselm. *Historia dedicationis ecclesiae S. Remigii Remensis*. PL 142, 1415–40.

The Ante-Nicene Fathers. Edited by Alexander Roberts and James Donaldson. 10 vols. Reprint: New York: Charles Scribner's Sons, 1903.

Augustine. *Confessions*. Translated by R. Pine-Coffin. Harmondsworth: Penguin Books, 1978.

Becker, Marvin. *Medieval Italy: Constraints and Creativity*. Bloomington: Indiana University Press, 1981.

Belisle, Peter-Damian. "Primitive Romualdian/Camaldolese Spirituality." *Cistercian Quarterly* 3 (1996), 413–29.

———. "Overview of Camaldolese History and Spirituality." In *Privilege of Love*. Edited by Peter-Damian Belisle. Collegeville, Minn.: Liturgical Press, 2002.

Blum, Owen. "The Monitor of the Popes, Peter Damian." *Studi gregoriani per la storia di Gregorio VII*. 2:459–76. Rome: Abbazia di San Paolo, 1947.

———. *St. Peter Damian: His Teaching on the Spiritual Life*. Washington, D.C.: The Catholic University of America Press, 1947.

———. "Alberic of Monte Cassino and Hymns Attributed to St. Peter Damian." *Traditio* 12 (1956), 87–148.

———."Alberic of Monte Cassino and a Letter of St. Peter Damian to Hildebrand." *Studi gregoriani* 5 (1956), 291–98.

Bois, Guy. *The Transformation of the Year 1000*. Translated by J. Birrell. Manchester: Manchester University Press, 1992.

Bonizo of Sutri. *Liber ad amicum*. Edited by Ernest Dummler. MGH, Libelli de lite imperatorum et pontificum (1891). 1:568–620.

———. *Book which is entitled "To A Friend."* In *The Papal Reform of the Eleventh Century: Lives of Pope Leo IX and Pope Gregory VII. Selected Sources*. Translated by I. S. Robinson. Manchester: Manchester University Press, 2004.

Boswell, John. *Christianity, Social Tolerance and Homosexuality*. Chicago: University of Chicago Press, 1980.

Bouchard, Constance. "'Feudalism,' Cluny and the Investiture Controversy." In *Medieval Monks and Their World*. Edited by David Blanks, Michael Frasetto, and Amy Livingstone. 81–91. Leiden: Brill, 2006.

Brooke, Christopher. *The Age of the Cloister*. Mahwah, N.J.: Hidden Springs, 2003.

Bruno-Boniface di Querfurt. *Vitae quinque fratrum*. MGH SS, 15, 709–38. Also in *Monumenta Poloniae Historica* n.s. 4, 3. Warsaw: Panstwowe Wydawnictwo Naukowe, 1973.

Bruno of Querfort. *The Life of Five Brothers*. Translated by Thomas Matus. In *The Mystery of Romuald and the Five Brothers*. Big Sur, Calif.: Source Books and Hermitage Books, 1996.

Bruno of Segni. *Concerning Simoniacs*. In *Papal Reform of the Eleventh Century: Lives of Pope Leo IX and Pope Gregory VII. Selected Sources*. Translated by I. S Robinson. Manchester: Manchester University Press, 2004.

Burchard of Worms. *Decretum libri xx*. PL 140, 537–1058.

Bynum, Caroline Walker. "The Spirituality of Regular Canons in the Twelfth Century: A New Approach." *Medievalia et humanistica*, n.s. 4 (1973), 3–23.

———. *Docere Verbo et Exemplo: An Aspect of Twelfth-Century Spirituality*. Missoula, Mont.: Scholars Press, 1979.

———. "Did the Twelfth Century Discover the Individual?" *Journal of Ecclesiastical History* 31.1 (1980), 1–17.

———. *Fragmentation and Redemption.* New York: Zone Books, 1991.
Cacciamani, Guiseppe. "La fondazioni eremitiche e cenobitichie di S. Pier Damiano: Inizi della congregazione di S. Croce di Fonte Avellana." *Ravennatensia* 5 (1976), 5–33.
Cafardi, N. *Before Dallas.* New York: Paulist Press, 2008.
Calati, Benedetto. *Sapienzo Monastica.* In *Studia Anselmiana* 177 (1994).
Capecelatro, Alfonso. *Storia di S. Pier Damiano e del suo tiempo.* Florence, 1862.
Capitani, O. "Esiste un' età gregoriana? Considerazione sulle tendenze di' una storiografia medievistica." *Rivista di storia e letteratura religiosa* 1 (1965), 454–81.
Catalogus Sanctorum Hiberniae. In *Councils and Ecclesiastical Documents.* Edited by Arthus W. Hadder and William Stubbs. Oxford: Clarendon Press: 1869–78.
Chenu, M. D. *Nature, Man and Society in the Twelfth Century.* Translated by Jerome Taylor and Lester K. Little. Chicago: University of Chicago Press, 1968.
Cowdrey, H. E. J. *Pope Gregory VII, 1073–85.* Oxford: Clarendon Press, 1998.
———. "Pope Gregory VII and the Chastity of the Clergy." In *Medieval Purity and Piety.* Edited by Michael Frassetto. 269–302. New York: Garland, 1998.
Cricco, P. "Monasticism and Its Role as a Liminal Community in Medieval Society." Ph.D. dissertation, West Virginia University, 1981.
Cushing, Kathleen. *Papacy and Law in the Gregorian Revolution.* Oxford: Clarendon Press, 1998.
———. "Of Locustae and Dangerous Men: Peter Damian, the Vallombrosans, and Eleventh-Century Reform." *Church History* 74 (2005), 740–58.
D'Acunto, Nicoangelo. *I Laici Nella Chiese e Nella Società Secondo Pier Damiani.* Rome: Nella Sede Dell' Instituo, 1994.
Dante. *The Comedy of Dante Alighieri the Florentine: Cantica III Paradise.* Translated by Dorothy L. Sayers and Barbara Reynolds. Harmondsworth: Penguin, 1962; repr. 1986.
Detler, Jasper. "Das Papstwahldekret von 1059." *Beiträge zur Geschichte und Quellenkunde des MA* (1986), 98–119.
De Vaux, Roland. *Ancient Israel.* 2 vols. New York: McGraw-Hill, 1965.

De Wulf, Maurice. *History of Medieval Philosophy.* Translated by Ernest Messenger. New York: Dover, 1952.

Dickinson, J. C. *The Origins of the Austin Canons and Their Introduction into England.* London: SPCK, 1950.

Dressler, Friodolin. *Petrus Damiani: Leben und Werk.* In *Studia Anselmiana* 34 (1954).

Dreves, G. M., and C. Blume. *Analecta hymnica medii aevi.* Leipzig: Fues's Verlag, 1886–1922.

Duffy, Eamon. *Saints and Sinners.* 2nd ed. New Haven, Conn.: Yale University Press, 2001.

Eliade, Mircea. *The Sacred and the Profane.* Translated by Willard Trask. New York: Harper and Row, 1959.

Elliott, Dyan. "The Priest's Wife: Female Erasure and the Gregorian Reform." In *Medieval Religion: New Approaches.* Edited Constance Berman. 123–55. New York: Routledge, 2005.

Endres, J. A. "Petrus Damiani und die weltiche Wissenschaft." *Beiträge zur Geschichte der Philosophie des Mittelalters* 8.3 (1910), 15–17.

Epistle of Clement. ANF 1:5–21.

Fichtenau, Heinrich. *Heretics and Scholars in the High Middle Ages 1000–1200.* Translated by Denise Kaiser. University Park: Pennsylvania State University Press, 1998.

Fliche, Augustin. *La réforme grégorienne.* 3 vols. Paris: Spicilegium sacrum Lovainiense, 1924–1937.

Foglietti, Raphaelis. *Sancti Petri Damiani Ecclesiae Doctoris Autobiographia.* Turin: A. Baglione, 1899.

Fornasari, Guiseppe. *Medioevo Riformato del Secolo XI.* Naples: Ligori Editore, 1996.

Freud, Stephen. *Studien zur literarischen Wirksamfeit des Petrus Damiani.* Hanover: Hahnsche Buchhandlung, 1995.

Furhmann, Horst. *Germany in the High Middle Ages, 1050–1200.* Translated by Timothy Reuter. Cambridge: Cambridge University Press, 1986.

Gall, James. *Layman's English-Greek Concordance.* Grand Rapids, Mich.: William Eerdmans, 1974.

Gerbert of Aurillac. *Die abriefsammlung Gerberts vom Reims.* Edited by Fritz Weigle. MGH Briefe der deuschen Kaiserzeit 2. Weiman: Böhlau, 1966.

Gilchrist, G. T. "Was There a Gregorian Reform Movement in the

Eleventh Century?" *Canadian Catholic Historical Association Study Sessions* 37 (1970), 1–10.

Golinelli, Jean. *Indiscreta Sanctitas.* Rome: Nella Sede Dell' Instituo, 1988.

Gonsette, Jean. *S. Pierre Damien et la culture profane.* Louvain: Publications Universitaries de Louvain, 1956.

Grandjean. Michel. *Laïcs dans L'Église regards de Pierre Damien, Anselme de Cantobéry, Yves de Chartres.* Paris: Beauchesne, 1994.

Gregory of Tours. *Historia Francorum.* Edited B. Krusch and W. Levisa. MGH Scriptores rerum Merovingicarum, 1 editio altera (1937–51).

Guerrier, L. *De Petro Damiano.* Aureliae, 1881.

Guillou, Andre. "Production and Profits in the Byzantine Province of Italy (Tenth to Eleventh Centuries): An Expanding Society." *Dumbarton Oaks Papers* 28 (1974), 89–109.

Gyug, Richard. "The Milanese Church and the Gregorian Reform." *Scintilla* 2–3 (1985–86), 29–65.

Hallinger, K. *Gorze-Kluny.* 2 vols. In *Studia Anselmiana* 22–25 (1950).

Hamilton, Sarah. "Penance in the Age of Gregorian Reform." In *Retribution, Repentance, and Reconciliation.* Edited by Kate Cooper and Jeremy Gregory. 47–73. Rochester, N.Y.: Boydell Press, 2004.

Howe, John. *Church Reform and Social Change in Eleventh-Century Italy: Dominic Soro and His Patrons.* Philadelphia: University of Pennsylvania Press, 1997.

Humbert of Silva Candida. *Libri tres adversus simoniacos.* Edited by F. Thaner. MGH Libelli de Lite (1891) 1, 95–253.

Hunt, Noreen. *Cluny under Saint Hugh 1049–1109.* Notre Dame, Ind.: University of Notre Dame Press, 1967.

Hurlbut, Stephen. *The Song of S. Peter Damian.* Washington, D.C.: St. Albans Press, 1928.

———. *Hortus conclusus.* Washington, D.C.: St. Albans Press, 1936.

Ignatius of Antioch. *Philadelphians.* ANF 1:79–85.

———. *Romans.* ANF 1:73–78.

———. *Smyrnaeans.* ANF 1:86–92.

Iohannis Gualberti auctore discipulo eius anonyme. MGH SS, 30, 2, 1104–11.

Jaeger, Stephen. *The Envy of Angels.* Philadelphia: University of Pennsylvania Press, 1994.

Jasper, Dether. "Das papstwahldekret von 1059." *Beiträge zur Geschichte und Quellenkunde des MA* 12 (1986), 111–203.

Jerome. *The Pilgrimage of the Holy Paula.* Translated by Aubrey Stewart. London: Palestine Pilgrims Text Society, 1896.

Jestice, Phyllis. "Peter Damian against the Reformers." In *The Joy of Learning and the Love of God.* Edited by E. Rozanna Elder. 67–94. Kalamazoo, Mich.: Cistercian Publications, 1995.

———. *Wayward Monks and the Religious Revolution of the Eleventh Century.* Leiden: Brill, 1997.

———. "A New Fashion in Imitating Christ: Changing Spiritual Perspectives around the Year 1000." In *The Year 1000.* Edited by Michael Frassetto. 165–85. New York: Palgrave Macmillan, 2002.

John Jay College of Criminal Justice. *The Nature and Scope of the Problem of Sexual Abuse of Minors by Catholic Priests and Deacons in the United States.* Accessed through www.jjay.cuny.edu/churchstudy/main.asp.

John of Lodi. *Vita b. Petri Damiani.* PL 144, 113–46. Critical edition, MGH: Studien und Texte. Hanover: Hahn, 1995.

Jordan, Mark. *Invention of Sodomy in Christian Theology.* Chicago: University of Chicago Press, 1997.

Kempf, Friedrich. "Pier Damiani und das Papstwahldekret von 1059." *Archivum historiae pontificiae* 2 (1964), 73–89.

Kleinermanns, M. J. *Der heilige Petrus Damiani: Mönch, Bischof, Cardinal, Kirchenchrer.* Steye, 1882.

Knowles, David. *The Monastic Order in England.* Cambridge: Cambridge University Press, 1940.

Landulph. *Historia Mediolanensis.* Edited by Ludwig Bethmann and Wilhelm. MGH SS, 8, 32–100. Hanover: Hahn, 1848.

Lawler, Philip. *The Faithful Departed.* New York: Encounter, 2000.

Lawrence, C. H. *Medieval Monasticism.* 3rd ed. London: Longman, 2001.

Leclercq, Jean. *Saint Pierre Damien: ermite et homme d'èglise.* Rome: Edizione di Storia e Letteratura, 1960.

———. *Love of Learning and the Desire for God.* Translated by Catharine Misrahi. 2nd ed. New York: Fordham University Press, 1974.

———. "Spiritual Guidance and Counseling According to the Rule of St. Benedict." In *Abba.* Edited by John Sommerfeldt. Kalamazoo, Mich.: Cistercian Publications, 1982.

——— "Traditions of Spiritual Guidance: Spiritual Direction in the Benedictine Tradition." *The Way* 27 (1987), 54–57.

Leyser, Karl. "On the Eve of the First European Revolution." In *Communications and Power in Medieval Europe.* Edited by T. Reuter. 1–20. London: Hambledon Press, 1994.

Leyser, Henrietta. *Hermits and the New Monasticism.* New York: St. Martin's Press, 1984.

The Life of Pope Leo IX. In *The Papal Reform of the Eleventh Century: The Lives of Pope Leo IX and Pope Gregory VII.* Translated by I. S. Robinson. Manchester: Manchester University Press, 2004.

Little, Lester K. "The Personal Development of Peter Damian." In *Order and Innovation in the Middle Ages.* Edited by William Jordan, Bruce McNab, and Teofilo Ruiz. 317–41. Princeton, N.J.: Princeton University Press, 1976.

———. *Religious Poverty and the Profit Economy in Medieval Europe.* Ithaca, N.Y.: Cornell University Press, 1978.

Loderchius, Jacob. *Vita S. Petri Damiani in VI libros distributa.* 3 vols. Rome, 1702.

Lokrantz, Margareta. *L'opera poetica di S. Pier Damiani.* In *Studia Latina Stockholmensia* 12 (1964).

Lucchesi, Giovanni. "Per una Vita di San Pier Damiani." In *San Pier Damiani nel IX Centario della Morte (1072–1972).* 4 vols. Cesna: Centro Studi e ricerche sulla antica provincia ecclesiastica ravennate, 1972–78.

McNamara, Joanne. "Canossa and the Ungendering of the Public Man." In *Rendering Unto Caesar.* Edited by Sabrina and Donald Treadgold. 131–50. Washington, D.C.: American University Press, 1995.

Macy, Gary. "The Theological Fate of Berengar's Oath of 1059: Interpreting a Blunder Becomes a Tradition." In *Interpreting Tradition.* Edited by Jane Kopas. 27–38. Chico, Calif.: Scholars Press, 1984.

Mandonnet, Pierre. *St. Dominic and His Work.* Translated by Marie Larkin. St. Louis, Mo.: Herder, 1944.

Mansi, Johannes. *Sacrorum conciliorum nova et amplissima collectio.* 54 vols. Venice, 1757–98. Reprint: Graz, 1960–61.

Ménager, L. "La 'byzantinisation' religieuse de l'Italie meridionale (ixe–xii^e^s) et la politique monastique des Normandi l'Italie." *Revue d'Histoire Ecclesiastique* 53 (1958), 747–74.

Mersch, Emile. *The Whole Christ: The Historical Development of the Doctrine of the Mystical Body in Scripture and Tradition.* Translated by John Kelly. London: Dennis Dobson, 1962.

Miccoli, Giovanni. "La storia religiosa." *Storia d'Italia* 2.1 (1974), 472–507.

Migliore, Daniel. *Faith Seeking Understanding*. 2nd ed. Grand Rapids, Mich.: William Eerdmans, 2004.

Miller, Maureen. "Masculinity, Reform and Clerical Culture: Narratives of Episcopal Holiness in the Gregorian Era." *Church History* 72.1 (2003).

Monumenta Germaniae Historica. Edited by G. H. Pertz et al. Hanover, 1826–.

Moore, R. I. "Family, Community and Cult on the Eve of the Gregorian Reform." *Transactions of the Royal Historical Society* n.s. 5, 30 (1980), 49–69.

———. *The First European Revolution c. 970–1215*. Oxford: Blackwell, 2000.

Morris, Colin. *The Discovery of the Individual.* London: Camelot Press, 1972.

———. *The Papal Monarchy.* Oxford: Clarendon Press, 1989.

Murray, A. *Reason and Society in the Middle Ages.* Oxford: Oxford University Press, 1978.

Neukirch, Franz. *Das Leben des Petrus Damiani.* Göttingen: Hofer, 1875.

Nightingale, John. *Monasteries and Patrons in the Gorze Reform.* Oxford: Clarendon Press, 2001.

Oakley, Francis. *Omnipotence, Covenant and Order.* Ithaca, N.Y.: Cornell University Press, 1984.

Oostermann, John. "Peter Damian's Doctrine of Sacerdotal Office: A Canonical Study of the Validity of Orders and the Worthy Exercise of Ordained Ministry." Ph.D. dissertation, The Catholic University of America, 1980.

Osborn, Ronald. "The Preaching of St. Peter Damian." Ph.D. dissertation, University of Oregon, 1955.

Otten, Willemien. *From Paradise to Paradigm.* Leiden: Brill, 2004.

Patrologicae cursus completes, series graeca. Edited by Jean-Paul Migne. 161 vols. Paris, 1856–66.

Patrologicae cursus completes, series latina. Edited by Jean-Paul Migne. 221 vols. Paris, 1844–64.

Payer, Pierre. *Sex and the Penitentials.* Toronto: University of Toronto Press, 1984.

Peter Damian. *St. Peter Damian: Selected Writings on the Spiritual Life.*

Translated by Patricia McNulty. London: Faber and Faber, 1959.
———. *Book of Gomorrah.* Translated by Pierre Payer. Waterloo, Ontario: Wilfrid Laurier University Press, 1982.
———. *Briefe des Petrus Damiani, Die.* Edited by Kurt Reindel. Vols. 4. Munich: Monumenta Germanica Historica, 1983.
———. *Sancti Petri Damiani Sermones.* Edited by Iohannis Lucchesi. CCCM 57. Turnhout: Brepols, 1983.
———. *The Letters of Peter Damian.* Translated by Owen Blum, vols.1–3, 5; and Irven Resnick, vols. 6–7. Fathers of the Church, Medieval Continuation. Washington, D.C.: The Catholic University of America Press, 1989–2005.
———. *The Life of Blessed Romuald.* In *The Mystery of Romuald and the Five Brothers.* Translated by Thomas Matus. Big Sur, Calif.: Sources Books and Heritage Books, 1994.
[Peter of Porto?]. *Regula clericorum.* PL 163.
Petri Damiani vita Beati Romualdi. Edited by Giovanni Tabacco. *Fonti per la storia d'Italia* 94 (1957).
Phipps, Colin. "Romuald—Model Hermit: Eremitical Theory in Saint Peter Damian's *Vita Beati Romualdi,* chapters 16–27." In *Monks, Hermits and the Ascetic Tradition.* Edited by W. J. Shiels. 65–77. Oxford: Basil Blackwell, 1985.
Pius XII. *Mystici Corporis.* Accessed through www.vatican.va/holy_fathers/pius_xii/encyclicals/docum.
Podles, Leon. *Sacrilege.* Baltimore: Crossland Press, 2008.
Poly, Jean-Pierre, and Eric Bournazel. *La Mutation féodale Xe-XIIe siècles.* 2nd ed. Paris: Pressus universitaires de France, 1980.
Poole, R. L. "Benedict IX and Gregory VI." *Proceedings of the British Academy* 8 (1917–18), 199–235.
Raby, F. J. E. *A History of Christian-Latin Poetry.* Oxford: Oxford University Press, 1927.
Radding, Charles. "Legal Theory and Practice in Eleventh Century Italy." *Law and History Review* 21.1 (2001), 377–81.
———, and F. Newton. *Theology, Rhetoric and Politics in the Eucharistic Controversy, 1078–79.* New York: Columbia University Press, 2003.
Ranft, Patricia. "Witness and the Twelfth Century Monastic Renewal." Master's thesis, West Virginia University, 1976.
———. "Role of the Eremitic Monk in the Development of the Medieval Intellectual Tradition." In *From Cloister to Classroom.* Edited

E. Rozanne Elder. 80–95. Kalamazoo, Mich.: Cistercian Publications, 1986.

———. "The Rule of St. Augustine in Medieval Monasticism." *Proceedings of the PMR Conference* 11 (1986), 143–50.

———. "The Maintenance and Transformation of Society through Eschatology: Cluniac Monasticism." *Journal of Religious History* 14 (1987), 3–29.

———. "The Concept of Witness in the Christian Tradition." *Revue bénédictine* 103 (1992), 9–23.

———. "A Key to Counter Reformation Women's Activism: The Confessor-Spiritual Director." *Journal of Feminist Studies in Religion* 10.2 (1994), 7–26.

———. *Women and Religious Life in Premodern Europe.* New York: St. Martin's Press, 1996.

———. *Women and Spiritual Equality in Christian Tradition.* New York: St. Martin's Press, 1998.

———. *A Woman's Way: The Forgotten History of Women Spiritual Directors.* New York: Palgrave, 2000.

———.*The Theology of Work: Peter Damian and the Medieval Religious Renewal Movement.* New York: Palgrave Macmillan, 2006.

———. "Franciscan Work Theology in Historical Perspective." *Franciscan Studies* 67 (2009), 41–70.

Regla tertia. Translated by D. de Bruyne. *Revue bénédictine* 42 (1930), 318–26.

La règle de Saint Augustin. Edited by Luc Verheijen. 2 vols. Paris: Etudes Augustiniennes, 1967.

Reindel, Kurt. "Zur handschriftlichen Überlieferung des Gedichte des Petrus Damiani." *Revue bénédictine* 67 (1957), 182–89.

———. "Studien zur Überlieferung der Werke des Petrus Damiani," *Deutsches Archiv für Erforschung des Mittelalters* 15 (1959), 23–102; 16 (1960), 73–154; and 18 (1962), 313–417.

———. "Petrus Damiani und seine Korrespondenten." *Studi gregoriani* 10 (1975), 203–20.

———. "Neur Literatur zu Petrus Damiani." *Deutsches Archiv für Erforschung des Mittelalters* 32 (1976), 405–43.

Resnick, Irven. *Divine Power and Possibility in St. Peter Damian's "Divine Omnipotentia."* Leiden: Brill, 1992.

Robinson, I. S. "The 'Colores Rhetorici' in the Investiture Contest." *Traditio* 32 (1976), 209–38.

Rosenwein, Barbara. *Rhinoceros Bound.* Philadelphia: University of Pennsylvania Press, 1982.

Rule of St. Benedict. Translated by Leonard Doyle. Collegeville, Minn.: Liturgical Press, 1948.

Russell, Kenneth. "Peter Damian's Whip." *American Benedictine Review* 41:1 (1990), 20–35.

Ryan, J. Joseph. *Saint Peter Damiani and His Canonical Sources.* Toronto: Pontifical Institute of Medieval Studies, 1956.

St. Benedict's Rule for Monasteries. Translated by Leonard Doyle. Collegeville, Minn.: Liturgical Press, 1948.

Sanford, Jonathan. "Peter Damian." In *A Companion to Philosophy in the Middle Ages.* Edited by Jorge Gracia and Timothy Noone. Oxford: Blackwell, 2003.

Saward, John. *Perfect Fools.* Oxford: Oxford University Press, 1980.

Semmler, J. "Die Beschlüsse des Aacherer Konzels im Jahre 816." *Zeitschrift für Kirchengeschichte* 74 (1963), 15–82. Also in CCCM 1. Turnhout: Brepols, 1963.

Sherman, James. *The Nature of Martyrdom.* Paterson, N.J.: St. Anthony's Guild Press, 1942.

Southern, Richard. *The Making of the Middle Ages.* New Haven, Conn.: Yale University Press, 1975.

Stock, Brian. *Implications of Literacy.* Princeton, N.J.: Princeton University Press, 1983.

Tellenbach, G. *Church, State and Christian Society at the Time of the Investiture Contest.* Translated by R. F. Bennett. Toronto: University of Toronto Press, repr. 1991.

Trites, Allison. "'Martus' and Martyrdom in the Apocalypse: A Semantic Study." *Novum Testamentum* 15 (1973), 72–80.

———. *The Concept of Witness in New Testament Thought.* Cambridge: Cambridge University Press, 1977.

Turner, Victor, and Edith Turner. *Image and Pilgrimage in Christian Tradition.* New York: Columbia University Press, 1978.

Vandermeersch, Patrick. "Sodomites, Gays, and Biblical Scholars. A Gathering Organized by Peter Damian?" In *Sodom's Sin.* Edited by Ed Noort and Eibert Tigchelaar, 149–71. Leiden: Brill, 2004.

Van Gennap, Arnold. *The Rites of Passage.* Translated by Gabrielle Caffee and Monika Vizedon. London: Routledge and Kegan Paul, repr., 1960.

Vogel, A. *Petrus Damianus ein Vortag.* Iena, 1856.

Wang, John. "St. Peter Damian, the Monk." Ph.D. dissertation, Fordham University, 1957.

Wickham, Chris. *Early Medieval Italy*. Ann Arbor: University of Michigan Press, 1981.

Willard, Henry. *Abbot Desiderius and the Ties between Montecassino and Amalfi in the Eleventh Century*. Miscellanea Cassinese, 37. Badea de Montecassino, 1973.

Wilmart, André. "Les prières de saint Pierre Damien pour l'adoration de la croix." In *Auteurs spirituels et textes dèvots du moyen âge latin*. Paris: Bloud et Gay, 1932.

———. "La recueil des poèmes et des prières de saint Pierre Damien." *Revue bénédictine* 41 (1949), 342–57.

Williams, Schafer. *The Gregorian Epoch: Reformation, Revolution, Reaction?* Boston: D. C. Heath, 1964.

White, Lynn. "The Historical Roots of Our Ecological Controversy and the Old Testament." *Bulletin of the John Rylands Library* 55 (1972–73), 9–32.

Wong, Joseph. "The Threefold Good: Romualdian Charism and Monastic Tradition." In *Privilege of Love*. Edited by Peter-Damian Belisle. 81–94. Collegeville, Minn.: Liturgical Press, 2002.

Wood, Charles. *The Quest for Eternity*. Hanover, N.H.: University Press of New England, 1983.

Woody, Kennerly. "Damiani and the Radicals." Ph.D. dissertation, Columbia University, 1966.

______. "Sagena Piscatoris: Peter Damian and the Papal Election Decree of 1059." *Viator* 1 (1970), 33–54.

INDEX

The Theology of Peter Damian: "Let Your Life Always Serve as a Witness" was designed and typeset in Tribute by Kachergis Book Design of Pittsboro, North Carolina. It was printed on 55-pound Natures Natural and bound by Sheridan Books of Ann Arbor, Michigan.